Praise for *Marooned: A Memoir of Fandom, Fatherhood, & the Far Side of the World*

'I loved reading *Marooned*. It's a heartfelt walk down memory lane shining its brightest light on the importance of family and of love.'
–John Eales, *Queensland Legend*

'By far the best book about State of Origin and all the emotions, memories and family interactions entwined with it that I've ever read. So much more than just a great book about a footy contest. If Origin means something to you, this book will hit you right in the heart. Very highly recommended.'
–Michael Gerard Bauer, *Prime Minister's Literary Award Winner*

'Not only did *Marooned* allow me to reconnect with some of my favourite State of Origin memories, it reminded me there are no straight lines in life, just a whole bunch of squiggles, and it's how well you handle the squiggles that will determine the quality of your life.'
–Ben Ikin, *Maroon Legend & CEO Qld Rugby League*

'A lively coming of age story by a Queenslander raised by State of Origin.'
–Joe Gorman, *Award Winning Author of 'Heartland: How Rugby League Explains Queensland'*

Praise for Darren Groth

'Groth's writing (is) continuously deft and striking.'
—*Australian Book Review*

'A superb sense of pace and timing.'
—*Australian Bookseller & Publisher*

'A wonderfully unique storyteller.'
—*The British Columbia Review*

'(Groth) writes with knowledge, compassion, maturity of vision and piercing humour.'
—*Vancouver Sun*

'Darren Groth shows an extraordinary ability to listen to the human heart: its fears, secrets, and telling silences.'
—*Prime Minister's Literary Awards, Judges' Comments*

'A writer who can pivot from heartbreak to humour without missing a beat.'
—*Vikki Wakefield, Davitt Award Winner*

MAROONED:

A Memoir of Fandom, Fatherhood, & the Far Side of the World

Darren Groth

HAWKEYE
PUBLISHING

First published in Australia in 2026 by Hawkeye Publishing

Cover Design by Isabella Lynch

Hawkeye Publishing recognises the Traditional Custodians of the lands where we live and work. We pay our respects to Elders past and present and extend that respect to all Aboriginal and Torres Strait Islander peoples. We celebrate more than 60,000 years of storytelling, art, and culture that continue to shape and enrich our world.

This book is based on real events. To protect the privacy of people included in this book, some names have been changed.

Aboriginal and Torres Strait Islander people should be aware that this book contains the names of deceased persons.

A catalogue record of this book is available from the National Library of Australia.

ISBN: 9781923105522
Proudly printed in Australia.
www.hawkeyebooks.com.au

For W, C and J. And especially for Dad.

FOREWORD

It never ceases to amaze me how rugby league, the greatest game of all, has impacted the lives of so many people in such a significant way.

Don't get me wrong, I love the game, my family loves the game, my mates love the game, and in some ways we all connect through the game, but it continues to fill me with joy when I hear stories of others who are infected by the game in the same way I am. *Marooned* is one of those stories.

Darren Groth takes us on a journey across multiple continents and decades sharing his love of family and rugby league, specifically his beloved Queensland Maroons.

Having played for the Maroons many years ago, it was always reinforced to me by my coaches and more experienced teammates, exactly who we were playing for. People like Darren and his father, Des.

What I didn't properly understand until I read this book was that people like Darren and Des don't just support the Maroons, feeling happy when they win and sad when they lose, they also lean on the Maroons legend and famous Queenslander spirit for motivation and inspiration when times get tough. That realisation had a profound impact on me.

But this isn't just a book for old rugby league players and fans, it's a story about a proud son, a loving husband and father, and an aspiring author who refused to stop chasing his dream.

Not only did *Marooned* allow me to reconnect with some of my favourite State of Origin memories, it reminded me there are no straight lines in life, just a whole bunch of squiggles, and it's how well you handle the squiggles that will determine the quality of your life. To that end, this is a story about a man who has lived a good life.

While Darren has clearly been inspired by our mighty Queensland Maroons over many years, there's much in Darren's story that inspired me, and I'm sure will inspire you.

Ben Ikin, Maroon Legend & CEO Qld Rugby League

2022

1

The Arm Wrestle

June 8, 2022

Origin Game #1, Stadium Australia, Sydney

First Half

Score: Qld 0 – NSW 0

It's an inevitable, untethered descent. Heart thumping. Nerves jangling. Inner voice setting out rules I'll comply with for the first five minutes then toss aside like a kicking tee after a conversion:

Do not yell.

Do not swear.

Do not lose your shit when things go wrong.

Do not be "Coach Groth", barking at everyone on screen about what they need to do and what they should've done.

Do not clap your hands, because your clapping is loud enough to startle animals and frighten children.

Do not be so bloody negative.

I breathe deep, tug the collar of my cherished 2006 Queensland Maroons jersey. All the lead-up is done. All the talk finished. Nothing left now but Ashley Klein blowing his whistle, the Steeden sailing into a night sky hazed with fireworks' smoke, and the best rivalry in Australian sport playing out in real time.

Except, this isn't real time.

It's 10:30am in Vancouver, Canada, my home since 2007. On the other side of the Pacific, it's 4:30am in Sydney, the day after. The game? All over, red rover. History has been made, heroes and villains etched into rugby league folklore. In this modest Ladner townhouse though, Destiny is on hold. Devices dark. Emails unread. Social media off-limits. I am oblivious to what lies ahead. I am an explorer fan venturing into the 2022 State of Origin outback, a forbidding landscape uncharted by my party but intimately understood by those who were here before us.

It takes me all of one minute to feel aggrieved.

First tackle of the match, Blues' lock Isaah Yeo reels out of the contact with Josh Papali'i and stumbles back towards the defensive line. It's obvious to everyone in the stadium he's had his bell rung. I'm excited by this development. The standard in the NRL this season has been clear and consistent: a player in Disneyland is quickly taken from the field by the independent doctor, undergoes a head injury assessment, fails, and takes no further part in proceedings. As I wait for Yeo's exit, I delight in the prospect of New South Wales down a man. And not just any man — one of their irreplaceable cogs in both attack and defence.

I wait.

And wait.

As Yeo takes a hit-up inside his own half, I lean forward in my maroon bean bag, arms outstretched like a Biblical prophet.

'WHAT IS THIS FUCKIN' BULLSHIT?'

'Darren!' chides Dad from the couch. 'The game's barely started, mate!'

'Dad, this is what I've been saying about concussion protocol all year! They're fine protecting players in a regular game, but if it happened in Origin to one of the Blues' stars, they'd do bugger all. And here it is! Happening right

now! Yeo should be on the sideline and gone for the night!' I scan the sea of faces in the living room. 'I'm right, aren't I? Aren't I?'

No response. Their expressions say it all: we've got seventy-nine more minutes of this.

'If he's not a hundred percent,' says Dad in his irritatingly calm voice, 'then that's bloody good for us.'

I reluctantly settle back into the bean bag, frowning, muttering about "conspiracies" and "disgraceful double standards". The situation is not improved when Valentine Holmes loses possession in the 12th minute resulting in a Jack Wighton try to open the Blues' account.

'I wish he'd signed with the friggin' Jets.'

My sour lament invokes Val Holmes' unsuccessful attempt to make a go of the NFL in 2019. It's a reference that maybe one other person in the room understands: Canadian brother-in-law, Cal, who is sitting next to my father on the couch. If everyone else is confused, so be it. In my millions of conversations since moving to Canada, too many have required explanation. "Yonks" means donkey years. "Cracker" means awesome. Toronto believes itself the centre of the universe, just like Sydney. Our version of The Tragically Hip is probably a combination of Cold Chisel and Midnight Oil. Yes, Australia has a lot of dangerous critters. No, drop bears aren't the most dangerous. Yes, Steve Irwin was the real deal. No, "The Simpsons" Aussie episode is not a documentary. There are two types of rugby — the awful kind, and God's own kind. Australian Rules is neither of those. What is State of Origin? Take the Battle of Alberta and times it by ten… Today, I can't be bothered with any explanations. They're luxuries for other sons, the ones who'll make many more Maroon memories with their cancer-free fathers.

If this is to be my final watch with Dad, at least it doesn't smell like a pasting. He's said many times he can tell when Queensland has come to play; it's obvious by their line speed and aggression in the first few minutes of the game. And I can tell when he can tell — he gives you this little nod that falls somewhere between assuredness and smugness. The nod has been working *overtime in the first half hour of the game, and with the score still at 4-0 down, Dad's proven yet again to have his finger on the Maroon pulse. While I'm comforted that we're well and truly in the arm wrestle, I'm at a loss to figure out where our points will come from.*

On cue, Queensland shifts the ball right to Kalyn Ponga. The Newcastle custodian's cut-out ball hits the turf but the bounce is kind for Brisbane wunderkind Selwyn Cobbo. In an instant, Cobbo is outside Brian To'o, streaking down the touch line and, with James Tedesco looming in cover, feathering a grubber more deftly placed than the garnish on a Michelin star steak. A second glorious bounce finds the hands of Dane Gagai, who crashes over to the right of the posts. I erupt, shouting and clapping, flailing to get out of the bean bag and onto my feet. When I'm finally upright, I vow not to sit again — an unwise affront to superstition given we just scored.

6-4 Maroons, following the Val Holmes conversion.

Somehow, after thirty-six minutes of willing but largely fruitless effort, we're in front. And we remain on top going into halftime (although there is a last-second heart attack to navigate — a Tedesco chip-and-chase after the hooter that requires Holmes' blistering speed to defuse). I take a deep breath and consider my father, now using the pause in proceedings to explain to a perplexed but attentive Cal why the penalty for a voluntary tackle should be brought back. He still looks confident.

I pray to the Goddess he's right.

The 1980s

2

Borne of Betamax

July 8, 1980
Origin Game, Lang Park, Brisbane
Score: Qld 20 – NSW 10

Like many Gen-X Queenslanders, I pledged my heart wholly and unconditionally to the Maroons the night State of Origin was born.

I was ten when the first game was played. The flowering of my rugby league love though traces back much earlier, to the age of three, the seed planted and tended on the hard-pan backyard of a flat in rural Queensland. In 1971, my father, Des – twenty-nine years old, Railways employee since the age of fifteen – arrived in the north-western town of Hughenden with wife, Kath, a toddler and a new baby, chasing promotion through the job of roster clerk for the train drivers, firemen and guards. The flat's backyard was unforgiving, but it was nothing compared to the role of the roster clerk. Consider the basic premise of the work: receive the work schedule from the trains clerk, assign work to seventy staff with an eye towards equalising everyone's time, run individual and group totals for the fortnight and the year, post the schedule, adjust the schedule when trains were late or broke down or took all weekend getting to Winton and back, re-post the schedule, wash, rinse, repeat... It was relentless, unwieldy. And then there was the politics. If the job itself was an all-day struggle in maths class, the politics was a hellish lunchtime in the schoolyard.

No matter what my father did or how he arranged the schedule, no matter how often he reached out or how inviolable his sense of fairness, people were pissed off. And a particular brand of pissed off: the steely disdain of small-town myopia, fired in the twin furnaces of big entitlement and narrow perspective. Rarely did it manifest as screaming and ranting and carrying on; most of the time it was pernicious, pecking away at my father's mental fortitude, eroding it like the foreshore of Surfer's Paradise during high tide. Dad recalls on one occasion, a bloke bailed him up in the office. 'Look at me, roster clerk!' When obliged, the bloke sneered: 'I've got cat's eyes from you working me so many bloody night shifts!' Another time, after an evening meal with one of the friendlier folk, Dad arrived at the office to find a message scrawled on the shift sheet:

Want to be a winner? Invite the roster clerk to dinner.

The bullying extended to Kath as well. The missus of a driver living next door would abandon her washing if Mum happened to come out into the yard. Another flat-out refused to have 'the roster clerk's wife' over for a Tupperware party. Through no fault of their own, Desmond and Kathleen Groth were the black hats of the Hughenden railway pantomime, and the emotional toll was considerable. More than once, Dad came home and shed the tears he dared not let flow between 9:00am and 5:00pm.

In trying life circumstances, distraction and validation can go a long way towards survival, and my parents – never ones to poison the soul with cynicism – sought them out in equal measure until their return to Brisbane in 1975. There were allies who would become forever friends. There was the brand new, Irish green Ford Cortina they bought. There were parties. There was drinking, occasionally to excess. There were picnics at Galah Creek. There was Sunday mass.

And there was rugby league.

Mum didn't want Dad playing football out west.

'We're here on our own,' she told him in Cloncurry, the twelve-month pit-stop prior to Hughenden. 'We can't afford for you to get hurt.'

Dad was more than prepared to honour Mum's plea. Challenging as his own lot was, mothering two tiny kids in a place as alien as the moon was next level. And his relationship to rugby league was shifting. ABC replays of the Sunday BRL game — preferably featuring his favourite team: the butcher-striped, leprechaun logo-ed, Catholic-approved Past Brothers — was no longer a solitary indulgence; I watched the games with him, propped on his knee, eyes like saucers, spongy brain soaking up every word of commentary, every black and white image. Passing along his passion for league, vicariously falling in love with the game all over again, shifting his footy identity to father instead of player... Dad enjoyed it. The fact that this all aligned with his beloved wife's wishes — it was the ultimate proof of concept.

Then, Jim Telford, manager of Cloncurry Railways, came calling.

Dad had been a fine player in the Brisbane Public Service throughout the 1960s. The Public Service comp, despite its procession of hilariously dull team names — Railway Institute, Main Roads, Titles Office, Stamp Duty, among others — was a solid football destination, featuring good young amateur talent and a smattering of former and current BRL professionals. In 1962 — his first year taking the game seriously — Des won a premiership with Housing Commission. In 1964, he was awarded the 'Best Forward' trophy playing for Railway Audit (Points 3, 2 and 1 were given out every Sunday by a randomly selected supporter on the sideline; Dad's teammates joked he only won the award because he had the most relatives in the crowd). The following year, repping Titles Office, he played alongside brother Roy and nephew Tom, the threesome acquiring the arresting nickname of 'The Dirty Groths', not for bad on-field behaviour but due to their penchant for skipping the post-game shower to be first to the pub. Bookending his time in the Public Service competition, he played in 1969 for Railway Institute and won a second premiership. It was his final season before the move out west.

My father's big-smoke resume was eye-catching, and it wasn't long before Jim Telford was on the doorstep, cap in hand, asking the new guy to join the local first 13. Did Dad refuse, waxing lyrical about prioritising his wife's wishes and his burgeoning commitment to parenthood? He did not. In fact, he agreed on the spot. Why the one-eighty? The simple answer might be incomprehensible to anyone my age and under: Dad played because he was *asked*. In recent years, I spoke with Mum about it, enquired if she was at all upset with her husband's backflip — she shrugged, her response matter of fact, resigned, completely free of the residue any simmering, five-decade resentment might leave behind:

'They *asked* him to!'

Chalk it up to the Silent Generation's profound sense of duty to community, or my parents' over-developed twin streaks of deference and politeness, or even a tactical move: promotion chaser wants to present as a team player in every way possible. My guess is that, on an unspoken level understood by both he and Mum, my father needed a square-up. To combat the colossal stress of overhauling one's life to move up in the world it was acceptable, even desirable, that Dad get some of it out of his system by belting a few blokes on Sunday.

There's evidence to support my claim. In one of his first Cloncurry games, Des did the unimaginable to anyone who knows him: he leapt up from a tackle and started throwing haymakers at a hapless opponent, causing an all-in brawl. When the dust had settled, the incredulous referee motioned the livid import from the big city over for a chat.

'What the bloody hell were you doing?' demanded the ref.

Indignant, my father stuck out his forearm. 'The bastard bit me, sir!'

Not about to take this slander lying down, the recipient of Dad's fisticuff barrage weighed in with something of a checkmate: 'I couldna bit him, sir!' he exclaimed, pointing to his abyss of a mouth. 'I got no fucken teeth!'

(The opponent would continue to plead his innocence post-game, trailing my father around like a blue heeler and pointing to his cavernous gob. His argument eventually proved persuasive and Dad apologised for attempting to knock his block off. If there was a biter, his true identity remains a mystery to this day).

Another example suggestive of my father's need to get out from under the thumb of his circumstances was on display in his third game with the team. Slotted into the front row after the prop was injured the previous week, Dad instructed the second-rower behind him in the scrum to bind with his inside leg, allowing a free strike at every ball and giving his team a huge possession advantage. It was thoroughly illegal, a blatant cheat, and way out of character for my father. And it wouldn't have occurred in a Brisbane game without a whistle, a penalty, a barrage of swearing, a flurry of punches, perhaps all of the above. But out here in the sticks, if you didn't do the time, why not do the crime? God knew Des was hardly alone. The first try he'd scored – against the Magpies in his second game – had been met with a firestorm of boots and fists; a "Welcome to country football" standard but, needless to say, a tad outside the lanes of fair play.

Cloncurry Railways went undefeated and won the premiership in 1970. It was Dad's last season pulling on a jersey; at the end of the year, he and Mum left Cloncurry and headed for Hughenden. Given the roster clerk horrors that awaited him, one could argue he pulled the pin too quickly on his playing days. Purging the workplace toxicity with a few weekend rib-ticklers and shoulder charges may well have resulted in fewer teary breakdowns. But in the end, nothing mattered more than honouring the earnest and well-founded wishes of his darling wife. And thankfully, no one asked him to play when he got to Hughenden.

How much did rugby league help my father cope during his time out west? It's tough to quantify. In my estimation, it wouldn't rank top five – in descending order, I would choose Mum, me and Sean, friends, faith and XXXX. But I'm convinced its presence wasn't insignificant. In the protracted, longform battle that was Dad's Country Queensland stint, his love of football – initially as a combatant by invitation, then as a fan passing on his passion – was a notable part of his pushback against a soul-sapping environment. And by the time fight had given way to flight, in the summer of 1975, he had at his hip an avowed disciple of the doctrine that footy was more than just a game: his eldest son.

If rugby league was an avenue of blessed escape for Dad, it was a portal of wondrous imagination for me. In the Hughenden backyard – a dry, gravelly, bindy-eyed field of dreams – three-year-old me would run up and down, ubiquitous brown plastic football in hand, throwing passes along the Western Suburbs Panthers' star-studded line-up of Richie Twist, Yogi Thompson and Wayne Stewart – me, me and me – until the money ball to fullback Peter Videroni (not a Wests player, still me) and his inevitable diving try in the corner. Not content to simply be the on-field talent, I commentated all the action as well:

'It goes out wide…Twist to Thompson…on to Stewart… to fullback Peter Videroni! VIDERONI! HE SCORES IN THE CORNER! Now let's see the action replay!'

(I'm not sure what it was about Peter Videroni that made him my favourite; as aforementioned, he didn't play for my beloved Panthers, and he wasn't a particularly gifted or decorated player. I suspect it had something to do with his name, the way it so gracefully rolled off the tongue. Considering I would spend much of my adult life trying to make words sing, I think it's as likely as any other explanation.)

I don't recall those all-me games in the Hughenden backyard. Not surprising – I was barely out of nappies. At that age, childhood memories are unreliable and vague; they can be altogether false, shoe-horned into the subconscious by a photo or a sibling's story or an old home-movie reel (say, one featuring a skinny three-year-old running around, passing to himself, commentating the action, scoring in the corner, then doing it all over again). My earliest rugby league recollection kicks in at six, after our family's return to Brisbane: me and Dad at Lang Park, 1976 BRL Grand Final, Wests battling cross-town nemesis Easts. I had donned my supporter gear – blood red velour jumper, black corduroy slacks – and, to my mind, this sartorial declaration of love had proved the difference in the game, the Panthers triumphing by the unlikely score of 16-1 (Easts had actually scored first, courtesy of a John Payne field goal in the first five minutes. I've always felt since that Payne and his

Tigers teammates got exactly what they deserved for this ridiculous strategy: an historical absurdity worse than if they'd been held off the scoreboard entirely).

The memories of that September afternoon are thick. The patchy grass of the Milton Road hill. The impossibly large forty-minute timer at the Caxton Street end. The melty goodness of my half-time Cornetto. The procession of old, tanned, nicotine-stained men sporting weathered leather pouches and shouting: 'First scorer! First try scorer!'. And the crowd. Its first seismic roar was scary, but not for long. I was safe and happy because rugby league was the greatest game of all, and Wests were winning, and Wests were winning because I was wearing red and black, and Dad was beside me, and Dad would always be beside me, there to protect me.

We were back at Lang Park the following year, a trio this time around with the addition of my thoroughly nonplussed younger brother, Sean. Lower section of the Hale Street Stand, afternoon sun shining in our eyes. Wests versus Easts again, 1977 Preliminary Final. No chocolates for the Panthers this time around, but I scored a Violet Crumble. And I recall Wayne Stewart kicking a goal from our sideline. The occasion was never going to reach the heights of the previous year – it wasn't a Grand Final, Wests lost, and that Fate-tempting little bastard Sean wore Tiger gold and black. But I had a grand time. And I remember it to this day.

I remember nothing about the Queensland Maroons in the '70s. Is it because they were routinely humiliated and, lacking any true suffering in my childhood, that humiliation was elevated to the status of trauma, burying itself so deep in my psyche it could only be accessed via therapy? I suspect so. In my adult years, Dad has assured me that, despite my absence of recall, the roots of my Queensland obsession were deep in my first decade and Maroon failure was a potent source of misery. More often than not, I was reduced to a blubbering mess. For one heartbreaking loss in 1977 – fifteen minutes to go, good guys leading comfortably; then Tom Raudonikis comes off the bench and bashes Greg Oliphant, Queensland melts down like a Paddle Pop in December – I took it particularly hard, venturing into the age-old "Divine Plan versus Chaos" debate, looking skyward and wailing at the supposedly just and loving God I prayed to at Sunday mass:

'It's not FAIR! We were SUPPOSED to win!'

It's possible this episode of shaken faith was the reason my father left me at home for the very first State of Origin game on the evening of July 8, 1980. More likely, he was looking out for his emotionally fragile eldest boy. Or maybe he was looking out for himself – I mean, what parent in their right mind would take their child to an event that could end with said child in the foetal position on the ground, sucking his thumb, weeping a-la Bob Hawke, and accusing God of being an arsehole? Whatever Dad's motivation, he caught the brand-new electric train to Milton while I remained in Mitchelton, facing the pivotal moment in Maroon history alone, in bed, under the covers, devoid of any comforting memory, imagining everything but Peter Videroni scoring in the corner.

I watched a replay of the victory the next day. The restoration of Queensland glory – I experienced it through the wonder of modern technology: our Sanyo Betamax VTC 9300PN Video Cassette Recorder.

Measuring in at slightly smaller than a Holden Barina, the Betamax was funded by a 1978 Melbourne Cup windfall (Kiwi thoroughbred Arwon took the prize and Dad jagged the big Queensland Railways office sweep, netting a cool $500 – the equivalent of a fortnight's worth of pay and then some). In its twelve-plus months distracting the Groth clan, the recorder was a revelation, supplanting Pong as the household's most beloved source of entertainment. My cultural consumption would be dictated by the content stored on its house-brick cassettes: those we owned and those we rented from the video store on Blackwood Street, the pithily named Jest-A-Movie. Fawlty Towers, Buck Rogers, Sean Connery's Bond in "Diamonds Are Forever", the Looney Tunes classic "Hareway to the Stars"… these were a few of the staples that shaped my late childhood and teen years. And, naturally, rugby league was a recording fixture. No longer was I a slave to the TV guide. Scheduled broadcasts of the Saturday Sydney game and the Sunday BRL replay? Ha! Schedules were for Luddite losers! I could watch any time: before dinner, after dinner, after school. I could even fast forward through the ads, though to do so required the deft hand of a safe-cracker and the exquisite timing of an orchestra conductor.

The taping of the inaugural Origin — it was about much more than entertainment-on-demand. This was history; or at least, the hope of history. Dad had carried that hope through the second half of the '70s. Like many of his Lang Park Outer brethren he had shown up, rain or shine, to the annual interstate clashes, just in case the Maroons produced a boilover. In a decade when Queensland's team of residents won two games — count 'em: *two* — of a possible twenty-nine, you didn't want to be the guy whose lottery numbers finally came up and you hadn't bothered to enter the draw. Origin 1 wasn't the Golden Casket, though. It was our best players coming home from Sydney to play for their rightful state. It was a contest. A fair fight. Potentially, a new age being ushered in. And if that was true, Dad wanted to ensure it wasn't all just some figment of his imagination. He would go to the game and see it with his own eyes. And in the event his eyes were deceiving him, incontrovertible evidence would be captured for all-time on our cutting-edge Betamax video recorder.

My father would lean on that evidence. In person, the game wasn't so much a spectacle as it was an immersion. Over capacity by anyone's guess, the crowd was cheek to jowl. (Dad's own presence, I found out many years later, was unlawful. A good mate with an insider contact at the official ticket printer had managed to procure a number of dummies, the precise number unknown to all but him. Des swears to this day he didn't know at the time his ticket was fake. As a chronicler, I desperately want his claim to also be a deception; as a son who's known his father for more than 50 years, it is my great lament to admit I believe him 100%).

From Dad's vantage – on the terraces at the Milton Road end – the action was often obscured by the surrounding mass of humanity. Much of the game experience was riding the wave of roars radiating out from sections with the best view of the biggest moments: Artie Beetson emerging from the tunnel, Artie Beetson clocking Parramatta teammate Mick Cronin, Mal Meninga potting penalty goals from all over the park, Chris Close carving up the Blues' ruck defence to score the match-winning try adjacent to the posts. In the end, attending the first ever Origin was more fever dream than witnessed reality. To understand how the game had played out, to appreciate how Queensland's prodigal sons had thrust a stake in the ground, Gandalf-like, and cried 'NONE SHALL PASS!' to any rugby league future without "Mate against Mate", one needed a large magical box to capture the eighty minutes for all eternity, right alongside the immortal footage of Bugs Bunny foiling Marvin the Martian's attempts to blow up the Earth because it obstructed his view of Venus.

I watched the game, and I watched my father watching the game. For the most part, Des is an all-or-none footy observer (the opposite of me: Coach Groth paces and gesticulates and talks over the top of the commentary. Unless you can reduce me to background white noise, I am insufferable). He spends the vast majority of the game quiet except for the odd comment, unmoved bar the frequent elbow-bending with a Carlton Mid-Strength or, when he's in Canada, a Kokanee. Then, in the biggest Maroon moments, he'll explode like Riverfire over the Story Bridge.

For the first Origin, Dad skewed one side of all-or-none, and not the side associated with triumph. No comments. No elbow bends. No eruption at the full-time hooter. He just sat on the couch, hands on knees, glistening eyes glued to the TV screen. Was his lack of animation because he knew the outcome? I don't think so. I suspect he still couldn't quite believe what was happening. He understood then as I do now; this was a small miracle. The future of State of Origin was comparable to giant pandas mating in captivity – everything needed to be just right to ensure the animal's ongoing survival. To his astonishment, Game 1 had played out perfectly. The pandas had got down to business and a future replete with Maroon redemption seemed possible. But one couldn't be complacent. Sitting there like a wax figure on the couch, he wasn't taking any chances. Any sudden sounds or movements, State of Origin might get spooked, escape captivity, and run off into the bamboo forest, never to be seen again.

I didn't realise how tenuous it all was, how a loss meant everything went away and, thus, Maroon failure was out of the question. I couldn't know that decades of my identity hung in the balance. I wouldn't appreciate until many years later that Chris Close's exhilarating try was the perfect metaphor for this fragile experiment: play going nowhere, gets a nothing pass from Mal

Meninga, flat-footed, near-slip; then purchase, progress, momentum, a burst through the line, a swerve around Graeme Eadie, the sealer right beside the posts. I just watched the game and cheered these mighty new Maroons on to victory, confident our best players would never again don a Blues jersey and that interstate humiliation would forever be in the rear-view mirror. I could dare to dream.

The divine balance had been restored. Life was fair and just. The Maroons were supposed to win, and they had won.

Perhaps God wasn't such an arsehole after all.

3

Uncle Eric and the Army of Groths

July 28, 1981

Origin Game, Lang Park, Brisbane

Score: Qld 22 – NSW 15

Credit for much of what I've done as a writer can be attributed to my grade seven teacher, Mr Wade. Many educators are memorable; some indelibly impact the young people they encounter. Mr Wade was all that and more. Balding, with one wonky eye, and a mudflap of a beard hanging from his chin, he was even-tempered yet no-nonsense, kind yet assertive, caring yet in command. He frequently participated in our lunchtime cricket matches, sending down a self-styled form of leg-spin that defied physics and never failed to confound the batsman. In class, he had a simple but effective system of incentive: do good work, get a crown stamp; the more crowns you got, the bigger the prize at the end of term. Bought out of his own pocket, prizes ranged from tuckshop fare – chips, Sunny Boys, Cherry Ripes, those tasty "space sticks" left over from the NASA Apollo missions – to more lucrative bounty such as key-rings and wallets and the odd bit of sports equipment. All this would've been sufficient for Mr Wade to leave a lasting impression, but his influence on me would extend far beyond googlies and crown stamps and Cherry Ripes. He would prove pivotal to a trio of important revelations in my life; the first two would bedrock my own thirteen-year career in education:

People will remember you much more for who you were than what you did.

To be a good teacher, you have to earn the respect of your students.

The third realisation came courtesy of his near obsessional focus on creative writing, manifest as every student penning a new short story every couple of weeks:

Writing is what you do.

Writing was what I was doing the evening of Origin 2. While Dad watched the live broadcast (he couldn't get a ticket in '81 – his inside man at the printer had gone straight), I was finishing my story for the fortnight: a diary-styled short of a soldier in Napoleon's army during the ill-fated march on Moscow. If completed before bedtime, I'd get to watch the taped Origin replay.

Dad's viewing wasn't too distracting. Once or twice, I time-slipped back from 1812 Russia and cupped an ear towards the action outside my closed bedroom door. The only sounds: faint, incomprehensible strains of commentary from Billy J Smith and Mick Veivers. And nothing from Dad; no noise that would hint at the unfolding result. So, I ploughed forward, head down / bum up, efforting to take my French soldier's tale to its tragic conclusion, itching to impress Mr Wade with my 500-word epic, desperate to get it done so I wouldn't have to go to bed without knowing the Maroons' fate. And get it done I did. Around 9:40, I left my soldier dying in the snow with an unceremonious "THE END" and ventured into the lounge room. Five minutes later, I was sitting cross-legged on the carpet, little more than arm's length from the TV, late night jam sandwich in hand, while a deadpan Dad brought the Betamax to life with its familiar *clunk* and *shunk*.

Converted try to the Blues.

Converted try to the Blues.

Converted try to the Blues.

New South Wales up 15 – 0, twenty minutes in.

Not good. Not good at all. I looked over at Dad, my eleven-year-old heart breaking, hoping for some sign of reassurance. He shrugged.

'Maybe we should've brought in more troops?' he asked.

He was referring to the fact that the Maroon selectors had picked only four Sydney-based Queenslanders: Mitch Brennan, Rod Morris, Paul McCabe, and Paul Khan. The surprising competitiveness of the all-residents' team in the two series losses – 10-2 and 22-9 – had convinced Queensland brass that assistance from south of the Tweed need only be minimal. At 15-zot, that decision was looking questionable at best.

Or maybe I was to blame? The events unfolding had taken on an eerie and disturbing resemblance to my short story of the French Invasion. Origin 2 was our Moscow – we were meant to be conquerors. Victory the previous year had ended the long march of Maroon futility and securing the Russian capital would signal the dawn of a new age to last generations. Yet here we were entering the city, only to find Peter Sterling had taken all the food, Ray Price had torched all the houses, and the only things left for us were desolation and misery and Les Boyd. We would freeze to death in the relentless winter laid on by Ted Glossop and his slick band of Tsarist Blues.

Or, maybe, we wouldn't? Maybe we could avoid the doom that befell Napoleon? Our "Little Corporal" was Wally Lewis, the 21-year-old kid from Fortitude Valley, thrust into the captaincy role with the withdrawal of Artie Beetson. He wasn't yet a King or an

Emperor, but he was on his way. He'd already broken into the Test team, acquitting himself well against, of all teams, France. Maybe he could inspire a comeback and save State of Origin from the guillotine?

I wasn't the only one plagued by distracting thoughts – towards the end of the first half, a daydreaming Les Boyd muffed a pass thrown his way, gifting Queensland fabulous field position. Three tackles later, Brad Backer was in.

15 – 5 at oranges.

'This is the start of the comeback, yeah?' I asked, spraying jam sandwich crumbs over much of Mitchelton.

Dad shrugged. His evasiveness was infuriating. I made a mental note that my next story for Mr Wade would feature my father, a football replay and some sort of truth serum masquerading as beer.

I wouldn't be mad at him for long. When Wally Lewis scored the first of ten Origin tries that spanned his glittering career, I knew we were back in the game. Then, not long after, it happened: the moment that has become Origin 2's most enduring memory, the moment emblematic of Queensland's pushback against decades of interstate inferiority, the moment I knew we were going to win.

And all that was required to engineer it was an assault on our family name.

⬭

It's remarkable how often "Groth" gets mangled, both in text and in pronunciation. Grot, Groff, Gross, Groat. In restaurant reservations, on junk mail. At events and over PA's. When I scored my first (and only) century in junior cricket, it was recorded in the Courier-Mail sports section under "D Grath". When I won my first (and only) state long jump title as an 11-year-old, the victorious youngster in the next-day paper was emo and clad in all black: "D Goth". Five little letters – that's all it is. *Five!* It's not a Welsh train station! And yet, to this day I wince every time someone new is about to say my name or write it down.

You may already suspect the most common gaffe with "Groth" is its pronunciation as "Growth" (As I write this, the *San Francisco Book Review's* very generous assessment of my new novel references the brilliant work of "Growth". I can't ever recall the mistake making it into print, so now I can die happy). During my youth, a big reason for this ever-present error was the work of one Eric Grothe Senior, bustling winger for the all-conquering Parramatta Eels of the '80s; "Guru" as he was known to fans around the country, presumably because of his beard, his long hair and, in service of rugby league irony, his anti-peace, anti-love, anti-flower-power, wrecking ball style of play. We Groths weren't averse to claiming Eric as one of our own. Anytime there was an enquiry to shared lineage, Dad would launch into a treatise on family trees and genealogy charts, and records indicating the origins of Groth / Grothe may have dated back to the Finnish Groots / De Groots before gaining a foothold in Germany, all the while conveniently leaving out the name's verified meaning: "A large or corpulent man".

'Basically, we're all the same mob,' he would say, as the enquirer struggled to stay awake.

Add in the fact "Eric" is my father's middle name and the Eels' finisher was practically a walk-up start for family barbecues. But what about when he played for New South Wales? Was he part of the clan when wearing the enemy's jersey?

Sort of.

Like any other Cockroach, he was to be despised. At the same time, he was *our* Cockroach. If he ran hard, did good, scored one of his signature bulldozing tries, it reflected well on all the large and corpulent men carrying his surname. Just as long as the Maroons beat his filthy stinking team, he could bring all manner of honour to the Groth(e) masses.

Twenty minutes into Origin 2, it was clear he had to be disowned. Of the three tries the Blues scored, the Guru had jagged two, one of them a soul-destroying ninety-five metre runaway after a misdirected Greg Conescu pass. I was mortified. How could I show my face at school? Not only had I sentenced the Maroons to death with my short story's dark literary magic, the executioner had been "Uncle Eric". Mercifully, he was kept in check after the early damage, and as Queensland began to claw their way back into the contest, I wondered what further role the Groth(e) name would play in the outcome.

It would be the starring role.

In the 65th minute, Queensland fullback Colin Scott sliced through the New South Wales' defence and set sail on a fifty-five-metre sprint to the try-line. Ten metres out, he was certain to score until, from the clouds, the Guru appeared and dived full-length, pulling off an incredible covering tackle, grassing Scott a body-length short of the stripe. As the Maroon fullback attempted to rise and quickly play-the-ball to teammate Chris Close, Grothe refused to let go of Scott's legs. He hung on.

And on.

And on.

What happened next is best described by the replay commentary of legendary Blues' caller, Rex Mossop (check it out on YouTube):

'*...Now, from that position... the hair was OHHHH! And a backhander to get him out of the way! Well, that's just not on. And it's a try to Close. I think I probably would've sent Close off for that if I'd have been the referee.*'

And after a second look:

'...Now there's the shot... the hair's pulled first... there's a smack in the mouth... a nasty bit of business which Close, in my estimation, Close... goes down very badly for. But they've scored the try, so one can assume they think the ends justify the means.'

Quite the scene. Choppy Close grabbing those lustrous Guru locks and yanking his head like it's a Christmas bon-bon, before a full-on slap to the moosh that sends sweat and dirt and IQ points flying. Then, discarding the Blues winger's corpse, Close picks up the play-the-ball and barges through New South Wales captain Steve Rogers to score.

15-15, after the kick in front to level-up.

I glanced over at Dad. 'Is Eric Grothe still part of the family?'

He lifted his can of XXXX, face a mix of ancestral pride and stoic sympathy. He nodded once.

'More than ever.'

As the glorious first entry in Queensland's storied Origin comeback canon was completed – penalty goal for a Ray Price headbutt on Chris Phelan; penalty try for Mal Meninga being tackled without the ball on an in-goal grubber – the truth of my Russian Campaign short story was revealed: it wasn't the Maroons who had come to Moscow after all. It was *us*. An army of Groths, Grothes, Groots, Goths and Groats. And who was my narrator? None other than the Guru, Uncle Eric. He'd believed himself a conqueror, but he was mistaken. He was a stooge, a patsy, a fall guy of history. His destiny was to die so that something great could live.

Final hooter: Queensland 22 – New South Wales 15.

I cheered, hugged Dad. Amidst the elation, I felt something else; something weird and alien and altogether loathsome: I felt sorry for someone wearing the sky-blue jersey. Turned out it wasn't accurate, though. With the wisdom of years, I've come to understand the true source of the sadness, the true inspiration for the melancholy:

I felt sorry for myself.

Mr Wade loved my French soldier story. He loved it so much he promised to enter it in some local contest for young writers. I don't know if he ever followed through – I never asked him about it, and I never received any word of entry or acknowledgement. It didn't matter. The fact that he'd thought so highly of it was satisfaction enough.

And let's face it: had Mr Wade put it in, and had it miraculously managed to get up like the Maroons in Origin 2, the certificate mailed to McConaghy Street would've read:

YOUNG WRITERS COMPETITION
BEST SHORT FICTION
WINNER
DARREN GOAT

4

The Jaws of Victory

June 28, 1983
Origin Game #3, Lang Park, Brisbane
Score: Qld 43 – NSW 22

The decider in '83 was my first in-person experience of Origin.

It was time. I was thirteen years old, grade nine, no longer a child, officially a teenager. I'd survived my first eighteen months of Marcellin Boys' Secondary, leaning heavily on a combination of studiousness, sporting aptitude, fear of authority and lunchtime wall-ball. The library was also a godsend. While many of the school spaces made me feel small and wary, the library was a welcome site of curiosity and excitement. My first time walking through the door – a skinny, bowl-cut streak of nervousness in grey pants – I spied Peter Benchley's *Jaws* on the display rack. Without knowing the story (I hadn't seen the movie), I plucked it off the rack, sat down and read an opening chapter that featured a beach party, a beautiful woman getting naked, said beautiful naked woman having a swim, and said beautiful naked woman getting chomped by a shark. As I reluctantly replaced the novel back in the rack, I thought: a) this is the greatest school day ever; and b) I'm not a little kid from McConaghy Street anymore.

Not being a little kid meant, in theory, I was better equipped to cope with the disappointment of Origin defeat. To date, there'd been very little need for coping skills. The triumph of the inaugural tilt in 1980, the comeback in '81, the delicious Sigsworth / Duke calamity that secured the first series win in '82. All the north-of-the-border talk that State of Origin would reveal the true balance of power in interstate rugby league had proven true. Okay, we were coming off a loss – a 10-6, two tries to one letdown on a muddy SCG track – but there were reasons to feel confident going into the '83 decider. We were back at Lang Park, which was surging towards its much-deserved moniker of the future: "The Cauldron". New South Wales headed into the game without two players I feared for vastly different reasons: the injured Peter Sterling; who'd been masterful in winning man-of-the-match honours in Sydney; and the suspended Les Boyd, who'd been rubbed out for twelve months after the dog act of breaking Darryl Brohman's jaw in the series opener. And, of course, we had Wally Lewis: the best player in the world and, thanks to Ron McAuliffe and QRL money, still running out for the Valleys' Diehards each week in the Brisbane Rugby League comp. The prevailing Maroon vibe was "Bring on the fight – she'll be right."

I wasn't so sure. What if we got done? What if my first live experience of Origin was despair? It was all well and good being more mature, but I was already figuring out that maturity didn't lessen pain – it just meant you were better at hiding it. Did *anything* lessen pain? My best guess would become a lifelong, and ultimately futile, strategy of self-care:

Distance.

Many years later, it would be literal, measuring thousands of kilometres. In 1983, it was figurative and arm's length, the textbook definition of cognitive dissonance. And it invoked the voice of my mother:

It's not the end of the world if they lose…

The sun will come up tomorrow if they lose…

It's only a bloody game of football… Remember that IF THEY LOSE!

It was unfair to Mum that she was the wet blanket on my brain. In 1983, she was doing more to benefit my mind than should be reasonably asked of any mother. She'd moved on from the god-awful part-time job of Ascot Cabs night dispatcher to the god-awful part-time job of TAB phone betting operator. She was getting her hair cut by a friend of a friend in the 'burbs. She was sewing her own clothes. Excepting the once-a-year birthday request of a bottle of Tweed perfume, she was foregoing the purchase of anything nice for herself. All this sacrifice to ensure there was enough money to provide her sons with a good education. It was apparent to me even as a new teenager nurturing solipsism: there was nothing she wouldn't do to help her three boys get a better crack at life. And maybe that's why it was echoes of Mum that night – it was yet another way she was attempting to safeguard her eldest's future. Or maybe it was simply because her attitude towards rugby league ranged from begrudging tolerance to simmering hostility. Whatever the reason, it made sense the caveats I had about the decider would carry her matriarchal stamp.

So, with Dad by my side and Mum in my head, I boarded the train to Milton and a destination that, in a very real sense, I would never fully return from.

There are many differences between the State of Origins of yesteryear and today. One of the most obvious is the colours in the crowd. Tune into a modern Origin at Suncorp Stadium and you'll witness a sea of maroon, home supporters decked out in all manner of merch and gear and bling. No argument, no ambiguity; Queensland allegiance, passion and pride clearly articulated and on full display. Cynics would argue it's crass commercialism, the triumph of brand over history and integrity. They'd bring up Australian cricket and their protection of the test cap as the model: 'You don't find Joe Bloggs, apprentice sparky from Inala, wearing the baggy green!' I see their point, but I'm not a cynic. A sea of maroon is a beautiful thing.

Contrary but no less beautiful is the lack of uniformity characteristic of the old days. Watch a video of an early '80s Origin – there's the odd bit of maroon clothing, a few maroon flags here and there. The rest of the crowd is all the colours. And oftentimes the colours belong to the club they follow year-round. The team might be in the BRL or the State League. It might be from the big smoke or out of town. Inner city or the 'burbs. It might be the team they played for in their heyday, or the team their kid plays for now. It's all the diversity and inclusivity of footy, the splendid shades and hues of the greatest game of all. The magnificent rainbow that is Queensland rugby league.

The train into town rode the tracks of that rainbow. At every stop on the Ferny Grove line, people piled in wearing their football hearts on their sleeves and on their chests and on their backs and on their heads. Wests, Norths, Brothers, Valleys, Redcliffe. Disembarking at Roma Street and on the walk to Lang Park, the representation extended well beyond the borders of Brisbane: Ipswich Jets, Toowoomba Clydesdales, Central Queensland Capras, Emerald Tigers, Calliope Roosters, Roma Cities...

'Look,' said Dad, pointing out a bloke with a handlebar mo, inhaling a sausage roll and holding a small transistor radio to his ear. 'A Mt. Isa jumper from the Foley Shield.'

What was I wearing? I had no official Western Suburbs gear, and I didn't play for any junior club, so I was in street clothes. But wearing civvies didn't have me feeling like an outsider when we got to the ground. Quite the opposite: I belonged because *everyone* belonged. There was, however, something else that gave me a distinct sense of unease.

It's not the end of the world if they lose…
It's not the end of the world if they lose…
It's not the end of the world if they lose…

Looking around, no one – *no one* – was entertaining the prospect of defeat. Folks were smiling, laughing. Shouting hellos at people they knew ten rows down. A bloke nearby on the terraces was so reclined reading the game program it was like he'd brought along the banana lounge from his back verandah. The mood wasn't just "she'll be right" – it was "we've got this in the bag". Believing I represented the young new generation of grounded, educated Maroon fans, I was appalled. A taste of Origin success had gone straight to our heads. A few years' compensation for the wretchedness of the '70s and we were already taking it for granted. Weren't we better than that? Weren't we more *grown up* than that? We'd survived the '74 floods. We'd rolled out electric trains that were air-conditioned – *air-conditioned!* – in 1979. Just last year, we'd wowed the world with an unforgettable Commonwealth Games. Where was our sensibleness? Where was our humility?

The sun will come up tomorrow if they lose…
The sun will come up tomorrow if they lose…
The sun will come up tomorrow if they lose…

The wisdom of many years has taught me how wrong I was. The crowd at the '83 decider wasn't big-headed or taking it for granted. Their happiness wasn't overconfidence drawn from inevitability – it was *comfort* drawn from *possibility*. Unlike the preceding decades, we were always in the fight now. We were always a chance. A *real* chance. And, regardless of any single Origin's outcome, that was reason enough to celebrate.

As Mal Meninga kicked off to a thunderous roar, I might've been the only Queenslander in Lang Park not drawing comfort from possibility. And that was unfortunate, because the idea of what's possible would forever be redefined in the eighty minutes that followed.

Prior to Game 3 of the 1983 State of Origin series, Queensland's last – and only – time scoring 40+ points occurred in 1940. The last time the Maroons had won by 20+ was a 34-12 triumph in 1955 (a mere two years later, we would suffer the biggest loss in interstate rugby league history: a 69-5 humiliation at the SCG). Despite the festive atmosphere, I can't imagine anyone at Lang Park that night believed we had a date with the record books. I didn't. I knew how Origin worked – it was tough and tight and the result would only be decided in the last twenty. Thrashings were a relic of the past, and the idea of Queensland delivering the thrashing was preposterous.

In accordance with this understanding, the Mum in my head – now informed by the action on the field – was keeping it real:

On top early.

But Mal Meninga misses the sitter in front.

Greg Conescu scores, giving us a 6-0 lead.

Then they lose the ball the set of six straight after.

Mal Meninga pots a penalty for 8-0.

But it should've been 12-0 after Mark Murray came up short.

Then it *was* 12-0, Steve Stacey flying through the air like Superman, scoring in the corner after a Steve Mortimer error led to a brilliant Maroon shift to the right. Then it was 14-0, Mal Meninga slotting the conversion from the sideline. Then it was 20-0, Mitch Brennan receiving a saloon passage to the line from a brilliant Brad Tessman offload. Then it was 21-0, Wally Lewis capping forty minutes at his imperial best with a cheeky field goal.

It's not the end of the world if they lose…

The sun will come up tomorrow if they lose…

Mum, if we lose after leading 21-zot at oranges, it *will* be the end of the world, and the sun *will not* come up tomorrow.

I looked around at the crowd. They were buzzing. Along the lengthy line-ups for the toilets and the bar and the pie stand, people were clapping and cheering, eyes wide, brows high on their foreheads. A pocket of fans in blue and green beanies were reviving the chant that had spontaneously started up after the Stacey try: 'QUEENSLAND!' (clap-clap-clap) 'QUEENSLAND!' (clap-clap-clap) 'QUEENSLAND!' (clap-clap-clap). Dad wasn't outwardly participating in the celebrations, but I could tell just from his body language – shoulders back, chin high, face beaming like a kid on Christmas morning – he was having a moment.

'I was hoping your first Origin would be good,' he said, turning to me. 'I didn't think it would be this good.'

I didn't really believe him. In the way a young boy views his father as omniscient, I felt like he'd known all along this was the game for me. He'd kept me in cotton wool until he was certain the Maroons weren't just competitive, but a force to be reckoned with. He'd shielded me from this rite of passage until both Queensland and I had come of age, and until the outcome was more coronation than contest. He'd waited until Origin mirrored that first chapter of *Jaws*: New South Wales – attractive, bold, brazenly naked, fearlessly entering the waters of Lang Park, oblivious to the Great White of Queensland prowling below the surface; in the span of forty minutes, the Blues monstered, dismembered, carcass left to wash up on Bondi where the Sydney media would be waiting.

Mum's voice faded away when Bryan Niebling went over and the scoreboard read 33-0. She didn't return when the Blues ran in four late tries to cut the deficit to 15, preventing the last seven minutes from being purely academic. At 43-22, the unthinkable chant commenced on the Milton Road terraces – 'WE WANT FIFTY! WE WANT FIFTY! WE WANT FIFTY!' – and my father and I added our voices to the chorus. We would settle for 43. When the full-time hooter sounded, I asked Dad if I should run onto the field.

'Don't you want to get home and watch the tape before bed?' he replied.

I answered yes, that is exactly what I want to do.

5

The Hater's Paradox

July 7, 1984
Third Test, SCG, Sydney
Score: Australia 20 – Great Britain 7

The great French writer and philosopher Simone de Beauvoir has a memorable quote about identity:

Self-knowledge is not knowledge, but a story one tells about oneself.

Sums up this book to a tee. There is no knowledge in these pages, no great insights to be gleaned. There is merely a story. But beyond de Beauvoir's assertion is a curly question worth pondering: Am I telling this story about myself, or was it told before I typed the first word? This Maroon character of mine: is it of my own design or is it something imprinted from the very beginning? Could I have been one of those normal people who watch Origin without forgetting that other things exist in the world (wife, children, friends, food, water, air…) or did I never stand a chance?

Like any enduring ontological query, there is a case to be made for both sides. Consider those early years in Western Queensland when I was a toddler, sitting on Dad's knee, watching the Sunday afternoon BRL match of the round. Those who favour personal experience over pre-wiring would argue this is clear evidence of the clay child being shaped and fired in the kiln of a dad's influence and environment. At such a formative age, and perhaps with the echoes of a little Confucian finger-wagging thrown in — *The father who does not teach his son his duties is equally guilty with the son who neglects them* — is it any wonder the boy grew up to be a Queensland Origin tragic? Ah, but what about the child's own blueprint, cry the behavioural geneticists. He didn't have to stay on his father's knee; he could've run off and helped his mother or climbed a tree or found a box of matches to play with. Something within the boy — something at his very core — compelled him to stay on that knee, absorbing the spectacle of rugby league. Furthermore, when the child was left to his own devices, free to do anything in the world that moved him, what did he choose? He ran up and down the yard playing pretend footy like it was the one thing everyone should be doing every second of every day.

Is my Maroon devotion the product of Nature or Nurture? Until "23 and Me" turns up a Queenslander gene, I'll never know for sure. The source of that devotion's flip side, however — my disdain for New South Wales — is no such mystery. On the graph of my identity, there is an incident that firmly fixes it on the axis of "Born This Way".

◯

Trophy presentation, third test against Great Britain, 1984. Wally Lewis — by now, well and truly ensconced as the "Emperor of Lang Park" — had just concluded his first campaign as captain of the Australian Kangaroos, piloting the team to a hard fought and, at times, brutal 3-0 series win over Ye Olde Enemy. With victory achieved, the only task remaining was to collect the spoils. Lewis mounted the stage, lifted the Ashes prize and, as is customary for the national skipper, launched into a speech. A stirring ensued amongst the Sydney Cricket Ground crowd. Then a low murmur. With each passing syllable from Lewis, the noise grew louder. And then it began to take on a collective shape. Watching the TV broadcast, I was confused. *Is there a problem with the sound?* The thought was barely complete when the truth began to dawn. *Bloody hell, is that…? Are they…?* I turned to Dad. He was sitting forward in his armchair, arms folded, the disenchanted look in his eye the same as when he'd caught me out in various lies over the years (no, I didn't get wet falling into the local creek I was forbidden from exploring; no, I really had to go to the loo when you asked me to dry the dishes; no, I didn't kick the footy onto the roof of grouchy Mrs Byrne's greenhouse…). He sighed and muttered a solitary word:

'Sad.'

It was confirmation. I wasn't hearing things. The indefensible scene happening on the box was, in fact, happening for real.

The Sydney crowd was booing Wally Lewis!

Booing the Australian captain!

BOOING *THEIR* CAPTAIN!

'They don't get it,' added Dad, delivering the decree that would become synonymous with New South Wales Origin. 'They never will.'

And with that, he up and left, headed for the backyard and some quality time attempting to start our lawn mower.

I couldn't believe he'd brushed it off so readily. I kept watching, infuriated. I wanted to put a foot through the TV, but with my Saturday morning job at the fish-n-chips shop on Camelia Avenue only paying $5 a shift, quitting school would've been necessary to afford a replacement. This boiling blood – it wasn't the standard anti-New South Wales sentiment I'd known to this point in my life. In past instances of Blue treachery – Bob Fulton calling the first Origin the 'non-event of the century', or Les Boyd breaking Darryl Brohman's jaw; or, a mere three weeks earlier, this same SCG crowd chanting 'WALLY SUCKS!' during the Origin 2 national anthem, to name a few – my reaction had fallen within a range of emotions generally considered acceptable for sporting fandom: ticked, disappointed, aggrieved, eyes rolled back far enough to see my brain stem. This was something else. Something deeper. Etched on the bones. Threaded through the marrow.

This was hate.

I hated that crowd. Their petulance. Their arrogance. Their unchecked privilege. I hated their stupid faces. Most of all, I hated this feeling of hate. Heart pounding. Guts roiling. Head spinning and tumbling like a car on the Zipper at the Ekka. So full of rage I wanted to scream and then cry and then scream again. These booing bastards – they'd done this to me. They'd made me feel this way.

They hadn't, though. In the darkest corner of my mind, I knew the sobering truth. The SCG crowd wasn't responsible for my descent into odium. They hadn't created a monster. The monster was there from the get-go. It was all me. I was a hater; I'd always been a hater. And now that I understood who I was, there was a choice to be made: embrace the low road of my true self or take the high road of personal temperance.

Just shy of four decades on, can I say which path won out?

To be honest, neither.

And both.

○

I try my best to keep Mr Hyde reined in. I'm able to admit there are things I can't hate about New South Wales. Sydney Harbour. Double-decker trains. The 2000 Olympics. Hunter Valley Shiraz. Authors such as Kate Grenville and Tara June Winch and Matthew

Reilly. Most of all, the little Northern Rivers town of Casino, near Lismore, site of some of my best childhood memories visiting Uncle Ralph, Aunty Dot and their house across the street from the Norco dairy factory. I can't hate Byron Bay and their wonderful Writers' Festival where I pretended to be famous for fifteen minutes. I've even come to terms with the idea that New South Wales has produced Origin combatants worthy of admiration: Tom Raudonikis, Steve Mortimer, Laurie Daley, Brad Fittler, Andrew Johns, Danny Buderus, James Tedesco. But what of the ultimate barometer of personal growth: forgiveness of that SCG crowd in 1984. Have I been able to reconcile their actions with commonplace human frailty and move on?

Paradoxically, I am very ashamed and very proud to say I've done no such thing.

Why, after all this time, does the incident still inspire such a visceral response in me? There are two reasons, and both speak to the DNA that, for better or worse, makes me who I am. The first is that quintessential Australian ideal: a fair go. Those booing punters, confronted with a worthy challenge to their longstanding "right" as the golden child of rugby league, sided with spitting the dummy over sharing the sand pit, punching down rather than extending a hand. I railed against that lack of a fair go at the tender age of fifteen and, as my life's journey attests, in subsequent years too, when the stakes were much higher and much more important than respect for the role of Kangaroos Captain.

The second reason is simple: they insulted my father. All through the decades-long trial of Maroon exodus and embarrassment, he never once booed a Blue wearing the green and gold, let alone captains like Graeme Langlands and Bob McCarthy and Max Krilich. The thought of it never even occurred to him. There's no hate in his heart. He was then, and remains now, a fundamentally good person with a grounded perspective and a generous spirit. He's better than most. Better than me, for sure.

I still aspire to be as he was that fateful July 7 afternoon in 1984, viewing the scene with sympathy instead of anger, passing the gentlest of judgements upon a rabble undeserving of leniency:

They don't get it.

He could justifiably render the same verdict on his hater eldest son:

Darren, you don't get it.

Perhaps, with the best elements of his nature and nurture to lean on, I might one day.

6

A Note of Clueless Gratitude

July 1, 1986
Origin Game #3, Lang Park, Brisbane
Score: NSW 18 – Qld 16

Origin wasn't the be-all and end-all in 1985 and 1986. They were my grade eleven and twelve years and there were bigger priorities. Studies and the looming TE score to determine my after-high school pathway. Learning to drive. The awkward dance of easing out of an old friendship group and ingratiating myself into a new one. The prospect of Schoolies Week. And girls – by far the biggest point of emphasis during this time. Having spent the previous five years at an all-Bros Catholic school, negotiating the co-ed landscape of Mount Maria Senior College was a rollercoaster to rival the Thunderbolt at Dreamworld. So many vexing questions. How do you talk to girls? How do you fool them into thinking you're interesting and cool? How do you like a girl without it being painfully obvious to everyone? What do you say when it turns out she likes the guy you sit beside in English? And how do you not write pages of crap poetry as a result? More generally, how do you avoid presenting as a gormless, hormone-riddled loser 99% of the time? The answers were beyond me.

Dad was no help. For all his admirable qualities as a parent, he was loath to engage with my rampant puberty. Pulling me aside to talk female physiology, sitting me down to discuss risky behaviour, fireside chats about the birds and the bees… there was Buckley's he was doing any of that. Why would he? Why forego silence when you belonged to the Silent Generation? All the things you'd rather not talk about with your kids – you could keep your mouth shut and legitimately claim you were just being true to your historical moniker.

'Dad, what do I do if I get a stiffy in class?'

'I'm sorry, son. As a card-carrying member of the Silent Generation, I am contractually obligated to respond with a firm "No comment"…'

Consequently, I attempted to figure things out on my own or with the help of guy friends just as clueless as myself. It went about as well as you'd expect.

With the follies of adolescence consuming my every waking minute, there wasn't much energy left over for the Maroons. Fortuitously, in the end. The sting of our first series loss in '85, and then Origin's first 3-0 whitewash the following year, wasn't nearly as painful as it would've been in the past. Few memories from those two years have survived the test of time. Greg Dowling giving Terry Fearnley a spray. My father's constant reference to Noel Cleal as a "big girl's blouse". Wally Lewis' man-of-the-match performance in the '85 Game 2 loss (it didn't make up for the defeat, but it added to the King's legend). The traitor, Michael O'Connor, in sky blue, mocking his previous representation of Queensland in rugby union.

Amongst this gaggle of hazy recollections is the lone stand-out: New South Wales' incessant talk of Origin's demise following the Blues' Game 3 win in '86.

It doesn't mean more to Queensland!

We've figured it out now!

The natural order has been restored!

Get ready for a return to the '70s!

Though I was (and remain) a natural-leaning sports pessimist, invariably gravitating towards the worst possible imaginings for my teams' fortunes, I couldn't abide this guff. The '86 series was a toss-up; the margins of victory six, four and two respectively. We could just as easily have won 3-0 ourselves. Okay, there was no denying the Blues had unearthed a group of players with the requisite passion and belief to match their skill. Game 3 of '86 was compelling evidence of that fact. Facing a Maroon outfit playing at home and desperate to avoid the ignominy of a whitewash, they made a solitary penalty goal stand up as the winning margin, holding us scoreless in the second half for an 18-16 victory. But the whole business of claiming the death of the Origin experiment and the fallacy of the Queensland spirit – it was, to say the least, misguided.

In the decades to come, I would realise that 1986 was the first of three Origin obituaries New South Wales would gleefully peddle. The second was prior to the 1995 series, the third in the lead-up to the 2006 games. In all cases, the death knell was predicated on the Blues seeking an unprecedented triumph. In all cases, the triumph was considered a mere formality. In all cases, the only casualty was their arrogant assumption.

I look at those instances of eating crow and, though I delight in them as a Maroon fan, I also see them as a valuable lesson, for which I am constantly grateful. And here in these pages, on the public record, I'd like to express that gratitude with a brief heartfelt note.

Dearest New South Wales,

It's a sad fact: you were clueless at the end of 1986. A time of prosperity had you believing it would last forever. A period of wearing the crown had you proclaiming a divine right. That girl you were convinced really liked you — she didn't. She liked the guy sitting beside you in English. Not just in '86, but in 1995 and 2006 as well.

It's tough finding out you're wrong, especially when you were so certain of being right. But your mistake need not be in vain. The rest of us can carry forward the enduring lesson of your hubris: be humble. Resist the temptation to get ahead of yourself. Know when you don't know.

Thank you, Blues. Thank you for this priceless gift.

Yours cluelessly,

Darren

7

No Body

July 15, 1987
Origin Game #3, Lang Park, Brisbane
Score: Qld 10 – NSW 8

Exiting high school, my TE score was good enough to get into my first-choice degree: Bachelor of Human Movement Studies at the University of Queensland. I was pleased. The life goal captioning my mugshot in the Mount Maria 1986 Senior Yearbook – "My ultimate aim is to be a PE teacher" – was set for launch. At least, I thought that was my life goal. Truth be told, there hadn't been much thought put into the thought. The premise for the decision to study Human Movements – I loved sport and I was good at it – was hardly a deep dive into Fundamental Darren. The immutable understanding that writing was my true calling would not be clear until the PE teacher pathway was well established and, in many ways, too difficult to abandon. (One of my alternate course selections for uni was journalism, so perhaps my knowledge of self wasn't completely superficial. I wonder sometimes about where a journey in media might've taken me. Maybe this memoir would be a State of Origin crime novel instead? *A mastermind is murdering members of the Queensland Dynasty team, and the only clues to the killer are Tim Brasher's mullet and John Hopoate's index finger...Fortunately, Detective Adam Mogg is on the case...).*

If Dad had any inkling that I wasn't clued in to my destined gig, he never said. As always, he and Mum were content to support whatever decision I made. The closest he ever came to putting his foot down on my future was his insistence I sit for the Public Service entrance exam as a fallback option, which I duly did, passing with flying colours (I topped the state in dictation).

'You could be a walk-up start for a Railway clerk job tomorrow,' he assured me. 'If you needed it.'

I didn't need it. I was bound for the University of Queensland, and he and Mum were pleased as punch. Until then, no one on either side of the family had ever attended university. Both my parents had left school for the workforce well before graduation, Dad exiting after Year 8, Mum after Year 9. Des and Kathy Groth being the ones to have their eldest enter the hallowed halls of tertiary education – it was as much their achievement as it was mine. Through years of hard work and sacrifice, they'd ushered in a new era.

They weren't alone – breaking dawns were everywhere in Queensland in 1987. The Fitzgerald Inquiry commenced in May, paving the way for the state to purge the despotism and corruption of Joh Bjelke-Petersen's two-decade premiership. Construction for Expo '88 – the event that would prove Brisbane's coming-out party – was in full swing. A new wave of local writers including John Birmingham, Nick Earls and Andrew McGahan were honing their craft, readying to take the national literary stage by storm in the '90s. The pieces were falling into place for the Brisbane Broncos' celebrated entry into the NSW Rugby League. And for the Maroons, a pocket-size twenty-year-old rookie exploded on the scene, defying the many doubters who argued he wasn't built for rugby league, let alone State of Origin.

◇

I arrived at the University of Queensland (UQ) campus with a host of insecurities. *I'll get lost every day. I won't handle the workload. I don't have any friends from school in my course. I won't get another part-time job if I quit lugging trolleys at the Everton Park Coles.*

I don't like my body.

To be fair, UQ wasn't responsible for the anxiety about my physique – that delightful condition was years in the making before my first step off the bus at St Lucia. Throughout high school, I was hyper-conscious of my skinny, underweight frame, and how far it fell short of the prevailing male ideal. The fact I was a good athlete, and the fact I was a good athlete with traits traditionally associated with muscle – speed and power – made the situation worse. At district carnivals I invariably found myself on the starting blocks of the 100 metres sandwiched by "men" I envied; to my left a human fridge with a chest hairier than a stage production of "Grease", to my right a King Kong stand-in with thighs as big as my torso. Off the track, the message of deficiency was further reinforced, even when no malice was intended:

'You look like an athlete, Darren.'

'Thank you.'

'Long-distance, right? You have that marathon runner's build. Thin and bony.'

My "chicken" legs were a particular source of angst – in my eyes, more pipe cleaners than limbs, stamped with a pair of patellae the size of muffins, ankles so puny that gripping them would see thumb and forefinger form a closed circle. To give my legs the illusion of volume, I donned shorts down to my knees (fortunately, Stubbies were no longer *du jour*) and wore thick tube socks or two pairs of regular socks with my runners, preferably basketball high-tops. I might've been the only male in my time at Marcellin College and then Mt Maria Senior who relished wearing uniform trousers all year round.

The incident that best sums up the struggle I had with body positivity in high school occurred in Year 9. The scene: a work experience stint at Gary Duggan's sports store on Waterworks Road in Ashgrove. Duggan was a Wests alum who'd won a premiership with the team in 1975, the year before my first Panther-inspired visit to Lang Park as a six-year-old. He also owned a racehorse, which seemed to occupy 98% of his time in the store. While I went about tidying, dusting, alphabetising files and collecting lunch, Duggan would lean against the counter chatting with various drop-in buddies about his charge, how it was working with the trainer, its chances of winning on the weekend, and generally how bloody expensive it was to own a galloper. It was on one of these occasions that a member of Duggan's entourage noticed me testing the pressure of a Steeden on the shelf.

'Hey, this kid could be a jockey for you, Gaz!' he declared. 'We should get him in the saddle on Saturday!'

There were laughs and nods from the posse, then estimations of the meagre kilos I carried and whether I would need extra weight to ride Gary's nag. I smiled and shrugged, all the while dying inside. Why this comment at this time was such a blow, I can't say. There'd been numerous instances in the past, frequent bruises to the ego. My 'girl's wrists'. My 'xylophone ribs'. My 'monkey arms'. Maybe this one just caught me flat-footed, off-balance. Or maybe it was a last straw for a young teen still awaiting puberty's rescue. At home that evening, I locked myself in the bathroom and took off my shirt. Stared at my paltry upper body. The pointy shoulders, the slight chest. Collarbones jutting like shopfront canopies. I tensed, made a fist with my right hand and drove it into my stomach. I did it again. And again. And again. Then I cried.

Four years later at UQ, the punch to the guts was figurative rather than literal and not self-administered. Theoretically, uni was a place to feel more comfortable in your skin, especially when contrasted with the hellscape of high school. You could point to various campus locales where your physical appearance and attributes didn't seem so dire compared to the surrounding mix (the Anatomy faculty's morgue for example – I can say with reasonable confidence I looked better than 95% of the folks in there, living and dead). The Human Movements building, though, couldn't be counted among the safe spaces. Not because of any malignant culture – some of the nicest, most supportive people you'd ever meet were to be found in the HM Common Room. The reason was everyone looked so *good*. Conventionally good would be today's qualifier, but good nonetheless. And it was little surprise the résumés matched the physiques. Nationally ranked triathlete, state rep netballers and softballers, future Wallaby, A-grade QRL player, volleyball prodigy… It seemed everywhere I turned, there was a reminder that I was a "no body".

So, what was to be done about it? Thankfully, my skin had grown a little thicker since my Tyler Durden episode in the bathroom. I hit the gym, kicking off a life-long love affair with resistance training. I hung out with friends from faculties that weren't so tanned and buff. I avoided an esteem-crushing nickname (a buddy wanted to call me "Manto", alluding to a praying mantis-like appearance – I managed to get out of it by convincing him people would think he was referencing a new Toyota sedan). And in my rugby league fandom, I cheered loudest for players that achieved greatness without the leg-up of being built like Ian Roberts.

〜

When you're small, you must prove you can play.
When you're big, you must prove you can't.

I forget who is responsible for this quote, but its truth is self-evident. Sport history is peppered with both scenarios: legends driven by the questioning of their physical gifts; busts given the benefit of the doubt due to their perfect bodies. In State of Origin, the ultimate example of the former is Allan Langer. When "Alf" was plucked from the Ipswich Jets to wear the number seven for the Maroons in '87, plenty of people had reservations about his sixty-eight-kilogram frame, foremost among them Coach Wayne Bennett who'd wanted the more robust, Sydney-based Laurie Spina selected instead. Recognising a fellow no body, I desperately wanted Langer to prove he could play, and to my delight the proof was apparent from the get-go.

Alf was outstanding in Game 1 and probably would've won man of the match had Queensland not been defeated (aka robbed) by Mark McGaw's infamous fingernail touchdown and referee Mick Stone's seeing-eye dog decision. Game 2 would further confirm that Langer belonged. On the quagmire of the SCG, the twenty-year-old tormented the Blues with his jack-rabbit speed and deft grubbers; in defence he was pure courage, grassing New South Wales forwards with the judo-throw tackling technique that would become his trademark. The enduring image of the match – Langer walking off the field victorious, Wally Lewis' arm draped over his shoulder, the King's lips smooching the side of his head – appropriately summed up my feelings on Alf's effort.

And then there was Game 3.

The decider of '87 was when I first understood not only Alf's magnificence as a player, but his superpower beyond the game, the positive gravitational pull he could exert upon my orbit of insecurity and self-doubt. I watched the live broadcast of the match in, of all places, Cooroy, on the Sunshine Coast hinterland. A friend from high school had invited a group of her fellow Mt Maria '86 grads along for a reunion of sorts and, although a shared Origin viewing was not the purpose of the trip, we found ourselves huddled around the TV on the evening of July 15.

There is a raft of memories from that night. The game itself was a classic (many still consider it the greatest Origin tilt of all-time). No points were scored by either team in a monumentally tense, faintly Shakespearean second half, while a devastating hit delivered by the King on Michael O'Connor became emblematic of Queensland being "seen" through Origin (more on that later). Amongst our group, there were moments I recall with alacrity. A girl I'd never heard swear before transformed into a wharfie. Another kept leaping up from her chair, sledging and shadowboxing every time it was advantage Maroons. My buddy Glen, later to become a leading criminal lawyer in Brisbane, bowed and genuflected every time Wally Lewis touched the ball. A trio of friends professing to be ambivalent about the game shouted and screamed and clung to emotional-support cushions throughout the final excruciating ten minutes. When the final hooter sounded, the living room became a rave, all of us hugging and jumping and cheering and dancing and shadowboxing with unbridled ecstasy.

While these scenes live long in my memory, the standout remains Allan Langer and what he gifted me personally with his stunning man-of-the-match performance. Seeing a player like him – a mere two years older and five kilos heavier than me – slay the beast of State of Origin gave me a sense of possibility that wasn't there before his emergence. If a nobody, and a no body, like him could reach such heights, could I do the same? Could I reach peak Darren Groth, the maximizing of my potential?

As Fate would have it, my best Allan Langer impression wouldn't be in athletics or cricket or tennis or basketball or anything else my skinny, fast-twitch-fibre physique had shown a propensity for – it would instead be on the page. And while there are plenty of literary heroes I can point to as inspiration for the writing successes that came my way, the most influential figure may well have been the tiny blonde kid from the Ipswich Jets who became a towering figure in Origin folklore.

8

Canned Heat

May 31, 1988
Origin Game #2, Lang Park, Brisbane
Score: Qld 16 – NSW 6

In the 1988 series, I went to Game 2 at Lang Park without my father.

There was no earth-shattering reason for the decision, no flashpoint moment that brought about this new reality. The Hollywood scene where Dad pleads to go with me, just once more, for old time's sake, whaddaya reckon son, and I sigh, shake my head and depart, leaving my father slumped on the couch, clutching a photo of me as a child in one hand and a Carlton Mid-Strength in the other, tearfully watching old Betamax tapes of Maroon triumphs… it didn't happen. There was simply the natural drift of a young man stepping out of the patriarchal shadow and into the light of his own identity. Or, minus the poetic nobility, there was simply the distance initiated by a solipsistic son with less time and energy to spend with his old man.

If my separation tested the strength of our bond, it never approached the point of collapse. In all the years of our relationship, I can't recall a time when Dad and I weren't speaking to each other, or where I went out of my way to avoid him. There were arguments, sure. And incidents. If we had to do it all again, both of us would change a few things, and not just during the span of my adolescence. Dad has told me numerous times he regrets using corporal punishment on us three boys (although, he always qualifies the statement – accurately – by saying, 'I only whacked you when you deserved it'). He erred badly when he browbeat a reluctant Learner-Driver Darren to take on our tight squeeze of a driveway, resulting in a crumpled left fender and a withering spray from Mum about how he should've listened to his son. He's also admitted that he and Kath could've handled the stresses of work and money better, preferably without the shouting matches that rattled the house's foundations and gave me pause regarding the health of their marriage. For my part, I'd re-think several of my poorer decisions. I would not swim out too far at Coolum Beach, compelling a panicked Dad to come after me and almost drown in the process. I would not act like a petulant child when having to spend New Year's Eve with Aunty Mona in Rockhampton instead of with my year twelve mates in Brisbane. I would not chug ungodly amounts of vodka prior to Jenna Paterson's party, disgrace myself at said party by throwing up everywhere, require a hide-out when the cops turned up, stagger home, then throw up again in our living room while my shocked and appalled parents looked on, wondering where they'd gone wrong.

And I would absolutely, positively, not do the worst thing I ever did to my father.

Occurring on an otherwise unremarkable Sunday at our McConaghy Street home in 1985, it was a few seconds of blind heat triumphing over sanity. It was instantly regrettable. It remains infamous to this day.

For any fan acquainted with the 62nd minute of Game 2 in the 1988 Origin series, 'blind heat', 'instantly regrettable', and 'infamous to this day' may sound familiar.

Before it became Suncorp Stadium – Greatest Rugby League Venue in the World, the real Lang Park, the true nature of "The Cauldron", resided on the licensed terraces at the Caxton Street end.

Prior to 1988, I'd spectated in every part of the ground except the terraces: Frank Burke Stand, Hale Street Stand, on the hill at the Milton Road end. I'd been adjacent to the terraces a couple of times, the first as a wide-eyed youngster viewing Australia versus France and Wally Lewis' home debut in the green and gold number six, the second as a newly-minted uni student witnessing Brothers' BRL grand final win – the last one ever played – in 1987. On both occasions, particularly the King's turnout for Australia, the terraces were lively and joyous, a ramshackle collection of playful boozy diehards, their vibe not so radically different from the rest of the ground. Come Origin, they were a different animal. I realised how different when I was in amongst it for the first time.

The terraces were packed. Sardine-level packed. The primary effect of this cloying human proximity was hair-trigger tension. Mid-game, you dared not get some fresh air or head for the bar or visit the toilets for fear of spilling beers or stepping on toes or tripping over bodies. The consequences of such effrontery, though accidental, could be a tirade or a scuffle or an ejection or, surprise surprise, a shower of cans.

Let's be real about can-throwing at Lang Park: it happened all the time. Most often it was a random tinnie lobbing from one section of the masses to another. Invariably, the rando was empty and tossed without any intent beyond "my alcoholic beverage is depleted, ergo I have no compelling reason to continue grasping this receptacle". The one time you saw collective, targeted can action was when a brave (read: masochistic) New South Wales fan would gather up their flag and run what I called 'The Gauntlet': the concrete pathway at ground level that started in front of the scoreboard and ended at the cyclone fence separating the terraces from the Hale Street grandstand. As the Blues punter bolted past, a squadron of dead marines would fall from the sky seeking, at worst, to knock the runner off stride and, at best, to take out the flag. It reads like a nasty attack, but the Gauntlet runs were generally theatrical, even light-hearted. Blues' fans knew what they were in for, the terraces duly obliged. And the cans being thrown were for the most part empty.

There was nothing theatrical or light-hearted about the volcano that erupted when Wally Lewis was sent to the sin bin in the 62nd minute of Game 2, 1988. In the lead-up, it was obvious the already on-the-ledge crowd didn't need much encouragement to jump. Things were not going to plan. We'd dominated the opener in Sydney, leading 26-6 until two consolation tries for the Blues made the result respectable. More impressive than the score was the fact we'd done it minus Lewis, who'd sat out the first Origin of his career due to a shoulder injury. With the King returning and the Maroons back on home turf, Game 2 promised to be a victory lap. But here we were, entering the pointy end of the contest and the Blues leading 6-4. In my little spectator group, there were furrowed brows and folded arms. My buddy Carl was imploring Mal Meninga to 'Do something! For once!'. My mate Glen was asserting that we wouldn't be in this position if the selectors had retained Scott Tronc in the side (he appreciated the Souths Magpies forward more for his name than his footballing ability). I was contemplating the merit of these comments when a spat between Phil Daley and Greg

"Turtle" Conescu became an all-out melee. When order was restored, the 31,000-strong screams of 'OFF! OFF! OFF!' were answered by ref Mick Stone. Only, it wasn't the punishment we were craving.

As the Emperor of Lang Park trudged to the sideline, the cans came from everywhere. Stockpiles had seemingly been hoarded just for this moment. In the ten rows closest to the field, people ducked and weaved and covered up as the barrage bore down. A fan in a Redcliffe jersey and beanie wore a blow to the back of his head — he shook it off, picked up the offending missile and hurled it in the direction of Wayne Pearce. Awash in the red mist, I turned to Carl in time to see him wind up and unleash. He would later claim to have hit the corner post with his toss. I then stared at the XXXX in my own hand. It was two-thirds full, a decent weight. With my cricketer's arm, I fancied I could make it onto the field. I gripped the can tighter, blood thrumming in my ears, fury and indignation coursing through my veins. I wanted to throw. I *needed* to throw.

Nothing could hold me back.

I don't remember the reason I clashed with my father on that innocuous Sunday in 1985. After 40 years, it remains the only thing I can't recall about the incident.

He stands in the doorway of my bedroom; I'm next to my bed, facing him. The distance between us? Eight feet, maybe ten. There is back and forth. I want my way. He won't allow it. I demand a negotiation. He isn't falling for it. My emotional ascent is rocket-like, lifting off from a launch pad of confusion, surging through incredulity and frustration before entering the stratosphere of anger. Dad is unfazed, calm, resolute in what he requires of me. Before long, I've reached the line that must not be crossed.

I cross, egged on by unconscious rage.

The effect is immediate. Dad's eyes get big. His mouth falls open. His face sags, blurring at the edges. He is equal parts shock and defeat. Through traces of a quiver in his chin, he manages to ask:

'You really want to do that?'

A circuit-breaker. The molten heat is doused and self-awareness returns. I take stock of my body. Shoulders bunched. Feet planted. Toes curled like talons inside my Dunlop Volleys. The clenched jaw and gritted teeth are genetic hand-me-downs from Mum – Dad is all too familiar with these traits, though he's never witnessed them in such a disturbing context. I arrive at my hands. They're held at my hips. Balled tight. Unmistakably fists. Primed. Ready. Their intent as stark as the white of my knuckles.

What have I done?

It's clear now. Dad is wounded. Shattered. Heart torn from his chest. And for what? Some tawdry teenage hill-to-die-on that will dissolve in the test of time. I can see in his devastation: he blames himself. A son shaping up to fight his old man – this is what happens when fathers are bad. When fathers fail. But he isn't bad, and he hasn't failed. This isn't on him. This isn't karmic justice for those occasional whacks across the hand with the belt when I stuffed up. This is an immature boy obeying his amygdala rather than his frontal cortex, a young adult male pressing the nukes button when a grenade would've sufficed. This is on me. I know this is on me because, despite my temporary insanity, I know my father's heart. And his heart is broken.

Later in the day, I will apologise and beg his forgiveness. He will hide the last of his hurt, wave a hand, and invoke one of his own father's quotes: 'If it was raining mansions, I'd get hit with a dunny.' I'm not sure what he means, but I love him for saying it. The following month, he'll claim to have forgotten the incident.

I will never forget it.

Even if I wanted to, the 62nd minute of Origin 2 in 1988 guarantees its unflinching place in my memory.

⬭

Can in hand, I readied to add my salvo to the attack.

It was then that Dad's face appeared in my mind's eye. The look was instantly and painfully familiar: a flash of horrified disbelief followed by a rictus of crushing despair. And then the inevitable words:

You really want to do that?

I took in the surrounding scene. Cans were still flying, but in fewer numbers. Perhaps others in the crowd were now seeing the anguished faces of their fathers. On the field, the Blues, after receiving the penalty and kicking for touch, were milling about like lost sheep. We would later discover they were justifiably contemplating a walk-off. On the sideline, a ballboy in a Maroon tracksuit had taken it upon himself to return fire, heaving tinnie after tinnie back into the terraces. I took a deep breath, lowered my throwing arm. I brought the can to my lips and drank it dry, the last of the beer spilling over my chin. Then I sat on the hard concrete step and stood the empty can upright between my feet. When the game was settled – a Maroon come-from-behind win that many attributed to the events of the 62nd minute – I carried the empty to Roma Street Station before tossing it in a bin on platform 5.

Dad was watching his tape of the game when I got home. He knew my section had been in the eye of the storm.

'Did you throw one?' he asked.

'No,' I replied. 'I wanted to, but…no. And anyway, it was two-thirds full.'

He scrutinised my face for a moment then smiled.

'Yeah, you can't throw a full one.'

I take no pride in the fact I held onto my can in 1988. And I don't consider myself above those who acted on their worst instincts. But for the cautionary tale of three years earlier, I might've been one of the first to let loose. In the end, Game 2 in '88 merely confirmed the hard truth of my Maroon obsession: I would forever need external forces for good to deliver me from chaos. Left to my own devices, I would always give in to the dark side.

Today, the can-throwing riot is celebrated as much as scorned. In recalling the night on Channel Nine's "Great Origin Stories", Peter Sterling accurately sums up the incident's revisionist history by labelling it 'a bit unsavoury' and 'part of folklore when it comes to Origin football'. For what it's worth, I look back on the moment as the sad end to a more honourable era in Maroon fandom. Via a hail of XXXX, we showed that our days of passionate support without the threat of violence were through. Like me, the Queensland faithful would need checks and balances to avoid future disgrace. And they would come soon enough. The can would be banned. The serving of alcohol would be cut off midway through the second half. The terraces would be replaced by individual seating.

Perhaps if they'd shown my father's distraught face on the scoreboard in the 61st minute of Game 2 in 1988, it might've all been unnecessary.

9

This Is How It Will Always Be

May 23, 1989
Origin Game #1, Lang Park, Brisbane
Score: Qld 36 – NSW 6

June 14, 1989
Origin Game #2, SFS, Sydney
Score: Qld 16 – NSW 12

June 28, 1989
Origin Game #3, Lang Park, Brisbane
Score: Qld 36 – NSW 16

In 1980, the ardent, one-eyed Queenslander arguing for the Origin concept and supporting it from the outset was fuelled by a belief held as incontrovertible fact: Maroon players in their rightful Maroon jerseys would reveal the true balance of power in interstate football. Queensland – historically the doormat, in the '70s a laughingstock – would rise like Lazarus touched by the Footy Christ, and rule like Odin giving don't argues to all and sundry in Asgard.

By the end of State of Origin's first decade, those ardent 1980 fans seemed measured and temperate, their lone eyes in possession of 20-20 vision. The first game in 1989 was a smash-up. New South Wales had turned to Jack Gibson following five straight losses and hopes were high the master coach could end the Blues' streak of futility. The enormity of the task was summed up by the cheesy "Mission: Impossible" intro to the Channel Nine broadcast which featured a trench-coat clad Gibson listening to his taped instructions in a public phone booth, choosing to accept the gig, then dumping the tape in a nearby bin before it self-destructed. Regrettably for Gibson, the mission in Game 1 self-destructed the moment a 19-year-old Laurie Daley missed a sitter from in front in the 21st minute. After that, the Maroons rolled, piling on seven tries in a 36-6 walloping. At the time, it was the biggest ever margin of victory for a Queensland side.

I was on the Caxton Street terraces again for this tilt (needless to say, the natives were much better behaved after the fiasco of '88, despite the opportunity for mayhem afforded by – believe it or not – another Wally Lewis sin-binning by Mick Stone late in the first half. The score had a lot to do with the calmer response. So, too, the hordes of police patrolling the scene). My enduring memory from the game came courtesy of Mal Meninga. The future Immortal scored two tries that night, both in our section of the ground, both sensational efforts backing up the ball carrier. For each score, the big fella rolled over while grounding the ball, got to his feet, stood in a superhero-like pose and pointed a finger; the first time a quick acknowledgement of his celebrating teammates, the second a more demonstrative assertion directed towards the Milton Road end.

That second finger-point spoke to me. It said: 'Here's the way forward, and the way forward is more of the same.' The 1980s had started with scepticism and doubt; it was ending with validation and affirmation. In that first Origin "experiment", when Artie Beetson ran out to the deafening roar of my father and the rest of Maroon Nation, the naysayers' imagined best outcome was that Queensland might have a puncher's chance against the Blues in future. Pivot to 1989 and Mal Meninga's digit was telling the naysayers where they could go. Puncher's chance? No. The decade showed we were the better fighter. We wore the title belt.

Game 2 in Sydney suggested we might even be Muhammad Ali. Faced with an injury toll as devastating as George Foreman's left hook – Alf Langer broken leg, Mal Meninga fractured eye socket, Paul Vautin busted elbow, Michael Hancock dud shoulder, Bob Lindner broken ankle – and ending the game with only twelve men on the park, the phenomenal Maroons prevailed through a Trevor "Axe" Gillmeister special to Paul Harragon's ribs and a subsequent "rope-a-dope" run to the tryline by, who else, but Walter James Lewis. With the series secured so sensationally, and multiple changes required due to the injuries, one could've forgiven the Maroons for a below par effort in Game 3 back at Lang Park. Perish the thought. A patched-up Queensland squad finished full of running for a 36-16 triumph, ending the '80s with an extraordinary eight-game win streak.

Watching the King lift the shield for the sixth time in eight years, a thought landed in my mind, nestling among the questions I had about my own place in the world: this is right. This is the standard. Not the eight-in-a-row or the casualty ward win in Game 2 – those were spectacular rarities, glorious shooting stars in the Maroon night sky. They might happen again; such was Queensland's singular Origin DNA. But they weren't the standard. The fundamental fact underpinning the years ahead was much simpler, much more grounded: we had arrived.

We are here.

We are home.

There would, of course, be disappointments. Tough losses, heartbreaking finishes. As it is in life, things wouldn't always work out. It didn't change what was immutable. It didn't alter the abiding narrative of the story. We would eventually find a way. We would feast on the doubters. We would win more than our fair share.

We are here.

We are home.

This is how it will always be.

2022

10

Family Company

June 8, 2022
Origin Game #1, Stadium Australia, Sydney
Halftime (Part 1)
Score: Qld 6 – NSW 4

It's a big crowd at Chateau Groth. Not a sell-out, though. My own little family is absent: Beautiful Wife Wendy (at work), Gorgeous Twin #1 Chloe (upstairs, working on their comic), and Wondrous Twin #2 Jared (at his disability day program). In the fifteen years since leaving Brisbane, Wend — best person I will ever know and an empath through and through — has often lamented my lack of in-house company for Origin viewing. Nothing could be further from the truth this morning. My brother Sean and his son Riley have jetted in from the UK; they're seated, respectively, on the left edge of the couch and the armchair by the sliding back door. I'm surprised their positions aren't swapped. At some point the senior party will want a durry, and unfettered access to the courtyard would surely be his preference. Fifty-one years old, Sean — a compelling mix of scruffy and debonair, hard edges of his Aussie accent chipped away by three decades of Anglo-idiom — has never had a sliver of interest in State of Origin or the Maroons. But he's delighted to be here, on the other side of the world, in Vancouver for the first time since 1995, part of a family reunion delayed for two years by Covid, a new admirer of the Caesar (do not call it a Bloody Mary), in the midst of a hard-earned respite from the woes of his marriage separation.

Youngest brother Simon, forty-six, clad in a Regurgitator 'Tu-Plang' tee-shirt, has folded his six-foot-three frame onto one of our Bunya pine chairs. He was a late bloomer in the Maroon garden, his investment in the team largely due to the enthusiastic interest of his teenage kids: son Xavier and daughter Genevieve. Queensland is not his primary sporting love, however — that honour belongs to the San Francisco Giants of Major League Baseball. A Frisco writing gig in 2012 happened to coincide with the Giants' run to a World Series crown and Simon was instantly smitten. It irks me he went halfway around the world to find his fandom while ignoring a perfectly good obsession ten minutes' drive from his two-storey Queenslander in Newmarket. But I can't argue with how it happened. In searching for a life partner, we all hope to be struck by lightning.

Mum is at the dining table, open copy of my new novel at her elbow. She's performing her usual Origin role: loyal but detached sidekick to Dad. There are things she knows about the game — Queensland coach Billy Slater was once a trackwork jockey, nineteen-year-old winger Selwyn Cobbo hails from Cherbourg, retired legend turned Channel Nine commentator Cam Smith is a very good-looking man. None of that knowledge should be construed as anything beyond circumstantial and / or accidental. After all these years, Mum would still rather attend a funeral than watch Origin. Indeed, Mum has become something of an expert in funerals, particularly the ones she's put together for herself and Dad. Arranged and paid for so that 'my three boys don't have to worry', she's taken advantage of our first family get-together in nearly a decade to dole out a swathe of personal items prior to our parents' seemingly imminent departure. Among those handed to me: a portrait of my grandparents' house on Barton Road, Hawthorne, and a poem I wrote for Grandma Costigan about said Barton Road house. The piece de resistance? Dad's priceless 1987 Queensland game guernsey. Bobby Lindner's number eight, signed by the man himself. I never asked for the jumper — it never occurred to me that it could be given away. I was certain Dad would be buried in it at his meticulously planned-in-advance funeral.

Rounding out the family rollcall is the rugby league patriarch himself: the Mitchie Maroon, former backrower for the Railway Institute, number thirteen of fourteen kids sired by George and Cecelia, the one, the only, Desmond Eric Groth. Dad is in the middle of the couch, wearing the 2021 iteration of the Queensland jersey, "DES 80" emblazoned on the back. The shirt clings so snugly to his Grandpa bod I fear he may need a crowbar to remove it. This genial gent is the source, the cradle, the origin of my state. Queensland is in his blood. So, too, cancer. During lockdown, Dad was diagnosed with multiple myeloma, an incurable condition in which cancerous plasma builds in the bone marrow and overwhelms healthy blood cells. To the infinite relief of all in the room and hundreds more friends and family around the globe, it was caught early enough to carry a sentence of life rather than death. Each month since diagnosis, he's been receiving infusions of Zoledronic Acid to strengthen his bones and, thus far, the situation has remained stable, to the point of Dad finding himself on the trip he and his health insurer thought could never happen. I'd like to think it's the Queenslander in his veins stopping the disease in its tracks. I'd like to think we have many more Maroon triumphs in our future.

Who am I kidding? In cancer, as in Origin, nothing is guaranteed. Dad's blood could turn on him tomorrow. His immune-compromised system could succumb to Covid on the flight back home, proving Mum's funeral fixation to be depressingly prescient rather than a running joke. As for the game, Queensland may have gone to the sheds up 6-4, but we're coming off the worst statistical defeat in the Origin era; the aggregate for the 2021 series 94-26, despite a brave Maroon victory in Game 3. Who's to say this won't be another gut punch? And if it is, I have no choice but to sit here and watch it — a singular wretchedness I've largely avoided in Canada due to the 2:30am game times and the pain-limiting pragmatism of a look at the score first thing next morning. But there's no escape hatch today, no ejector seat. Like the famous snap of

Gorden Tallis and Terry Hill, I am nose-to-nose with the potential for torment: the Maroons could get rolled, and this might be the last game I ever watch with my father.

As I exit the lounge room and head for the loo, it dawns on me: in a very real sense, Queensland Origin has been the connective tissue of my life. For years, dates circled on the calendar with two million Sunshine State kin; in more recent times, an annual dose of identity in a foreign land. A jumping off point with new acquaintances; a safe place to land with old friends. Glorious affirmation that dreams can come true; crushing realisation that suffering is inevitable. And, not least of all, the gift of a precious, reliable, indestructible space built for two: me and my dad.

I need to write about this. For myself and my family, but for others too. Not just fellow Queenslanders or league tragics or sports obsessives. For anyone putting their hand up, anyone doing the hard yards. Anyone familiar with complete and irrational love. Anyone far from their literal or figurative home, clinging tight to the things that feed them, that make them who they are. I need to honour these well-travelled roads with a few words on the page.

Before it's too late.

The 1990s

11

I've Got a Little Girl to Look After Now

June 12, 1991
Origin Game #3, Lang Park, Brisbane
Score: Qld 14 – NSW 12

I was stunned.

A glance around the hill revealed many others similarly floored. Some were staring at each other, eyes wide, brows high on their foreheads. Some were airing an anguished cry: 'NOOOOOOO!'. One row down and to the right, a young girl wearing a jumper with Channel Seven's "Agro" screen-printed on the back was leaning against her father's hip, sobbing.

I turned to my own father. For the first time in seven years, we were together at Lang Park, Milton Road end, for a decider. Other Origins we'd attended had been special, but this one was set to stand on its own, courtesy of the just delivered bombshell over the PA.

Tonight was Wally Lewis' last game for Queensland.

I studied Dad, gauging his reaction. His arms were folded tight across his chest, blocking the passage of some internal surge, damming a wave beneath his ribs that was desperate to break. His grim gaze was fixed on the action, but there was a stirring behind the eyes. A film reel of unforgettable Lewis moments, no doubt. So many; almost too many to count. I was loath to interrupt his quiet reverie, but I couldn't ignore what had just happened. I couldn't pretend that our world hadn't just tilted on its axis.

'The end,' I said, pushing the incomprehensible words past the stone in my throat. 'All the talk during the week… it didn't seem real. But it is. This is the end.'

Dad leaned towards me, attention still on the game.

'Better make sure we win then.'

He spoke as if it were up to me, as if I could make it happen. And maybe I could. Maybe we all could. Wasn't it the reason the announcement had been made in the 70th minute, Maroons clinging to a 14-12 lead? Wasn't it the intent that the fabled Lang Park crowd should carry the boys to victory in the King's final ride? I was contemplating a pair of ill-advised pitch-invasion options to help ensure a win — streak across the field if the Blues looked likely to score? Coat hanger Ricky Stuart in a sneak attack at the next scrum? — when a chant of 'WALLY! WALLY! WALLY!' swept over the hill. And then, just as it was dying down, Dad revived the momentum by bursting into song. Borrowing the tune of "Tis the Season to be Jolly", it was a tribute he'd debuted to rave reviews seven years earlier, in the 1984 series:

'WALLY LEWIS WALKS ON WATER, FA-LA-LA-LA-LAAAA, LA-LA-LA-LA… WALLY LEWIS WALKS ON WATER, FA-LA-LA-LA-LAAAA, LA-LA-LA-LA… WALLY LEWIS WALKS ON WATER, FA-LA-LA-LA-LA-LAAAA, LA-LA-LA-LA… WALLY LEWIS WALKS ON WATER, FA-LA-LA-LA-LAAAA, LA-LA-LA-LA…'

(I know what you're thinking: it could really do with a second line. To my knowledge, Dad's never entertained one. I have. The best I've been able to come up with in forty-plus years are 'HE BELTS THE BLUES JUST LIKE HE OUGHTA, FA-LA-LA-LA-LAAAA, LA-LA-LA-LA…' and 'ALFIE TOO ALTHOUGH HE'S SHORTER, FA-LA-LA-LA-LAAAA, LA-LA-LA-LA…'. Hey, I never claimed they were *good* lines.)

I sang at the top of my lungs, summoning the difference-maker my father had challenged me to be. For sure the King could hear my voice above all the rest. Not because I was unique, or that I was any more deserving to be heard than the next Maroon fan. It was due to the news that had broken earlier in the day: Lewis' youngest child Jamie-Lee had been diagnosed as profoundly deaf. This revelation – it was the reason for the unfolding curtain call. And it had brought me closer to the King, within shouting distance of his circumstance. In this last hurrah, I was convinced: subsequent to my own recent insight into disability, I'd been granted, if only for this moment, a direct line to the great man.

◯

Coming out of university, the expectation for a first-year graduate teacher entering the state system was to spend their initial school stint in one of Queensland's country locales, build up service "points", then be transferred back to the capital when a place became available. Perhaps influenced by those hard formative years in Cloncurry and Hughenden, I wasn't keen to go country. Consequently, I was without a job when the 1991 school year commenced. By April, with friends settling into their posts in Cooktown and Gladstone and Mt Isa and Chinchilla, I was starting to wonder if I'd erred holding out for a local opportunity. Then word came through from one of my University of Queensland lecturers: a PE position was available in Ipswich. The proviso? It was teaching kids with disabilities.

I'd never envisaged myself in a special school role. I'd completed one education subject with a disability focus during the four years of my degree. Apart from a single session working with two kids for a total of ninety minutes, I had no practical experience teaching disabled youth. These were sound reasons to look beyond me; the Principals of Ipswich Special and Claremont Special weren't fazed. I was young, enthusiastic and wanted a job. And whispered with a hand over their mouths, I was that rare breed in the special school sector: a male. As far as they were concerned, I was over-qualified.

By the time I was in the Lang Park outer for Game 3, I'd been teaching all of eight weeks, but already it felt like I was part of something essential, something fundamentally shaping my world view for the better. I was getting to know kids I would remember for the rest of my life. Sam: the boy with Down Syndrome whose lips were always blue due to a hole in his heart; Chris: the lad on the autism spectrum who knew the flag of every country on the globe; Jenny: the girl who spoke in squeaks and required social distancing at all times due to unpredictable aggressive outbursts; Margie: the teen with the massive head scar and permanent smile. I was observing parents of all persuasions: the ones who were brilliant, the ones who were plugged in; the ones who were checked out, the ones who were nowhere to be found. I was learning that special schools were an afterthought in the education system, but that being an afterthought had its advantages, particularly the freedom and creativity it offered a teacher. I was gaining insight into a community that knew struggle on a daily basis and saw success in the things we take for granted.

The sense of all this new perspective was heightened when the news of Lewis' daughter broke. Of course, the challenge of deafness isn't directly comparable to that of Down Syndrome or spina bifida or autism. And teaching a disabled child is a YouTube clip next to the full-length feature of parenting said child. Nevertheless, I suddenly felt *sympatico* with the King. We were both at the start of a defining journey with disability and we both wanted a win in the '91 decider to propel us into this brave new world.

Our desire wouldn't be met without drama. The final minutes required heroic scramble defence, a timely Rod Wishart knock-on, and one last piece of brilliance from Lewis: a kick in general play that found touch a metre out from the Blues' line. When the final hooter sounded, we had prevailed. All of us, together. Seventeen brave, on-field combatants and three million shouting, screaming, royally bowing Queenslanders, thirty thousand of whom had helped Lang Park go supernova. The saying goes: it takes a village to raise a child; on this night, the Maroon village had helped to raise Jamie-Lee Lewis the only way we knew how: by sending her father out a winner.

In the post-match interview with Darrell Eastlake, it was no surprise to me that prioritising his disabled daughter's future framed the King's immortal, parting words:

'Yeah, that's it, mate… I've got a little girl to look after now. I love her very much.'

Watching on from the outer, I felt like I understood those words better than most.

I would understand them more than I could ever fathom in the years to come.

◯

Here's to Wally Lewis / For lacing on a boot
Sometimes he plays it rugged / Sometimes he plays it cute
He slices through a backline / Like a Stradbroke Island shark
There's glue on all his fingers / He's the Emperor of Lang Park

Along with the above song made famous by the XXXX TV commercial, the Lewis resume includes: thirty-one State of Origin games for Queensland, thirty as captain; thirty-four times wearing the green and gold of Australia, and Kangaroos skipper from 1984 to 1989; Golden Boot winner as best player in the world; named in rugby league's "Greatest 100 Players" and in the Kangaroos' "Team of the Century"; crowned rugby league's sixth "Immortal" in 1999.

The numbers and the recognitions don't come close to telling the tale. It's stating the obvious that Lewis meant much more to Queensland than his status as the state's greatest ever rugby league player and, arguably, the greatest to ever play the game. How much more? I doubt it can ever be properly assessed. What is the true measure of restoring hope and instilling pride, the chance to witness magic and the privilege to reign supreme? On his watch, we weren't the feckless backwater of the nation, Australia's Deep North. We could be anything. We could be anyone. We could be Thea Astley and Oodgeroo Noonuccal and Eddie Liu and Duncan Armstrong and Ted Smout and Powderfinger. We could be great.

For me, the perfect symbol of Lewis' gift to Queensland is his famous tackle on Michael O'Connor in the 1987 decider. O'Connor was the embodiment of our southern neighbours: slick, polished, fast, built to step around us and make us look like fools. We feared him, and every time he had room to move, I prayed for divine intervention. On that night, God not only answered my prayers, He wore the number six jersey.

O'Connor, in open space, plants his left boot in the Lang Park turf, unleashing his lethal jink. We knew the drill — our defender wrong-footed, embarrassed, grasping at thin air. We'd seen it so many times before. And so had the King, with eyes different to ours. Lewis doesn't over-commit; he somehow defies physics, tracking the step rather than being beaten by it, then lowers his shoulder. The hit is thunderous, collecting all that Blue arrogance in the ribs, sending Michael O'Connor's dancing toes skyward towards the tropical Brisbane night.

The tackle is talismanic. It is Queensland defiance, a line drawn in the Coolangatta sand. We are not yours to ridicule, to sneer at. We are not your "gone troppo" cousins to the north. Try to make us look foolish? We'll hit you with everything we have.

Wally Lewis was a sporting genius, the greatest footballer to walk the Earth, and one of us. He loved us, wholly and unapologetically. In the eternal words of rugby league's supreme ambassador, Tina Turner: he was simply the best.

It is said that disability is the one experience of diversity and marginalisation reserved for us all. Whether physical or cognitive or both, no one is immune.

Not even an Emperor.

In July 2023, Lewis revealed he is suffering early-onset dementia, more than likely the result of chronic traumatic encephalopathy (CTE). At the time of writing this, he'd recently delivered a speech at The National Press Club. In his address, he provided wonderful insight into his on-field greatness; how he could see the play before it happened, how his mind could process exactly what was needed: a kick early in the tackle count, a run at a tiring opponent, a big hit to change momentum. He also revealed that, in his day-to-day life now, the confidence and control he exuded as a player has been replaced by fear, forgetfulness and embarrassment. His love for us – it has come at a colossal price. The question begged of this tragedy: Will we step up for him, just as he did for his daughter in 1991? And will we heed Lewis' call to arms and do right by the four hundred thousand-plus Australians with a similar diagnosis to the King, but without his platform?

In many ways, this is our Origin decider. In the interview post-match, when the metaphorical microphone is placed under our chin, will we channel our hero and deliver a response that will make him proud?

We've got a King to look after now.

12

A Farewell Guernsey

May 31, 1993
Origin Game #3, Lang Park, Brisbane
Score: Qld 24 – NSW 12

I wouldn't say Queensland coming up short in 1992 and 1993 was expected, but it certainly wasn't a shock. As every sports team can attest, success in the years immediately after any GOAT's goodbye can be hard to come by. There were memorable moments to savour though, Game 2 of '92 notable among them. A stalwart survival of two sin-bins (Marty Bella and Peter Jackson, marched by Bill Harrigan), debutant Billy Moore's try soon after the sin-bins were over, and ultimately Alf's winning field goal at the death.

(A brief aside: what is it with these full-of-themselves Cockroach refs always sending our brave boys to the sheds for trivial indiscretions? Maroon whistleblowers never spoiled a contest by letting ego influence their decisions. Hell, David Manson defied all logic permitting Mark Geyer and his swinging-arm buffoonery to stay on the park in '91. And Barry "Grasshopper" Gomersall merely penalised Les Boyd for transforming Darryl Brohman's jaw into a set of Jenga blocks in '83. New South Wales can have no complaint when it comes to outright dismissals over the span of Origin history. Indeed, a fan of the unhinged persuasion might be tempted to suggest a conspiracy.*)

(*It's a conspiracy.)

Game 3 in '93 was also one for the Maroon scrapbook. Although the Blues had secured the shield with narrow wins in Brisbane and Sydney, the return to Lang Park was anything but a dead rubber. All-in brawls, multiple sin-bins, and a tasty Andrew Ettingshausen blunder that sealed a superb 24-12 Queensland victory stamped the game as a highlight. One thing made it unforgettable, though: Bobby Lindner's final go-round. In the Groth circle, the long-serving forward was a favourite for many reasons. His fearlessness as a ball runner. His courage to play with a fractured foot in the epic Game 2 of '89. His off-field profession as an optometrist. And, above all, his guernsey.

Or, more accurately: Dad's guernsey.

I'll let Des himself explain…

I won Bobby Lindner's jumper in a raffle at Mt Maria College in 1987.

It was a sports night and the guest speaker was Cyril Connell, former Queensland great, ABC radio commentator, and legendary scout for the Brisbane Broncos. He told many amusing tales from his playing career and his days searching for rugby league talent. I remember one story, in particular, about captaining the Maroons at the Sydney Cricket Ground in 1957. After Queensland scored the first try and led 5-0, he turned to the team and said 'Boys, this is going to be our night'. They went on to lose 69-5 — still the greatest ever defeat endured by a Queensland side.

Towards the end of the evening the raffle was drawn. First prize was a wheelbarrow chock full of beer, wine and spirits. Second prize was a fair dinkum Origin jersey, number 8, personally signed by Bobby Lindner. The winner of the 'barrow was announced — a delighted woman at a nearby table leapt up, declaring it was all hers. Then came the draw for the guernsey. I promised God I'd head straight to confession tomorrow if he jagged me a win. He must've been keen to hear my sins because, lo and behold, my name was announced! It was joy all round, and not only from our table. Bear in mind that back then you couldn't go into a sports store and buy a rep jersey — you either earned it, or it was donated to raise funds for charity events like the one at Mt Maria.

Fast forward to the end of the night and we were on our way out. Barrow Lady was leaving at the same time as us. She turned to me with a boastful look in her eye.

'I won first prize!' she crowed. 'And all you got was a crappy jumper!'

I had a little glance at Bobby Lindner's signature then pointed to the mobile AA meeting by her side.

'When all your grog is gone,' I replied, 'and your wheelbarrow has rusted out... I will still have my Origin jersey.'

I had it for thirty-five years, despite it never seeing a clothesline until sometime around 2010 (with the collar turning yellow, I finally gave in to Kath's decades-long pleas to wash it). Now, I've passed it along to my eldest son — an equally passionate Queenslander — so I reckon it'll be around another thirty-five years at least.

When I imagine the Maroon number eight on someone's back, I don't first think of Bob Lindner. Or Paul Vautin. Or Martin Bella. Or Shane Webcke. Or Steve Price. Or Matt Scott. Or Josh Papali'i. I don't think of those great players. I think of my father. And so do all our family and friends. Evidence supporting this claim has been in abundance over the years, but it was especially on show at Dad's 60th birthday in 2001. To celebrate that grand occasion, I wrote a Rupert McCall-esque poem: *Ode to Des Groth or The Greatest Origin Story Never Told* (read it at the end of the book); it contained the line *This "everyone's mate" with the stretched number eight.* The hundred or so people in attendance roared and applauded. They needed no explanation. They knew. The players who wore "8" on the field — they weren't its custodians. They were just borrowing it from Des for a time.

It's an irresistible fact: every Queensland player must eventually give up their guernsey, abandon the number on their back. But us fans never do. We are the true keepers of those guernseys and those numbers. We are the stewards of all that is Maroon. Through us, the players are never forgotten, never left behind. We carry them and their deeds with us like heirlooms. In photo albums and smart phones. On VCRs and PVRs. At the highest point of bridges and buildings. Across car bonnets and shop front windows. In our heads. In our hearts.

And, always, on our backs.

13

Heaven Sent

May 23, 1994

Origin Game #1, SFS, Sydney

Score: Qld 16 – NSW 12

Dear reader, if you've managed to reach this point in the book without tossing it aside, and you're Maroon to the core, and you've been keeping tabs on my timeline, and you perused the title of this instalment with a knowing grin, you'll be keenly aware that it's time to unpack a miracle:

How my beautiful wife came into my life.

(Okay, you were expecting THE miracle, THE try, immortalised by Ray Warren's call and a must in every Origin highlight package that ever was and ever will be? Don't worry – I'll get to it in due course.)

Unless you're a devotee of the destined soulmate, the chances of any two random people meeting and falling in love can be considered at best remote, at worst nigh impossible. My connection with Wendy Fraser sits squarely in the latter category. Our paths crossed on a Great Adventures tour boat to Green Island in far north Queensland. Alongside two other teachers, I was supervising a camp group of older intellectually disabled students; it was our last day of the trip – the following morning we'd be up bright and early to catch the Sunlander back to Brisbane. Wend was one of the staff working on the boat, which carried a name we would later reference with thinly veiled innuendo: "Mandalay". On the ninety-minute journey out to the island, she caught my eye. Cascades of dark, wavy hair. Mischievous smile. Gorgeous, tanned skin accentuated by her bright white uniform shorts. On the trip back, she was serving behind the bar. Could she have been any more attractive?

We started talking. She was from Vancouver, Canada, and came from a family with Metis and First Nations heritage. She'd arrived in Brisbane in 1988, by way of a six month stop in Hawaii. She'd worked the staff canteen at Expo before heading north to Cairns. She loved scuba diving and bungy jumping. She was intrigued by the campers in my care and figured I must be "a nice guy" to be doing such important work. She liked my blue eyes, listened politely when I opined (ill-advisedly) that Julian O'Neill would be our next Origin great, and didn't seem put off by the fact that I wasn't wearing a shirt.

This mystery woman was fixing me with beers, but it was her that was intoxicating. The ease of our conversation, her spirit of adventure, that accent… I couldn't end things by shaking her hand, saying 'Have a nice life' and walking away, as if this nigh impossible moment had been nothing more than a pleasant diversion. With the Mandalay nearing dock in Cairns, I threw a speculator out to the wing:

'Would you like to do something tonight?'

She said she would and wrote her number down on a vomit bag. I took it as a positive sign that the bag was empty.

I rang her on the hostel pay phone as soon as our group got back. I asked again if she'd fancy getting together and she, again, replied in the affirmative. She said she'd pick me up at the hostel at 7:30pm and then we'd head to a local bar called Gypsy Dee's. I hung up and a thought occurred to me, puncturing the balloon of giddiness enveloping my head: *Umm, you're here as a teacher, champ. You're supposed to be looking after your students, not cracking on to beautiful tour boat strangers.* Sheepishly, I approached my two teaching colleagues – both older married women – and explained the situation. They didn't hesitate. Go on, they declared. We'll hold the fort. Three years later at our Australian wedding reception, they would claim it was more obvious than a Mills and Boon ending that Cupid had shot me right between the eyes.

7:45pm arrived and no sign of Wendy. Did I blow it? Had I been too eager on the phone? Perhaps she'd realised she could do better. Sure, I might be a "nice guy", but she could get with any number of nice guys who looked better without a shirt on, made more money, and didn't live a Sunlander journey away. I was debating whether to call again – women love desperation, right? – when she rocked up at the hostel front desk.

'Sorry, I'm late,' she said.

'No worries,' I replied, acting cool. 'It's not like I was going to phone you over and over again to make sure you were coming.'

(Many years after we were married, Wend would reveal the reason for her lateness. She was recovering from fifteen rounds of a long-term relationship gone bad and wasn't inclined to step back into the dating ring. Arriving on the dot at 7:30pm, she'd driven around the block several times, wondering if she could be bothered to go through with the night, and whether she should just bail now to save herself further trouble. In the end, something convinced her to front up. Maybe it was the money I owed her for the Mandalay beers.)

A gentleman doesn't kiss and tell, so I'll describe the evening that ensued thus: it went as well as any first date ever has in the long and sordid history of first dates. When I got back to the hostel — sometime around 2:00am — I knew I wanted Wendy Fraser in my life. Who cared if we were fifteen hundred clicks apart? I was committed to seeing how the miracle might unfold.

By the night of Origin 1 in 1994, Wend and I were living together. That might seem quick (because it *was* quick) but establishing the *bona fides* of our love relied on time's quality more than its quantity. After my return to Brisbane, we did the long-distance thing for three months. Calls every day, sometimes twice a day. Often staying on the line for two hours or more — an occasional bone of contention in the single-phone Taringa house I was sharing with three other renters. We wrote letters, too — pages and pages, handwritten. There was a brief reprieve: a flight back up to Cairns for a glorious long weekend spent in each other's arms and, for one morning at Smithfield Bungy Jump, in the lap of the gods (an apt metaphor for our relationship if ever there was one). The rest of the time, all we had was conversation and correspondence. During those months, it was torture not being together in-person, but hindsight suggests it was the best way to grow our relationship, perhaps the best way to grow any relationship. We talked and wrote about anything and everything: family, history, politics, values, work, fun, life goals, having kids, the correct way to squeeze the toothpaste tube, the crime of having a toilet roll go under rather than over the top… Topics that may not have been on the menu for a while in each other's presence — we devoured them over the phone and on the page. Unsurprisingly, in amongst all those essential discussion pieces were the Queensland Maroons. I'd like to think Wend had some idea of what she'd encounter in our first shared Origin the evening of May 23. But as the esteemed Swedish physician and professor, Hans Rosling, famously said: 'nothing beats a firsthand experience'.

Our venue for the game was the old stomping ground on McConaghy Street. Dad and Mum were away, watching at a friend's place. They were disappointed to miss Wend; she'd made a strong impression in her initial visits, accepting Dad's offers of beer without hesitation, and laughing at his joke that the portraits of Joseph and Mary in the living room were 'Darren's grandparents'. And when his casual mention of the Broncos' back-to-back NSWRL premierships prompted Wend to refer to Glenn Lazarus as the "Brick with Eyes", Dad might've shed a little tear of joy. The burgeoning endearment of Wendy Fraser to my parents, though, would have to wait. Our only company for this Origin tilt would be a pair of buddies, Glen and Mark. With the four of us viewing the action in Des' prototype of the modern man-cave – a downstairs entertainment area he'd built from scratch in the late '70s, featuring a bar salvaged from the dump and a beast of a Westinghouse fridge built in 1952 – it promised to be an intimate and, from Wend's perspective, insightful evening.

Like the on-field combatants, I'd steeled for a special effort. Anything short of my best self would be unacceptable. No anger, no aggression. No shouting advice at the TV. No over-the-top antics of any kind; celebration, disconsolation or otherwise. The intent was that my Maroon lunacy would initially be fed to Wendy in tiny morsels, baby bird-like, soft and pre-digested as to be easily swallowed. Over time, as her resistance built up and her constitution strengthened, the diet could be expanded until she could stomach any amount of my Queenslander excess.

As the kickoff sailed away from Mal Meninga's boot, I mentally consulted my list of bad behaviour mitigations: sitting with Wend instead of my mates – check; sitting at the bar instead of six inches from the TV – check; first drink scheduled for half-time – check; inner voice reminding me of the Camus quote, 'Life is a sum of all your choices', and that the sum of all my choices tonight must not equal "utter pork chop" – check; inner voice also reiterating that I really, really, *really* dig this woman beside me – check. I was in good shape. So much so that when Laurie Daley strolled through our defensive line the first set of six, and Mal Meninga was bundled into touch on our second tackle of the match, my response to these calamities was merely a shrug, a pained smile and a small squeeze of Wend's knee. It really felt like I could be a man – and fan – worthy of the beautiful creature occupying the next barstool over.

12 – 4 Blues, five minutes to go.

Not the worst outcome. A big victory, a bad defeat – they carried the highest risk of me reverting to type. A tepid loss like this? It didn't move the needle too much. Naturally, there'd been moments of weakness. When Paul Harragon scored after a Daley play-the-ball that reeked of rugby union, I muttered a series of expletives under my breath. When a Queensland shift sent Willie Carne streaking down the sideline, I leaned forward far enough that I stumbled off the stool. When Julian O'Neill crossed in the corner to level the scores, I briefly joined Glen and Mark in their festival of high-fives. When Bill Harrigan missed a blatant Blues knock-on but then called back a line-ball Tim Brasher touchdown on the stroke of halftime, I blurted a sarcastic 'THANK YOU!'. When New South Wales went up two scores, a pitiful groan escaped my mouth before I could gulp it back down. On the whole, nothing too damaging in those lapses. Wend had taken it all in stride. She patted my hand after a disoriented Marty Bella played the ball towards the opposite try-line, kissed my cheek whenever I called Ricky Stuart a whinger, and wondered aloud how Gary Larson juggled "The Far Side" and football. And now, blessedly, we were almost at the final hooter. The first small dose of my Maroon madness had been administered to Wend without serious side-effect.

Thank you, boys, I thought. Thank you for prioritising my love life.

Perhaps the players were waiting for this acknowledgement, or it provided an epiphany that had escaped them to this point in the game. In the 75th minute, a brilliant hot-potato sequence involving Kevin Walters, Meninga and Steve "The Pearl" Renouf climaxed with a Mark Coyne basketball-pass to Carne for the four-pointer. As Meninga piloted the conversion between the sticks to make it 12 – 10, I sensed it: the existential threat to my shared future with Wendy. The landmine set in my carefully curated path to romantic fulfillment.

Hope.

Fight it, my inner voice barked, but the futility of the command was undeniable. I was powerless to stop the descent. Two minutes to go, Queensland with the ball. I was standing on the floor now, double-arm's distance from the TV, hunched and tense like a half-cocked jack-in-the-box. Gaze glued to the screen. When had I vacated the barstool? No clue. Suddenly, Ray Warren's rising voice was swamping me, lifting me off my feet and carrying me towards an unknown shore.

〇

'Coyne at the 79th minute is tackled…Langer pushing it wide…Walters onward…'

'Come on, lads!' I pleaded, fist punching my thigh, my world nothing but the next sixty seconds. 'One play!'

'Renouf down the touchline… beats one… gets it infield…'

Heart racing. 'Come on!'

'Hancock gets it on! Queensland are coming back! Darren Smith for Langer!'

Blood singing. 'COME ON!'

'LANGER GETS IT AWAY! HERE'S THE BIG FELLA! GETS THE PASS ON!'

Shouting. 'YES!!!'

'COYNE!!! COYNE!!! GOES FOR THE CORNER!!!'

Screaming. 'FUCK YES!!!'

'AND GETS THE TRY!!!'

Chaos. 'OHMYFUCKINGGOD!!!'

'THAT'S NOT A TRY – THAT'S A MIRACLE!!!'

What happened next was mindless ecstasy. Noise everywhere, bodies bouncing off each other. One of either Glen or Mark kept shouting 'I KNEW IT!' over and over and over again. Or maybe it was me, lying through my teeth? The three of us were one giant mass of jubilation, our own personal expressions of joy indistinguishable from the whole. And it might've continued unchecked for the rest of the night but for a single instance of lucidity that shattered the anarchy:

Wendy.

I clamped a hand over my still-bellowing gob.

Oh, no.

I've wrecked everything.

Pivoting away from the TV, away from the replay of a euphoric Wally Lewis monstering Dick "Tosser" Turner in the stands, I turned towards the bar. I knew what I would encounter: an empty stool. Wend had cleared out. Run for the hills. She was likely already on the Sunlander, slow-poking her way back up to Cairns. I couldn't blame her. She hadn't signed up for this circus. Heart heavy, I lifted my eyes to the tragic consequence of my Maroon disorder: the one that got away.

She was still there.

I stepped towards her, arms outstretched. She held up a hand, halting my advance. Gave a little shake of the head. Smirked. Then she stepped down from the stool and stood in front of me. I felt her soft hands. Her fingers interlaced with mine. Behind her Ray-Ban specs, her stunning brown eyes were communicating a clear message: "What's a girl to do?"

'That was something else,' she said.

'You mean me or the try?'

'I'll never tell.'

She smiled, kissed me then announced in a commendable Aussie accent that Phil Gould could suffer in his jocks. At that moment, I understood two things:

I would love Wendy Fraser for the rest of my days.

And on the night of May 23rd in the year 1994, I had, without question, witnessed a miracle.

14

A Neville Abroad

May 31, 1995
Origin Game #2, MCG, Melbourne
Score: Qld 20 – NSW 12

At various times during my life, people have erroneously considered me an outlier. The sprinter kid with the distance-runner body. PE teacher idolising Peter Carey and Gabriel Garcia Marquez. Sports junkie with an artist's heart. Novelist obsessed with rugby league. While such associations can be considered unlikely, they are not unique – others in this world possess them. Even the league-loving literary type is not such a rare breed. Thomas Keneally, anyone? Blow that whistle, Ref. Blow that whistle for the footy literati.

I'm also not an outlier as a reasonably intelligent, semi-articulate Maroons fan. Contrary to perceptions south of the Tweed, they are plentiful. I sat beside them in school. Went to uni with them. Taught with them. I've met them on the streets of London and along the Las Vegas strip and in the British Columbian outpost of Dawson Creek. I share a Facebook group with them: "The Raging Bull's Ragdoll". I've read their articles and books.

Watched them on TV. Listened to their podcasts. I was incredibly fortunate to be raised by one. They are educated, savvy connoisseurs of Queensland Origin, steeped in its history and deeply cognisant of its cultural significance. The fallacy that we're all mindless yobbos swilling kegs of XXXX at the Caxton before dragging our knuckles over to Suncorp is damaging. Not to us, mind you — to the Blues' cause. New South Wales' baked-in condescension towards Queensland represents a fundamental failure to understand both thy enemy and thy self. And as Sun Tzu teaches in *The Art of War*, 'If you know neither… you will succumb in every battle.' In my experience, whenever a Blues player trotted out the tired tropes of us having two heads (Paul Gallen) or being nutbag rednecks (Willie Mason) or — wait for it — having two heads (David Klemmer), I felt bullish about their chances of succumbing in the battle.

If there's one context I can be tagged an outlier, it is the fan living abroad. Not to imply I'm here on my own in Vancouver — Aussies abound in the Lower Mainland; even more up Whistler way, where the locals have dubbed it "Whistralia". A decent percentage of those Strayans are Queenslanders and, naturally enough, supporters of their footy team. Diaspora, though, doesn't figure much in my sense of outlier — it is shaped more by definition. The Oxford dictionary entry for outlier reads: "a person or thing situated away or detached from the main body or system". The word that hits home for me: detached. I am severed from the body of my sporting love. I'm a castaway fan, disconnected and adrift. A Robinson Crusoe on a *Mas a Tierra* of hockey and baseball and the Super Bowl and March Madness and Sportsnet and ESPN and the '72 Summit Series and Nathan Lafayette hitting the post in Game 7 and Sidney Crosby's golden goal in 2010. Ironically, for one-third of my fan-life and counting, I've been marooned.

I got my first taste of that detachment in 1995 – the year widely considered the ultimate Origin outlier.

At the '94 Ekka, somewhere between Sideshow Alley and the Showbag Pavilion, Wendy and I made the decision to spend 1995 in Canada. It was an easy call, much less fraught than the one we would confront twelve years later. Wend had been away for more than half a decade and was missing her family. After three years of splendid reward and soul-sapping struggle in the special schools, I was up for a bit of adventure. By the end of October, we were set with approvals, passports, plane tickets and my twelve-month work visa. We would be in Vancouver for Christmas.

From a footy supporter standpoint, it appeared an ideal time to exercise some distance. The Super League war was gearing up and lamentably my Brisbane Broncos were in the vanguard of the advancing troops. The back pages of the *Courier Mail* were a precursor to modern doom-scrolling: a constant stream of secret meetings and court cases and public sniping that felt like fatal damage to the game (thankfully, it wasn't). The newly named ARL comp was expanding; instead of adding only North Queensland and Auckland to the mix, they admitted the South Queensland Crushers and Western Reds as well, bringing the total number of teams to twenty – a decision I felt was lacking in fortitude, prudence and common sense (regrettably, I was right). Then there was the biggest kick in the guts: rumour had it the players aligned with Rupert Murdoch's rebel league would be excluded from Origin, which all but guaranteed New South Wales crushing a second-string Queensland side and securing an unprecedented fourth series win on the trot. The whole scene was depressing.

By contrast, the sports landscape awaiting me in the Pacific Northwest was new and shiny, painless and full of promise. The

Vancouver Canucks had just made the Stanley Cup Finals for the second time in their history. The Vancouver Grizzlies were set to launch their first season in the NBA. The San Francisco 49ers – the NFL team I'd developed a passing interest in – were on their way to another Super Bowl. Michael Jordan was still trying to make a go of baseball. This smorgasbord of foreign action could fill the rugby league-sized gap in my sporting diet. No North American offering would ever nourish me like my beloved Queensland Maroons, but they could serve as takeaway for one year.

The memo about reducing my footy focus in 1995 – Dad didn't get it. He had serious misgivings. How would I keep up with the game? Where was I going to get the match results? Could I even survive in such a rugby league wasteland? Compounding the situation was the imminent prospect of time to kill. Dad had done the unthinkable: he was taking a redundancy and leaving Queensland Rail after forty years. The combination of concern for his eldest's well-being and the uncertainty of his purpose post-QR saw him shift into pen-pal mode. Soon after our arrival in Vancouver, monthly care packages of newspaper inserts and clippings began turning up (the first one got there before we did). I gave the info enough attention to be familiar with the basics: Broncs near the top of the ladder, three teams – Balmain, Easts and Canterbury – now calling themselves "Sydney", breakaway comp not "if" but "when". And the rumour was now fact: Super League players were out of Origin. Oh well, I thought. Time to double-down on directing my energy elsewhere.

It wasn't much of a challenge. In addition to the local sporting diversions, there was a plethora of new world elements to occupy my time. Living with my in-laws. Working at the local Rec Centre gym. Driving on the right (i.e. wrong) side of the road. Learning to skate (not good) and ski (not bad). Wearing long johns all the time, even indoors. Sparked in part by the different surrounds, an idea for a novel was beginning to take shape in my head. And then there was the biggest factor of them all: our wedding. Knowing my parents would be leaving Australia's shores for the first time to come visit us in July, and unsure of when the Groth and Fraser clans would be on the same continent again, Wend proposed to me one late-April morning as we brushed our teeth.

'Wanna get hitched?' she asked.

'Orright,' I replied, spitting into the sink. 'Let's do it.'

From that ultra-romantic kickoff, we embarked on a frenetic, thrilling, often hilarious eleven-week journey to 'I do'. Scenarios arose that would send any self-respecting bridezilla to a padded room. Wendy settled on her dress two weeks prior to the big day. She purchased her shoes the weekend before. My best man, brother-in-law Doug, bought his kicks on the way to the ceremony. There were also unforgettable surprises, foremost among them Sean and Simon arriving on the doorstep unannounced, and Wendy's best mate Louise dropping everything and jetting over from Cairns to be maid-of-honour. In the end, though, no breakneck odyssey towards the wedding would've been complete without a brief acknowledgement of the sporting marriage I'd been in since age ten and had largely neglected since arriving in the True North. And who else but my father would ensure I was faithful to my Maroon vows. On July 9, to celebrate his fifty-fifth birthday — his first ever away from Oz — there would be a special viewing of the tape he'd brought over in carry-on. The label on its spine, written in Des' neat hand: "Game 2, 1994. Fatty's Neville Nobodies".

I bent down towards the VCR, pushed the tape into the slot and pressed "Play". Then I returned to the couch to sit beside Wend and my dear mum-in-law, Dorothy.

'Righto,' announced Des, as Billy Moore's shouts of 'QUEENSLANDER!' backdropped the boys' run out onto the MCG. 'Seat belts on!' He added: 'I hope the tape is good. It was a bugger converting it from PAL to NTSC.'

I knew what was to come, the most recent care package having clued me in. Coach Paul 'Fatty' Vautin and his merry band of "Nevilles" had not only won the game we were about to watch, they'd swept the series. *Swept!* A team the bookies had as rank outsiders for every game (even the third, when we were up 2-0 and playing at Lang Park); a team featuring a Papua New Guinean halfback, a lock from Kempsey, an eighteen-year-old bench player that Vautin didn't know from Adam, and, zero Broncos (Gavin Allen the exception), Cowboys and Raiders. They'd won three-blot against the Blues' best. The verdict of the folks who'd witnessed it first-hand? Unbelievable! Incredible! Unrivalled Maroon spirit! Every Queenslander's finest hour! On an intellectual level, I couldn't have agreed more. The sheer magnitude of the achievement was almost too much to comprehend. The question nagging me, though: here I was, on the far side of the world, two months after the fact, knowing the result, detached from the real-time at-home immersion… would I feel the same?

An innocent bystander might've thought it was a live broadcast. More than once, Wendy told me to settle down, assuring me everything would be okay and suggesting Queensland were a decent chance of winning a game they'd already won. Her rationality fought a losing battle. I yelled at Danny Moore to deck John Hopoate during the third minute all-in brawl. I called Paul Harragon a sook when he was felled by a swinging arm from Tony

Hearn. I asked Matt Sing what the hell he was doing not jamming in when Brett Rodwell scored for the Blues. I jumped out of my seat and attempted to high-five Wendy (she gave me the finger) when Adrian Lam crossed the stripe. And when the two end-game moments of destiny arrived – New South Wales' try disallowed for a forward pass, then a Brett Dallas dummy-half run of ninety metres to seal the deal – I stood, arms aloft, head back, face upturned to the heavens, like a martyr awaiting the first match on the pyre.

But it wasn't the same.

It wasn't... *visceral.*

Parsing the result afterwards, I was still wondering where these extraordinary eighty minutes would land in my Maroon psyche. To help the process, or at least advance a different perspective, I asked Dad how it was for him to be here watching the game. His answer surprised me:

'It feels like a present. Maybe it's because of the birthday, but I think it's given me something to take back to Brissie.' He paused, staring wistfully at the can of Kokanee in his hand. 'Leaving Queensland Rail was a big decision, mate. I was fifteen when I started there. It's all I've known for forty years. When you step away from something like that, when you're not a part of it anymore... you might start to feel like a Neville Nobody yourself.' He took a sip of his beer and waved a finger in the direction of the TV. 'This team, what they managed to do... It makes me more confident in the decision I made. They came out on top, and I will too.'

'Of course you will,' I replied, clapping his shoulder. 'You're a Queenslander.'

As we rewound the tape to watch the glorious action for a second time, I put aside my search for meaning in the fan experience and considered the life lesson on offer. The confidence my father was bringing back to McConaghy Street – was there a similar gift available to me? Perhaps that gift was the idea for a novel rattling around in my brain?

Could a literary Neville like me become a published author?

On July 24, Wend and I were married in a ceremony that had all the fun, family and chaos typical of the two-and-a-half months preceding it. A few weeks later, I received word I would no longer be teaching intellectually disabled kids back home – I'd been transferred to a school for migrant and refugee students in Chelmer called "Milpera". That same day, I wrote the first page of my novel. By end of year, I had a modest seventy-five pages – all handwritten with a 2B pencil – and I'd given the work a title: *The Procrastinator*.

Dad continued to send over all the rugby league latest. He also mailed me the tape of Game 3 which, along with Game 2, I played more and more as our departure date loomed. I didn't need any extra injection of hope – seventy-five pages was definitive proof I'd bought-in to the example set by the '95 team. Rather, I watched again and again in a bid to elevate the Nevilles to the place they deserved in my Maroon pantheon: the best of the best.

I wanted to overcome my detachment.

Predictably, I did not succeed. The emotional response was always tempered, never essential. Watching while secure in the knowledge we'd prevail – it was enjoyable. At times, satisfying. But it was never transcendent. Without the potential for failure, minus the live game's unknowable destiny and inescapable capacity for despair, a true sense of triumph was always elusive.

But hey, this "plight of the far away supporter" was set to become a footnote in my story. I was headed back to Queensland to resume being up close and personal to Origin. The twelve-month Vancouver experience – I was certain I would look back on it as a one-off, as the outlier in my lifetime of Maroon fandom.

15

Danijel

May 20, 1996
Origin Game #1, Suncorp Stadium, Brisbane
Score: NSW 14 – Qld 6

1995 had been a fever dream for both me and the Maroons, and expecting 1996 to match it in any way was pure fantasy. Coming into the year, my wish was for modest success on and off the field. A 2-1 series win for Queensland wasn't too much to ask, especially with the return of the Super League signees and two of the three games being played at Lang Park. (Even though it had been renamed Suncorp Stadium in 1994, I couldn't bring myself to call it that; not until its state-of-the-art, purpose-built makeover in the early 2000s. To this day, I still refer to it as Lang Park when mixing with fellow league tragics.) As for the new teaching gig at Milpera Special School, I'd be happy if the kids were manageable, the teachers were friendly, and the school day left me with enough energy in the evening to work on my novel.

I knew from the outset it was a privilege to be at Milpera and that it was "special" in the truest sense of the word. As a stand-alone, temporary stop for immigrants, it was the only school of its kind in Australia. At any one time, there were one hundred and fifty-plus students attending from forty countries, speaking forty languages. Their profiles varied wildly: business migrant to asylum seeker; ten-year-old girl to "eighteen-year-old" man who was clearly twenty-five; educated in the home country to completely unschooled; some grasp of English to no English whatsoever; excited to be in Australia to desperately wanting to go home; surrounded by loving family to parents killed during war; embracing a new beginning to traumatised beyond comprehension. In simple terms, my job was to assist these young people in developing their language skills within a HPE context before their move on to a mainstream high school with ESL support. Later, I would cultivate the other invaluable contributions of my classes: acculturation, inclusivity, teamwork, friendship, success, respite and healing. At the beginning of my journey, though, it was all about the English and my proficiency in helping the students improve.

It didn't take long for proficiency to be jettisoned for survival. I was out of my depth from day one. Apart from the need for ultra-simple, ultra-clear instructions, and a level of patience that would've tested a starving lion stalking prey, very little of my Ipswich experience with intellectually disabled kids was translatable. There was nothing practical I could bring over. No curriculum or units of work. No specific lessons. At my disposal were the resources used by my predecessor, but they were outdated and didn't make much sense (volleyball – tough to master at the best of times – as the chosen sport for the kids with the least English and, in some instances, least coordination? WTF?). I was starting this teaching set-of-six a metre out from my tryline, and cluelessness was muscling up to smash me.

The hard yards were made even harder by the constant change embedded in Milpera's operation. Take enrolments. Unlike regular schools where 99% of sign-ups occur prior to classes commencing in late January, Milpera had students on the doorstep all the time. It was the norm – calendars don't much matter to a Hazara teen fleeing Kabul to escape the Taliban – but that didn't make it any easier to manage. My first exposure to the randomness came in my third week on the job. On the Monday morning, I taught a basic basketball lesson to a class of six Beginner students. (Classes at Milpera were arranged by English ability: "Beginner", "Post-Beginner", "Intermediate" and "Senior". Consequently, due to comparable language skills, you might end up with a twelve-year-old bookworm from Taiwan and a seventeen-year-old soccer star from Croatia in the same PE class. And by "you might end up", I mean "it happened all the time".) The lesson went well, a fun series of dribbling and ball-handling activities then some shooting games. The kids were respectful, engaged, and didn't laugh too much at the exaggerated gestures I used to clarify my words. I was pleased. My next visit with them at week's end would build on this promising start. Fast forward to Friday – I turned up with my bag of eight balls (always be prepared with a couple extra), walked into the classroom and found myself staring at twenty-seven faces. Suffice to say, the session didn't pan out as well as the previous Monday.

Relentless change wasn't just reserved for Milpera's front door – it was at the exit as well. Twice a term, a group of students would "graduate", heading to high schools with ESL units like Toowong, Indooroopilly and Yeronga. Any teacher will tell you one of the bigger difficulties of the gig is students moving on after you've made a connection or a breakthrough. In the mainstream schools, parting of ways generally occurred at year's end – at Milpera, it was every five weeks. Just when you were getting a handle on Noor, the Sudanese girl from the refugee camps in Uganda; you'd gained her trust, and you'd seen the lightbulb flare over her head, and you saw her smile when you entered the classroom, and you knew this was just the beginning of the positive impact you could have on her future… poof! She was gone. And the next day, there was another Noor just arrived, and you were back to square-one.

Teaching at Milpera was akin to standing in a rushing river, and the initial months had me on the verge of being swept away. Arriving back at McConaghy Street in the late afternoon (we temporarily lived with Mum and Dad until we found a rental unit in Graceville), deluged by all the white water of the school day, too exhausted to even look at my novel draft, I frequently considered handing in my resignation. To endure, I needed things to hold on to, things to help me withstand the swirling currents and not be dragged under.

One of those helpful things was entirely unexpected: a message of sympathy arising from the first Origin clash of 1996.

A message from Danijel.

The morning of the game. The air had that upper cut of crispness standard to Brisbane's inner west in late May. A sprinkling of dew flecked the stretch of grass serving as Milpera's "sports field", enough that the Post-Beginner students finishing my class and heading for recess were lamenting the damp patches on their shoes. We'd just completed forty minutes of "tag rugby" – a heavily modified, foreigner-friendly version of touch footy that substituted flags for contact, allowed forward passes, and emphasised fun and participation over the final result. The session had gone okay. Everyone had seen the ball, no one had been injured, and I'd only shouted in angry frustration twice. Baby steps. The rest of the day might provide more reasons to quit, but for this period at least I'd withstood the rushing river.

I was packing up the gear when a gruff but friendly voice prompted me to pause.

'Your shirt, Sir.'

It was one of the Serbian students from my class. Danijel. Last name: not sure. Something ending in "itch". Sixteen-years-old. Tall lad. Had the Slavic look I was becoming familiar with: fair complexion, light brown, almost straw-coloured hair, round face, prominent cheekbones. I only knew the bullet points of his hard history (as I did for all the students; the home-room English teachers got the detailed brief), but I was aware his family had refused to participate in the atrocities of the Bosnian War and had fled to Australia to avoid repercussions. In the brief time we'd spent together, I understood him to be cooperative, quiet, and thoughtful. A "good" kid. The sort that could turn invisible in class if you didn't limit the tunnel vision brought on by the disrupters. He also typified every Milpera student in that, regardless of language ability, he'd gained a solid grasp of English swear words.

'Your shirt,' he repeated. 'I fucking like it, Sir.'

It was the 1995 jersey. I'd seen it a few weeks before in, of all places, the Brookside newsagent. I bought it on the spot. As the first Maroons guernsey I'd ever owned, it wasn't a bad place to start.

'My team, Queensland,' I said, pointing out the badge on the chest. 'We play a big game tonight.'

He nodded enthusiastically. 'Ah, yes! I see on TV. Orange-in.'

'Origin.'

'Ori-gin.'

'That's it.'

'Why is Ori-gin big fucking game?'

I glanced at my watch. Delighted though I was by his interest (and his swearing), recess was disappearing fast and I needed to set up for the next class. I told him if he really wanted to chat about Queensland we could meet at the start of lunch on the bench beside the basketball court. He said he'd be there and, sure enough, at 12:30 he was waiting. I sat beside him. His eagerness was palpable.

'Tell me about the Ori-gin, Mr. G!'

In the simplest language I could muster, I explained the basics. Three games every year between two states, Queensland ("Us") and New South Wales ("Them"). Maroons versus Blues. The result — very important. If we win, everyone in the state is proud for the year, our hearts are happy. If we lose, we are very sad, but we always love our team. At the end of my spiel, Danijel nodded and applauded, as if I'd delivered a performance he'd paid good money to see.

'Queensland like Partizan,' he said. 'Partizan my football team. Play Red Star.' He balled his hands into fists and knocked them together. 'Partizan-Red Star… crazy!'

Given the bigger picture in the Balkans, "crazy" seemed like an understatement. As a sporting rivalry, I imagined Partizan-Red Star on par with India-Pakistan in cricket rather than Queensland-New South Wales in rugby league. He continued:

'Partizan-Red Star game is *večiti derbi*. It mean…' He clicked his fingers, cinched his face. 'In English, like… enemies long time. Very long time.'

'Like, forever?'

'Yes! Forever. Partizan-Red Star forever enemies. And Partizan, *Parni valjak*…' He patted his chest, 'My team forever.'

His eyes softened and his gaze drifted languidly towards the students kicking a soccer ball on the grassed area. I recognised the look's source — my old friend from '95: detachment. I toyed with the idea of telling him I could relate. It was a ridiculous notion. The Canadian dislocation of my fandom, my identity, my life, had been popped back into place, no damage done. Danijel's injury was likely irreparable.

Any trace of the pain was absent when he turned back to me. His face was all twinkling eyes and cheeky grin.

'Blues are shit, like Red Star,' he announced. 'Fuck Blues!'

He offered up his hand for a high-five. I duly accepted.

'I want Queensland is winner, Mr. G!'

Queensland was not the winner.

We never looked likely. From the opening whistle, New South Wales was quicker, stronger and… well, better. Two early penalty goals to Andrew Johns felt like a let-off; going in at halftime down 10-nil felt like a victory. Actual victory, though, was a pipe-dream, despite the obligatory Maroon bravery: a magnificent goal-line stand in the thirty-first minute that somehow denied successive surges at the stripe by Andrew Ettingshausen and Paul Harragon; Alf besting Tim Brasher by sheer force of will to post our only try; debutant Wendell Sailor diving head-first at a grubber to prevent an Adam Muir four-pointer. Courageous deeds that merely delayed the inevitable. When the final hooter sounded, I felt we were fortunate to not get beaten by twenty.

The 14-6 loss made the fairytale of 1995 something of a paradox, simultaneously more and less incredible, a logical marriage of 'Can you believe they did that?' and 'Of course, they did that!' The Nevilles had been a Maroon perfect storm, but as with all storms there is wreckage in the aftermath. Questions following the Game 1 defeat centred on the Super League prodigals. Should they have been picked? Should we have stuck with the '95 heroes? Were there tensions within the team? Regardless of any truths, I didn't care to buy into the debate. I was too busy wallowing in a misery beyond the traditional standards. It wasn't my flagrant over-investment in Maroon victories, my unfair leaning on them to help me feel better in times of personal difficulty. And it wasn't the prospect of resisting the Milpera white water without the respite of a Queensland triumph. It was the altogether unfamiliar state of being gutted for someone other than myself.

Next day, Danijel was waiting outside the teachers' office at recess. Approaching, I figured he now regretted asking about my shirt. And I assumed he had some of his wharfie-worthy swearing set aside for me. He didn't. His message was curse-free and a complete surprise.

'I'm sorry, Mr. G,' he said, shaking his head. 'I'm sorry Maroons did not win for you.' He lifted a hand and patted my shoulder. 'Next one… win for sure. Things will be better.'

I stared at this young man displaced from his country, his language, his childhood, his memories, his Partizan; an innocent dealt the toughest of Life's cards, who had every right to view optimism as fool's gold. He was trying to make *me* feel better. And succeeding. He was right. Things would be better. The rushing river would ease. My novel would resume. The Maroons would win the next one, or the one after that, or the one after that. Things would be better.

I wanted to cry, I wanted to laugh, I wanted to hug this kid. In the end, I opted to swear:

'Fuck the Blues.'

Danijel grinned, applauded then pretended to spit on the ground.

'Yes! Fuck Blues forever!'

16

Dog Act

June 25, 1997
Origin Game #3, SFS, Sydney
Score: Jamie Goddard's Fist 1 – Andrew Johns' Lip 0

Like many, I consider 1997 the most forgettable of all the Origin years and arguably the low point in the series' storied history. Please indulge me a barest of bones explanation as to why. (For a comprehensive history of this period, and the entire Super League saga, I thoroughly recommend the epic podcast series put together by Michael Adams and Andy Paskin at The Rugby League Digest.)

1997 saw the long-feared schism in rugby league become reality, culminating in two separate but parallel competitions: the ARL and the breakaway Super League. The player talent pool was split. Clubs scrambled to survive. Lawyers and agents made out like bandits. Casual fans turned their back on the game and into the waiting arms of rugby union and the AFL. For the hardcores keeping the faith, allegiance tended to follow in step with the club. If you were a Manly, Newcastle or South Queensland Crusher supporter, you sided with the establishment ARL. If Canberra or the Bulldogs or North Queensland was your team, you bought into the vision of Super League. As a devotee of the club at the heart of the upheaval – the Brisbane Broncos – I had more of a stake in the rebel comp, and I was pleased the Broncs dominated the Super League season, ultimately lifting the inaugural Telstra Cup trophy after a win over Cronulla in the grand final. In the end though, I was never all-in. I felt this was World Series Cricket 2.0. Rugby league would re-unite, sooner rather than later, hopefully without too many scars.

My indifference to the '97 season was best illustrated with Origin. To this day, I have few recollections of the traditional ARL fixtures and Super League's poor facsimile of the concept, the Tri-Series. I vaguely remember New South Wales winning the latter with a late Noel Goldthorpe field goal – a bummer to be sure, but no heartbreaker. More prominent in my memory is how ugly the Tri-Series jerseys were (age has not improved them – they still look like the love child of a lava lamp and a Rorschach test. If you stare at the design long enough, you might see Nate Myles doing a Mad Monday nudie run). As for the ARL Origin "proper", my Maroon mind's standouts are few and far between. The poor crowd at the MCG for Game 2. The missed penalty goal by Julian O'Neill that would've kept the series alive. Ben Ikin's brilliance in Game 3. Amidst all this hazy recollection is the one exception, the highlight prized in every '97 retrospective: the infamous "Cattledog" stoush in which Jamie Goddard towelled up Andrew Johns.

Watching the brawl in real-time on TV, my response was no doubt familiar to fellow Maroons tuning in: instant rage at the Mark "Spud" Carroll cheap shot that knocked out Craig Smith and started the melee; a demand for vengeance, preferably Billy Moore dispensing the justice; then the *schadenfreude* of Johns' capitulation. At the time, I wasn't aware that the violence was pre-ordained, that legendary Cockroach coach "Tom Terrific" Raudonikis had instructed his players to bung on a blue when he issued the command "Cattledog". Discovering this fact – perhaps the day after – not only resuscitated the real-time feelings I'd had, it supercharged them to eleven. Spud Carroll? The grub of all grubs! Andrew Johns? Got exactly what he deserved! Jamie Goddard? The greatest Queenslander who ever lived! Cattledog? The literal definition of a dog act!

Three decades on, attitudes have softened towards the incident. In much the same manner as the Lang Park can-riot of 1988, Cattledog and the Goddard-Johns fracas are symbolic of the Origin mythos, viewed through the lens of a Reg Reagan-esque, misty-eyed nostalgia. I assess it differently nowadays too, although to say I've softened would not be accurate. I've sought to step back and consider it with a more objective eye, seeking to unpack its true legacy. And while some might accuse my objective eye of wearing a Maroon monocle (it does), what I observe at the kernel of Cattledog is yet more evidence that New South Wales, to quote my father and many others since, 'doesn't get it'.

The motivation is now commonly understood. Raudonikis, Carroll, Johns and other members of the Blues squad are on record as saying Cattledog was instituted as a response to the legendary "Queenslander" call. To quote Johns from an SEN interview in 2021:

'It was arranged during the week that the first guy to yell out, 'Queenslander!', Tommy said he wants someone to yell out, 'Cattledog!', which is the (code for) all-in brawl.'

Carroll offered further insights in his colourful sit-down with Fox Sports in 2020:

'Tommy got us together and he stood up in front of everyone and said, "I fucking hate these blokes," he said. "We're going to have a call, when I call Cattledog, it's on." Joey Johns says, "We can't do that Tommy, we can't just go up and whack blokes." And he goes, "Mate when I call it, it's going to be on.' And that was the end of it.'

Putting aside Johns' salient and very sensible point about not whacking blokes out of nowhere, let's consider the source that deemed this "strategy" necessary: the cry of 'Queenslander!'. Conceived by Wayne Bennett's team in the 1987 series and made iconic by Billy Moore's impassioned tunnel delivery in 1995, Queenslander is understood as much more than a rallying point or a call to arms. It's a vow of fidelity, a promise to be true. It's a declaration of undying love. As Wally Lewis stated in Wide World of Sports' "Birth of Origin" podcast:

'It only took one word to instantly inspire (us), that chant, every time, and you knew you weren't just playing on behalf of the twelve other guys on the field with you, and the reserves on the bench, and the coach and manager. You were playing for the entire state, for all the people who had been so loyal to you.'

So, what does New South Wales have to rival Queenslander? What mighty bellow do they invoke that perfectly articulates their adoration of jersey and place? Insert the sound of crickets here. After forty-plus years, all they can point to is Cattledog: a sad, cynical response to the Maroon mantra they wish could be replicated in their own identity but will always be out of reach.

Cattledog is entrenched in Origin folklore, but by any measure it was a failure. It didn't undermine the opposition. It didn't shake their resolve. It didn't result in a victory. It didn't bury the Queenslander call, ensuring it was never heard again. And the biggest loser of this Raudonikis brainchild? His own man: Andrew Johns, future Immortal, voice of reason, and recipient of a busted lip that needed twenty-seven stitches.

Cattledog should be seen for what it is: indicative of the character flaw in New South Wales that allows them to recognise Origin's Holy Trinity – Hate, State and Mate – but compels them to worship only one.

17

Hail Mary

May 22, 1998
Origin Game #1, SFS, Sydney
Score: Qld 25 – NSW 24

The clock showed two minutes left. New South Wales five out from our line, five tackles gone, five up on the scoreboard. A try here and the game was over. Hell, a repeat set and the game was over. At dummy-half, Geoff Toovey threw a long pass to Andrew Johns for the grubber into the in-goal. A ricochet. Momentary confusion. A knock-on? All over bar the shouting? No. We'd defused it. Shane Webcke was in possession. Ninety seconds to go. The Maroons were still alive. We were close enough if good enough.

I was in my customary down-to-the-wire position: on my feet, leaning forward, crowding the TV, shouting instructions. There was a new wrinkle to my Coach Groth act tonight – I was wearing a pair of oven mitts to muffle my inordinately loud applause. Buddies Michelle and James, at whose house we were gathered for the tilt, had brought out the mitts with great fanfare just prior to kickoff. I'd laughed and told Shell it was a funny joke. She'd assured me it wasn't a joke. I'd dutifully worn the mitts from that point on, ditching them only at halftime to avoid calamity in the loo. The absence of ear-splitting applause for seventy-nine minutes had been appreciated by the group and the surrounding neighbours, but with sixty seconds to go it was implicitly understood – all mitts were off if magic came to pass.

Second tackle, the ball found Kevin Walters. The shift was on. Spreading it wide, looking to offload and constantly backing up, a-la the Miracle Try in '94 – it was our best shot. We could go the length of the field in five plays. Walters glanced outside then edged forward, seemingly intent on drawing his defender and passing left.

He didn't draw his defender. He didn't pass.

He kicked.

It was an awful shot-duck of a punt. Couldn't have looked worse if he'd booted a bag of White Wings flour. As it tumbled gracelessly through the air, a chorus of groans filled the room. My voice wasn't among them. Yes, Kevvie's roost downfield had literally taken the chances of a win out of our hands and given them to a bounce of the ball. It was a "Hail Mary" – a popular sporting term I'd discovered during my year in North America. But Hail Mary's weren't pleas to St. Jude, they weren't a lost cause. They'd been known to come up trumps.

And not just on the footy field.

By February of 1997, I'd finished the draft of my novel. Titled *The Procrastinator*, it was the story of an accidental hero who wishes to free himself of his unearned life of public adoration by jumping off a bridge. Writing it had been a tale of two halves: the first, I'd written longhand, and Wend – bless her – had typed it out on a word processor; the second, I'd knocked out the pages myself on our whizz-bang entry into the technology top grade: a Pentium 4

IBM PC. Holding the printed manuscript in my hands, I couldn't be sure it was any good and, by extension, if I was any good. I'd made colossal mistakes along the way, writing great swathes of pages only to realise they had no place in the story. They hadn't stopped me reaching the finish line, though. And it had been largely fun to write, if that counted for anything.

The question was what to do next with this novel-in-waiting.

The answer was to channel future Kevin Walters: kick it downfield and pray it gets picked up.

In the second half of 1997, I sent the manuscript to the biggest, most prestigious literary agencies in Australia. To be fair to Kevvie, my Hail Mary wasn't close to his in terms of *cojones*. I was young and naïve to the unforgiving ways of the publishing world. The chances of a complete unknown receiving a personalised response, let alone being signed as a client – I understood they were slim. I was blithely unaware that "slim" meant the odds were shorter on Fine Cotton saluting the judge in the Melbourne Cup. Of course, my submissions weren't being broadcast live on Channel 9 to millions of viewers across the country. And I wasn't in danger of breaking millions of Queenslander hearts – just my own little artistic ticker was on the line. Nevertheless, sending my creative toil out into the world placed a sizable chunk of my self-esteem firmly in the crosshairs of dismissal, doubt and pessimism.

The rejections started arriving in April. A form letter would accompany the returned manuscript, both bundled inside of the stamped, self-addressed envelope I'd provided with my submission. In today's doorstop delivery universe, coming home to a package is a thrill – not so for me back then. I dreaded the sight of a yellow bulge in the mailbox; it meant another member of my brave literary search party had returned empty handed. As the "thanks, but no thanks" slips piled up, I retained little hope for my prayer of a kick. Instead of finding a teammate, it had sailed out over the touchline. No surprise then that the package arriving eighteen days before Origin 1 sat unopened on my desk for a full afternoon.

After dinner, I tore the bag open. It was a rejection – as expected. One of the premier targets, top 3 in my ranking, home of some serious hitters. Form letter. Thank you for submitting your novel *The Procrastinator* blah blah blah. We receive hundreds of submissions and sign very few yada yada yada. Unfortunately, this one wasn't right for us and so on and so forth. I was about to crumple the letter up when I noticed blue biro scribbles peeking over the top of the folded section. I opened the fold to find a handwritten message. It was from the founder, the name on the masthead of the agency.

Darren,
We aren't signing this one, but your work is impressive.
You've got something here. Don't stop. I think you're a writer to watch.
I look forward to your next submission.

I read the message again. And again. And again. A dozen times in all. I carried the letter into the lounge room and handed it to Wend. She read it then looked at me, eyes dancing.

'Wow!' she said.

'I know,' I replied.

'I mean, this is someone who really knows books.'

'Yes.'

'And they're impressed. They think you're someone to watch.'

'Apparently.'

Still holding the paper, she wrapped her arms around my neck. 'My clever husband!' She kissed me, released me then read the note again. 'Do you feel awesome?'

I thought for a second. 'I feel relieved. I was afraid I'd been kidding myself the last couple of years. Wasting my time. This is proof I'm not.'

Wend nodded, hugged me. She folded the letter and tucked it into my shirt pocket. 'So, what are you standing here for? Go write the next one!'

I might've looked at that letter every one of the eighteen days preceding Origin 1. As I began toying with the idea that would eventually become my second novel *Most Valuable Potential*, the letter was a constant reminder: contrary to prevailing logic, a Hail Mary could succeed. A kick and a prayer could deliver.

◯

Walters' mongrel punt found open space. The first bounce was kind; the Steeden stood on its point instead of veering left to where Laurie Daley was motoring across in cover. The second bounce was a dream. Ben Ikin, leading the chase, didn't break stride or change direction. He didn't even bend down — the ball was on his chest before he could imagine any other scenario. A tackle from behind by Adam MacDougall brought him to ground ten metres into Blues territory. Under a minute remained. Sensing the hand of the Divine, I stood up straight, brought my mitts together and offered a silent, slightly modified devotion that merged with Ray Warren's frenzied call on the TV.

◯

Hail Alfie, full of pace, the King is with thee...

'SAILOR GETS A PASS AWAY TO LOCKYER... LOCKYER TOWARDS THE THIRTY METRE LINE...'

Blessed art Dell among wingers, and blessed is the boot of thy Locky genius…

LANGER… LANGER COMES TO BRASHER… GETS IT AWAY TO WALTERS… IT'S WITH DARREN SMITH…

Holy Kevvie, brother of Kerrod, make us winners now…

QUEENSLAND WILL NOT LIE DOWN…IT'S WITH LANGER AGAIN… LOCKYER IS PUT DOWN…

Right at the death…

IT'S WITH JASON SMITH… HE HOLDS THE PASS UP… AND HERE'S WALTERS GETTING IT AWAY! THEY'RE OVER AGAIN!! QUEENSLAND ARE IN!!! WELL, WHAT A GAME OF RUGBY LEAGUE!!!

Amen.

With time expired, Darren Lockyer piloted the conversion through to seal the win. The spectacle in our lounge room mirrored that on-field, on the Queensland sideline, and throughout the state: fist pumps, shouts, hugs, unrestrained glee, never-in-doubt declarations. One scene was unique to our gathering, however – the sight of a man in his late-twenties shaking off a pair of oven mitts and readying his hands for a sonic-boom barrage of applause.

'Someone say a prayer for us,' said Shell, covering her ears.

'How about a Hail Mary?' I replied and brought my hands together.

18

Impasse

June 23, 1999
Origin Game #3, Suncorp Stadium, Brisbane
Score: Qld 10 – NSW 10

There was no denying: regardless of the '99 decider's outcome, the decade belonged to New South Wales. Half a dozen series wins and a chance to make it seven at Suncorp. While our trio of victories were the standouts of the ten-year span, and the one-off triumphs of Game 2 in 1992 (Alf's wobbly winning field goal) and Game 1 in 1994 (the Miracle Try) added to the Maroon legend, the numbers didn't lie. The Blues were Origin's team of the '90s. It was a bitter pill more easily swallowed if we prevailed in the final game of the 20th century. 6-4 in the series ledger looked a whole lot better than 7-3.

Des had insisted we watch the game together. I wasn't sure why (he might've been worried Y2K would take us all out), but I was happy to oblige. I had a delicate subject to broach with him and doing so while watching the footy was the ideal forum. A safe haven was what rugby league and the Maroons always offered. When important, sometimes difficult conversations with Dad were needed, I knew the wheels of our talk could be greased by a Broncos recap or a Queensland selection dilemma or yet another whinge from Phil Gould about the state of the game. Footy was our catalyst, our connector and our cushion. The '99 decider needed to be all those things.

For almost a year, I'd wanted to tell my parents about Wend and I experiencing fertility issues. Soon after our return to Australia in 1996, we'd tried to get pregnant, casually, then with more intent. With nothing to show for it by mid '97, we went for testing. There were problems with both of us. Immediately, we sought solutions within our control. Wend changed her diet, I cut back on the booze. Wend took herbs, I took pills. Wend had acupuncture, I wore boxer shorts. Entering the spring of '98 – still no hint of success. It was clear we needed serious medical intervention.

Until you're in the thick of it, imagining the singular misery of struggling to conceive is impossible. Something so fundamental, so natural, easy as falling off a log for most people… it stabs at your soul when it isn't happening. For Wendy, the emotional trials I was suffering were multiplied by ten. Two events in the early months of '99 offer some insight into her colossal pain. The first occurred at her job working on the phones at Centrelink. Arriving home from a day's teaching, I discovered Wend had ended her shift early. She was in tears. One of her afternoon calls had been a pregnant 16-year-old and unsurprisingly the girl hadn't intended to get knocked up. Her attitude to bringing a child into the world? Little more than an irksome inconvenience made worthwhile by the money she was entitled to receive on the dole. The second torment was instigated a few weeks later by a scandal in our social circle. A lesbian couple of our acquaintance had split due to one of the women having a one-night stand with her male boss. The result of this dalliance (you guessed it): she'd fallen pregnant. When the news reached Wend's ears, she could barely contain her anger and despair. It took all her waning resilience to stop herself retreating to our bedroom, locking the door and never coming out. This pair of incidents may have been uniquely cruel and painful, but they were also part of a constant stream of day-to-day heartache, a seemingly endless loop of taunts from the universe about our failure to fulfill the most basic function of the human species.

They didn't know it, but Mum and Dad were part of the problem. In the three-and-a-half years since our return from Canada, grandkids had been on the folks' conversational radar. It was often alluded to, if not referenced outright, during Wednesday night family dinners. Over plates of salmon rissoles and shepherd's pie and, for vegetarian Wend's benefit, Dad's earnest but dodgy attempts at nut loaf and lentil burgers, the topic of a baby on the horizon was apt to find its way into the chat. Our standard response was to smile and shrug. Say 'maybe in the future'. It was wearing, wearying. It was also within our power to change the situation. In a grind where so much rested in the lap of the gods, limiting the grand-kiddy chatter was something we could influence. Such was the tightrope of a talk I'd prepared for Dad over the safety net of the decider.

◯

As the boys emerged from the sheds and ran out through a pom pom-waving guard of honour, I shied away from the *fait accompli*. If we won, I'd tell; if we lost, I'd wait until another time. A little voice in my head was reminding me of the Des Groth MO: gold-class softie, unabashed crier at my wedding, the man who valued family above all. The hurt and guilt he would feel at having caused us grief — it would be bad enough without a Queensland loss piling on. And that was discounting the sad leap he would make, the same one I'd made on the drive over: this Maroon bond between my father and

I, this wonderful gift of shared passion that communicated our love for each other like nothing else… it might never be passed down. There was still a distance to go in the fertility journey, stages to be explored and options to be exhausted, but I was already prone to thinking I would never be a father and nights like this would never be replicated in my life.

The prospect of a childless future faded once the game was underway. It was cold and wet at Suncorp. The track, though, was fast. So, too, the Maroons' early attack. In the second minute, a crisp exchange between the Smith brothers saw Robbie O'Davis go close to scoring in the corner. In the fourth minute, Wendell Sailor pinballed his way to within arm's length of the line.

'Positive start,' I said, catching my breath.

'No cigar,' replied Dad.

Proving my father's words prophetic, the Blues were first to post points. A shift right, some exceptional hands from Laurie Daley, and Matt Geyer was in untouched. Ten minutes gone, Cockroaches in front 4-nil. It should've been 10-nil in the 23rd minute when Darren Lockyer slipped in the wet, allowing Ben Kennedy to retrieve a towering Andrew Johns bomb. Blessedly, Kennedy panicked and pushed an ill-advised offload, resulting in Luke Ricketson dropping his lollies with the line wide open. It was the invitation we needed. In the 27th minute, after a barnstorming carry from Shane Webcke, Paul Green darted out of dummy-half, powered through three Blues defenders and plunged over next to the posts. Maroons 6-4 after the conversion. Although we would surrender the lead via a 31st minute penalty goal, the halftime scoreboard of 6-6 felt like a win.

Stretching the legs during the break, my thoughts returned to the Dad talk. Still a go if we got up, and postponed if we lost. If pressed to put money on the result, my bet was on Queensland delivering like the proverbial stork that kept bypassing our home. I rehearsed the scene at the final hooter: Des lifting a coldie as our Maroon man-of-the-match was interviewed (I pictured Adrian Lam); me asking him to turn the volume down on the TV then launching into the news like Gorden Tallis on the charge:

Dad, Wend and I may never be able to have kids.

I was ready. The movie was in the can, set to screen in vivid Technicolor.

At no time did I entertain the possibility of a twist ending.

10-10 and one minute to go when Robbie O'Davis coughed up the ball on our twenty. I dropped my head, unwilling to watch the final ignominy. I listened to Peter Sterling's plea to the Blues – 'One more to the posts then a Daley field goal!' – and waited for the dagger. It came. But the body wearing the fatal blow wasn't ours. A messy play-the-ball cruelled New South Wales' chance at the one-pointer and forced them to run it. Seconds later, the pass was spilled, Queensland came up with possession and the game was over.

A draw!

A *draw?*

I was celebrating – as defending series winners from '98, we retained the shield – but I couldn't quite wrap my head around it. Origin outcomes weren't left to the imagination. They were clear-cut, definitive. It was like pregnancy: all or none. I was still grappling with this turn of events when I felt Dad's hand on my shoulder.

'Still ours,' he said, patting his chest. 'They can't take it away from us.'

I studied his round face, his affable smile that held a hint of the rogue. The '90s had aged him – his hair had thinned and greyed, and his jowls were beginning to resemble Dali's melting watches. His spirit, though, was younger than ever. He'd run with the confidence acquired from the '95 Nevilles and had lived his best life ever since. Golf with buddies. Wednesday drinks at Fihelly's Arms. Trips with Mum to Hong Kong, Canada, New Zealand and Tasmania. A return to Queensland Rail via a contractor before taking up comfy, on-my-terms positions with Public Works and Housing and then the department of Transport and Main Roads. With the curtain coming down on the decade, Des Groth was a winner rather than a survivor.

It might've been the time to reveal our troubles to my father but, like the status of our reproductive efforts, the moment was much closer to impasse than opportunity. In the end, I could only repeat his words back to him:

'Yes, Dad. They can't take it away from us.'

I vowed to have the chat after the next Brisbane victory. I figured on a little breathing room (the Broncos had famously begun the season with one win in their first ten games), but the wait was only three days. Following the 19-6 triumph over Penrith, I sat him down and told him. He took it hard, but he took it well. His only concern was for the welfare of Wend and I. And he did as always: he chose light over dark, assuring me that things could turn around and that the past wasn't a predictor of the future. There was a new millennium on deck – with it came new hope. The '90s were done and dusted, and the scoreboard couldn't be changed. The 2000s, though, were starting at nil-nil. Maybe they would be better than their predecessor.

Maybe they would be the best yet.

2022

19

The Man-Child in the Mirror

June 8, 2022
Origin Game #1, Stadium Australia, Sydney
Halftime (Part 2)
Score: Qld 6 – NSW 4

In the bathroom, I have a nervous number one, which soon detours into a nervous number two, and then concludes with an encore nervous number one. I wash my hands before spying the sorry countenance in the mirror. Blotchy skin. Bags under the eyes. Some of the tiredness can be put down to hosting my family the last fortnight and the constant parade of late nights, boozy sessions and epic karaoke. The lion's share, though, belongs to this game and all its attendant weight. I press two fingers to my neck, checking my pulse. It's tap-dancing like Fred Astaire. I try some box-breathing to settle down but the necessary concentration fails me. I keep thinking of Dad's cancerous blood circumnavigating his body, dropping poisonous cells like breadcrumbs, corroding the bone marrow as if it were acid rain. I splash my face with water. Sit for a bit on the toilet.

You know what might help, Darren?

You could check the final score.

Tempting. Not because it would help, but because I am, as I've always been, a coward. It will hurt big-time if we lost and, like calling off a wedding before walking down the aisle, a pre-emptive strike might limit the pain. There are also the wonderful implications of a win: I'll be able to watch the second half stress-free, revelling in my surety of triumph.

Go on, Darren.

Relief is at your fingertips.

I reach into my pocket and extract my phone. Type in my pin. "Watch NRL" is up on the browser — a tap of the icon will access it. From there, the final score is only a screen refresh or two away. Alternatively, I could just do a quick search: "Maroons Origin". The headlines of the found articles will reveal all.

My index finger stalks the icon, jinking back and forth like Cam Munster probing the defence.

Go on.

It's better this way.

There's a knock on the bathroom door. Then a voice that could justifiably claim to be my conscience.

'You alright, son?'

'I'm okay, Dad.'

'You haven't fallen in, have you?'

'No, I haven't fallen in.'

'Good. We need you for the second half.'

I hear retreating footsteps, then Des' voice back in the living room. He begins discussing the Maroons' prospects, assuring Cal he has 'no idea' in an accent intended to be Canadian but closer to the American Midwest. I sigh and return the phone to my pocket. I can't do it. Whatever lies in wait — soaring joy or crushing disappointment — I wouldn't be able to hide the knowing from my father. I haven't changed from the little boy who would ruin every delayed footy telecast by blurting out the score pre-game if his team got up and flatly refusing to watch if his team came up short.

Fine – be a grown-up then.

Be a stupid, present adult.

I rise from the toilet and adjust my 2006 jersey, ensuring it properly covers my 52-year-old stomach. I exit the bathroom without a second glance at the man-child in the mirror.

The 2000s

20

Rock Bottom's Grenade

June 7, 2000
Origin Game #3, Stadium Australia, Sydney
Score: NSW 56 – Qld 16

In a world where sports fandom is lifelong woe punctuated by the occasional instance of delirium, Queensland Origin is a splendid anomaly. A cursory look at the numbers tells the story. At the time of writing this, we lead the titles count 24-17. We lead overall games won 70-60. We've never lost more than three series in a row and, as any Maroon die-hard will gleefully tell you, we jagged eight consecutive series from 2006 to 2013. In forty-plus years of living and dying with the team, I've lived much more than I've died.

There are no such gaudy levels of gratification in my other sporting passions. The Brisbane Broncos have won six titles in three-plus decades with the NSWRL / Super League / NRL – a creditable return for loyalty if one forgets that the last premiership was in 2006 (best not to mention the two epic grand final losses since, unless you want to witness a grown author cry). The team in North America I chose to make my own, the NHL's Vancouver Canucks, would kill for six titles. Actually, we would kill for just one. Entering the National Hockey League in 1970, the Canucks have made the Stanley Cup Finals three times, losing all three (the city rioted after the last two). The championship drought is one year younger than yours truly. The day the Canucks lift Lord Stanley's mug, I may well be in the ground.

As a Queensland supporter in the State of Origin era, I am spoiled. I worship a team that not only defies the odds and wins more than its fair share, it wins more, period. The inevitable suffering brought about by the losses — it's a pittance compared to the accepted sports fandom price. Maroon rock bottom will never be a Canuck-like fifty years without the ultimate reward or, as my father endured in the '70s, two wins in twenty-nine games.

So, what is rock bottom? Many argue it was the 56-16 Game 3 shellacking during the 2000 series, and in particular the notorious "grenade" try celebration by the Blues. I concur, although my opinion is skewed by the additional burden I carry with that game. In the eerie way Queensland Origin has often imitated the prevailing circumstances of my life, Bryan Fletcher's grenade charade was a perfect, horrible metaphor for the event that laid me lower than I'd ever been before.

I can't recall the exact date Wend told me she was pregnant, but it was sometime in late February of 2000. Five months previous, we'd had our second attempt at ICSI: Intracytoplasmic Sperm Injection, in which fertilisation is done in a lab, then one or more treated eggs are implanted in the uterus. When the procedure failed to produce a viable pregnancy, we decided to hit pause and take a break. Family and friends assured us it was a good idea. They mused that it might even be our remedy. They'd heard the story: old mate and missus struggle to get pregnant, step back, let go of expectation then, Bob's your uncle, they're up the duff! We knew the story too, but what had happened for others was no guarantee it would happen for us.

Then it did happen for us. No drugs. No procedures. No laboratories. The way it's supposed to. I was stunned. Tearing up, I grabbed Wend and held her in an embrace that might've lasted hours. When I finally let her go, my mind galloped off across the plains of parenthood's joyous and daunting unknowns. What will our kid's first word be? What school should our kid go to? How will we teach our kid to drive? Will our kid's first live Origin be an epic Queensland win, as it was for me? I was giddy with the thought of it all, but I also knew I was getting ahead of myself. We were eight weeks along and standard practice was to wait until twelve weeks before treating the pregnancy as the real deal. Until then, it was best to be circumspect.

Wendy wasn't circumspect – she was sceptical. And afraid. We were pregnant, yes, but it didn't feel good. It didn't feel right. She arranged an immediate appointment with the gynaecologist. What he discovered was the worst possible outcome: our pregnancy was ectopic. Instead of descending into the uterus, the fertilised egg had implanted in the fallopian tube. Left untreated, the growing egg would cause a rupture – a potentially life-threatening situation. It had to be removed and, in doing so, the fallopian tube would be destroyed.

Devastation doesn't begin to describe the fallout. To go from being pregnant to not being pregnant in a 24-hour period was awful enough; having our already compromised fertility cut in half as well… it felt like a knockout punch. I blamed myself. I'd been too excited, too soon. I hadn't respected Mother Nature. I'd forgotten to be humble. Consequently, this was on me. I'd brought this bombshell down upon our heads.

I deserved to be punished.

I watched Game 3 alone, slumped on the couch of our New Farm rental house on James Street. For perhaps the first time ever in Origin, I hadn't bothered to call any mates or arrange a get-together. It wasn't because New South Wales had already won the series — as every Queenslander knows, there's no such thing as a dead rubber. I just didn't feel like being around people. Prior to kickoff, Wend asked me if I wanted a watch buddy; I told her I was fine and that she should continue in her quest to beat Tetris on our Nintendo GameBoy.

From the moment Ryan Girdler intercepted Julian O'Neill's 17th minute pass and streaked away, the game had the smell of a Blues rout. Mat Rogers pouncing on a Tim Brasher mistake in-goal made the score 10-6, and a Darren Smith four-pointer in the 30th minute saw us hanging on 18-10 at oranges, but it was only delaying the inevitable. By the 60th minute, New South Wales were up 38-10. At other times, in other years, I would've switched off and skulked away, hoping to assuage the pain with a good book or a few beers or some trash TV or all three. Not tonight. Mental shackles had chained me to the couch more assuredly than a sentence of house arrest.

And then came Bryan Fletcher's try celebration in the 65th minute. After being mobbed by teammates, Fletcher instructed them to scatter before cradling the ball in one hand and lifting it to his mouth. He then bit an imaginary pin from the top of the ball, lobbed the "grenade" at the throng and covered his ears. When the ball hit the turf, the "explosion" levelled Fletcher's teammates, in particular Ben Kennedy who took a dive worthy of Greg Louganis.

Like Choppy Close, who refuses to let it go to this day; like Gorden Tallis, who believes it was the reason Queensland turned the result around in 2001; like Darren Lockyer, who in 2020 called the incident 'a dark day for Queensland'; like every Maroon fan witness to the disrespect, I should have been livid at Fletcher & Co's antics.

I wasn't.

From where I sat, it felt appropriate.

Inside the darkness of the new millennium's first months, it felt deserved.

21

Babies

May 6, 2001

Origin Game #1, Suncorp Stadium, Brisbane

Score: Qld 34 – NSW 16

Had both the Maroons and Wendy taken their cue from my defeated response to the adversities of 2000, the aughts might've panned out along these lines:

Queensland loses in '01.

Loses again '02.

We lose every series of the decade.

We fail to win a game after '04.

In 2010, State of Origin is abandoned due to lack of interest.

The Suncorp Stadium statues of Arthur Beetson and Wally Lewis are relocated to the Gaythorne RSL and used as hatstands.

The Caxton Pub becomes a vegan restaurant called "Wattle Ya Have".

My beautiful wife comes to her senses in late 2000.

She ditches me for Ewan McGregor (a massive upgrade from yours truly, but still not on Wend's level).

She lives out a life of blissful happiness, hob-nobbing with Hollywood's A-list, unencumbered by writer wannabe dreams and obsessive rugby league parochialism…

Thankfully for all but Ewan McGregor, the Queensland Maroons and Wendy Fraser are made of more Churchillian stuff than I — *"If you're going through Hell, keep going"* — and rock bottom would prove to be a launch pad rather than a crash site.

In December of 2000, conditions aligned for another attempt at assisted pregnancy. Stalwart Wend didn't hesitate and the gynaecologist performed our third ICSI procedure, implanting a pair of fertilised eggs under the rationale of two chances being better than one. The agonising wait to pee on a stick then ensued. Over Christmas. Through New Year. Into early January. The week before Australia Day, six weeks after the procedure, we chose the venue for our fate's discovery: the campgrounds of Mapleton Falls. If it turned out that Mother Nature had failed us again, at least we could give Her an up close and personal gobful.

On a pristine Sunshine Coast hinterland morning, Wend walked from our tent to the toilet block, test in hand. I waited, distracting myself by chatting to our golden retriever, Cheyenne.

'Hey, pup. You sleep well? Mum's just gone to the loo. She'll be back in a tick…'

Wend returned fifteen minutes later, unzipped the tent and crawled in. Her eyes were red-rimmed, raw. I scrambled out of my sleeping bag and went to hold her. She shook her head, held up a hand. She scanned my face, as if the consolation she needed was hiding somewhere in my features. The search ended when she met my worried gaze. She handed me the stick and smiled.

'We're pregnant.'

The celebration this time was muted and brief. The lesson of the ectopic – I wasn't about to forget it. Rather than projecting into a parental future, I would stay in the moment, quiet, humble, respectful, not getting too high or low, doing what needed to be done without any fuss or fanfare. In rugby league parlance, I was taking it one game at a time.

That commitment to even keel would be essential in the three months of surreality that followed. Back from camping, we booked a follow-up with the gynaecologist to confirm that we had a little embryo growing.

'Embryos,' he corrected. 'Both eggs were successful.' He noted our stunned, open-mouthed reactions. 'Surprised?'

'We're just taking it one game at a time, Doc,' I replied.

Bigger tests of our equanimity were to come. The interminable wait to reach the magical 12-week mark. The euphoric reveals to loved ones, starting with Des and Kath (Dad was so blinkered by delight he offered Wend a beer for the obligatory toast). Then the sternest examination of our level-headedness: a major scare just shy of the 5-month mark. A bout of cramping – possible precursor to miscarriage – prompted an urgent medical consult. To our eternal relief, the babies were fine. And to ensure they stayed fine, Wend was placed on modified bed rest. By the time we'd reached 24 weeks – the threshold deemed the floor for newborn survival – my even keel was tilting towards the positive. After everything we'd been through, was it too much to suggest we'd paid our dues, that we'd earned a little support from the universe? It wasn't. It was a very reasonable request. After rock bottom, I was confident things were looking up. The page was turning.

Bring on the babies!

Bring on the babies!

It might've been master coach Wayne Bennett's command to Des Morris and the selectors when choosing his squad for Game 1. Ten debutants came into the side, most of them twenty-five or under. After the throttling of 2000, changes had to be made. So many though? And so young? It was undoubtedly the good pregnancy vibes colouring my footy goggles, but I was upbeat. To my mind, this was the Queensland Origin comfort zone: rank outsiders, everyone writing us off, the Blues crowning themselves before a ball is kicked in anger. It had ambush written all over it.

The game viewing reflected my optimism. Gone was the one-man, self-flagellating act of the previous year — a dozen family and friends were in attendance at our home. Ensuring everyone could see the TV required a few creative chair placements and body positions due to the couch being reserved for one. Wend was laid out across its expanse, modified bed-resting, my 1995 jersey stretching over her twin bump (by July and Dad's birthday — his 60th — the bump would be a grand belly, worthy of competing with Des' own carefully cultivated midriff. The side-by-side comparison produced a photo finish with Dad edging out the Canadian challenger). Every two minutes, someone from the group — more often than not Mum — would check in with her. Can I get you anything? A water? Something to eat? Do you need an extra blanket? More cushions? Never one for the spotlight, Wend was a little embarrassed by all the attention; I thought it was great. And fitting. On this night of a new buzz in the Maroon hive, it made perfect sense that Wend was our Queen Bee. Or more accurately: our Queensland Bee.

I've never sat down and figured out my all-time top-five most enjoyable Origin wins. If I did, Game 1 of 2001 would be right up there. From the second minute when Darren Lockyer put Lote Tuqiri away down the Hale Street sideline then backed up to cross beside the posts, the atmosphere in our New Farm Queenslander was loose and lively. Even Coach Groth was tolerable, exhibiting a level of obnoxiousness more in keeping with sports fandom than clinical diagnosis. Very little stress, very little tension; so many smiles and cheers and high-fives and fist-pumps. And when Bennett baby Carl Webb scored the best solo try in Origin history just before halftime, the misery of the previous year felt like a bad dream fading from memory.

The rest of the game was a party. During the break, I popped Regurgitator's Sydney Olympics "tribute" EP in the stereo and cranked up the lead track, "Crush the Losers". After North Queensland Cowboys' rookies John Doyle and John Buttigieg scored in the 45th and 49th minutes respectively, Texas-like YEE-HAWs resounded out of 150 James Street. When the scoreboard reached 32-4 following Chris Walker's touchdown, we re-enacted Bryan Fletcher's "grenade" toss, only with a Maroon-styled correction: all of us standing, none of us felled. Two late Blues' tries tempered the scoreboard smash-up, but it took nothing away from the thrill of the win nor the monumental scale of the twelve-month turnaround.

Post-game, the TV broadcast flipped from the on-field celebrations to the dressing sheds where Wayne Bennett paced alone, a proud parent awaiting the return of his seventeen triumphant sons. I made my way to the lounge, knelt down and took Wendy's hand in mine. She'd been confined to the couch as a precaution, as a counter to her supposed fragility; to me, she was the epitome of strength. As tough and brave as the players who'd soon be joining Bennett in the sheds.

'You happy?' she asked.

'Couldn't be happier,' I replied.

'The kids came through.'

'They sure did.'

She brought my hand down and placed it on her baby bump. 'A lot can happen in a year, eh?'

I kissed her then spoke directly into her tummy. 'Bloody oath!'

For most fans, the 2001 series is iconic for Allan Langer's return from England in Game 3 and his extraordinary performance in Queensland's series-sealing 40-14 romp. There is no denying that Alf answering Wayne Bennett's SOS and playing the game of his life at age thirty-four thoroughly deserves its place on the list of all-time greatest Origin deeds. To this day, I wish I'd witnessed it first-hand (it wasn't possible; in addition to Wend's modified bed rest, we were a week away from moving to our new house in Arana Hills). To have seen Langer weaving his old man magic, guiding the kids home to their eternal place in rugby league history… it would've been incredible. But here's the thing about Game 3: it doesn't happen without Game 1. Take away the blinding brilliance of the team with ten debutants, there is no stage set for the decider, no series up for grabs, no call to Langer, no fairytale finish, no exorcising the demons of 2000. Without the arrival of Bennett's Babies, there is no sense that we can look forward to the years ahead, no thought that we can withstand the inevitable grenades tossed in our direction.

The same can be said for the arrival of Chloe Lee Groth and Jared Fraser Groth, born at 33 weeks, via caesarean section, three minutes apart on July 21st, 2001. Their mere existence was marvellous, miraculous, the ultimate reward for five years of painful toil. And though more pain would come, shadowing the twins' early time in this world – they would spend three weeks in hospital following their birth; they were eight weeks old when the World Trade Center towers fell on September 11; they were six months old when Wend had a second ectopic pregnancy and required emergency surgery – our babies would always be living proof that the darkest hours are followed by the dawn.

22

Maroon Munchhausen

June 26, 2002
Origin Game #3, Stadium Australia, Sydney
Score: Qld 18 – NSW 18

I shouldn't remember anything about Origin 2002. With a pair of infants occupying every waking (and sleeping) moment, my recollections should only be of feeds and baths and slings and giggles and nappy changes and bottle rinses and days without showering and singing Spiderbait's "Ultralite" as a lullaby and daily entries in the twin journals and drives out to Albany Creek to settle screaming lungs and teaching in quicksand at Milpera and using car capsules as weights to work out and moving Operation Offsprings to the downstairs rumpus room because it was Brisbane's hottest summer in eighty years… somehow there was still room in the brain for footy. That it looms quite large in my memory to this day says something about the 2002 series. Or me (most likely me… okay, definitely me).

Game 1 is a standout for all the wrong reasons. Queensland was poor, going down 32-4 in Sydney. It wasn't as catastrophic as the 2000 Game 3 debacle, but it didn't bode well for the rest of the series. Had the debutants of '01 been a flash in the pan? Were they good enough to back it up? What really stamped the game as unforgettable was the night that unfolded post-match. Chloe woke soon after the final hooter and started to cry. On its own, the scenario wasn't abnormal; Chloe was a challenging bub when it came to sleep. What was unusual on this occasion concerned Twin #2. Relied upon to be our night-time rock, Jared crumbled as well. The moment his sibling settled – a state achieved only after a patting, cooing, cuddling process that took thirty minutes or more – he would start up. And so began a game of "my turn, your turn" that would last for the next seven-plus hours; a span that, in its entirety, never failed to have one or more of us in tears. When I collapsed into bed around 5:15 am, aware on some astral plane that I was required to teach young, non-English speaking minds in a very short while, I wondered if this was all of my making. Had the sleeping twins absorbed my gloom from the Origin drubbing? Was this the first evidence of me burdening the kids with my Queenslander baggage?

Wend was taking no chances with Game 2. She was okay with having people over – she might've viewed them as a means of escape if things went sideways again – but the gathering would take place in the rumpus room (we'd moved Operation Offsprings back upstairs at the end of the summer). And to further safeguard the twins from disturbance, the oven mitts would once more be in effect, only this time with the additional buffer of cricket inner gloves under the mitts.

Given what transpired over the eighty minutes, one might assume a gag would've also been a wise choice. This was the infamous Justin Hodges debut in which he gifted New South Wales two tries with errant passes in his own in-goal before being yanked from the field by Wayne Bennett. Surely my response to those calamities must have woken the dead, let alone two little babies? Nope. I can't say for certain why, but amidst all the opportunity for regrettable actions afforded by Hodgo's mayhem, I produced one of my calmest, most even-tempered Origin displays. In fact, I never thought for a minute we would lose the game.

And we didn't. A Blues four-pointer in the 68th minute – the only one they managed to score without Hodges' generosity – reduced the deficit to two, but that was as close as they got. Andrew Johns hit the upright with his conversion attempt and, after Jason Moodie knocked on inside his 10 with a minute to go, Lote Tuqiri barged over to claim a hat-trick of tries and seal the deal. Final score: 26-18. Making the win even sweeter: the twins slept through the night. Again, questions arose in my mind. Were the kids taking their cue from my Maroon elation? Had my Origin happy place helped them achieve the same state?

Two games, two contrasting experiences… two babies tapping into their Dad's emotions? I felt the decider would offer definitive proof one way or the other.

◯

I was sick for Game 3. Nothing serious – just a cold, likely new parent-itis. Because I didn't feel too bad, I wanted company for the viewing. A few hours before kickoff, I made my case:

'Game 2 we had people over,' I said to Wendy, wiping a stray strand of snot from the collar of my '95 jersey. 'And we won, even though Hodgo shat the bed. We should do everything the same, so we don't upset the ju-ju.'

Wend considered me through narrowed eyes. 'How many drugs have you had?'

'Just a couple of Codral.'

She made a sceptical 'mmph' sound. 'Stick to one.' She picked up Jared's current favourite toy – a Thomas the Tank Engine that aggressively and relentlessly played the show's theme song as it rolled along – and stashed it in the nearby tote. 'We're not having people over because they don't want to catch your man-flu. Queensland will have to make the ju-ju on their own tonight.'

I started to protest then had a sneezing fit, which took all the resistance wind out of my sails. Wend was right. Although I had no qualms about doing whatever it took for the Maroons, the dedication of family and friends – even Des – likely fell short of communicable disease. And in a decision I fully supported, Wend wasn't about to fill the void created by my soft, bandwagoner, plague-free, absentee buddies. The last thing our little family needed was for Mama to get sick; it was a not an insignificant mercy she'd evaded my illness flick pass to this point. So, there I was at the opening whistle, alone on our inadequate-for-social-distancing couch, mug of chamomile tea in hand, box of Kleenex by my side, nose running more freely than Chris Walker with a hint of daylight.

The first half was a distillation of the extremes witnessed in the first two encounters of the series, lurching from joyous high (Tuqiri wins the race to a deft Darren Lockyer kick; 4-0 after seven minutes) to anguished low (Steve Menzies plunges over beside the sticks; Blues on top 6-4), back to ecstasy (Gorden Tallis ragdolls Brett Hodgson over the sideline and into origin folklore) then plunging again into ennui (Trent Barrett carves us up and sends Jason Moodie in under the black dot). 12-8 Cockroaches at the break. Dumping my tumbleweed of used tissues in the bin, I asked Wend if she'd heard any stirring from the kids' rooms.

'So far, so good. You're all behaving yourselves.'

I nodded, heeding the thinly veiled warning. I might've been unsure if my fandom was seeping into our babies' consciousness but Wend was erring on the side of caution. And the implication was clear: keep the kids out of it, Darren, for all our sakes.

Fulfilling that brief would be much easier with a win, and it looked likely when Shane Webcke bulldozed over in the 59th minute to give us the lead. Even more so in the 69th minute when a moment of Lockyer genius saw him snatch a Langer grubber from Brett Hodgson's grasp and touch down a hair inside the dead-ball line. But Fate wasn't about to give me a free ride. The video ref ruled that Locky had knocked on (a travesty) and New South Wales made the most of their let-off by scoring in the 75th minute to lead 18-14.

With sixty seconds to go, I felt all of it rising like bile in the back of my throat. Anger, frustration, dejection. Somehow, I had to temper it. If I didn't, Game 1's Worst Night Ever would repeat. On that occasion I'd poisoned the twins with my negative vibe, a case of Maroon Munchhausen by proxy. Without their consent, I'd prescribed them a hefty dose of disappointment and their tiny immune systems hadn't stood a chance. I couldn't let it happen again. As per the standard applied to all my non-Origin parenting, I needed to sacrifice my feelings, my needs, my indulgences for the good of my kids. I needed to swallow my medicine and be the adult in the room, the bigger man. I needed to be a father.

I needed to be *my* father.

As much as anyone who's ever tried balancing optimism and realism, Dad had always sought to buffer his children from personal dismay. If he had misgivings about Douglas Adams' *life, the universe and everything*, about raising a family; about shepherding three sons into the world; and yes, about football too, because football is a lens through which all of the above may be observed… I wasn't aware of them. Dad never hid his vulnerability, but he also made sure his boys weren't needlessly exposed to his own fears and doubts.

I can do this, I thought. With my father's example, I can inoculate the twins from my disease.

Five seconds later, it all went out the window.

○

I shouted when Dane Carlaw beat Moodie one-on-one and broke free.

I cheered when the big second-rower powered through Hodgson's covering tackle and crossed the line.

I yelled expletives as Gordie gave the crowd his legendary spray and two-fingered salute.

'What. The fuck. Are you *doing*?'

I turned. Wend had the look of a serial killer who relished the idea of just murdering the one person multiple times. I gave a thin smile that was closer to a grimace and pointed a limp finger at the Queensland rapture on TV.

'We won! In the final seconds! Actually, we tied it. But because we won last year, we get to keep—'

'Just stop!'

'Sorry.'

Wend cupped her ear, listening for any unhappiness in the bedrooms, any grounds for instant divorce. I muted the TV and held onto a sneeze, nearly popping my eyeballs out of their sockets.

Silence.

Blessed silence.

'Sleeping easy,' I whispered. 'Thanks to the lads.'

'Of course.' Wend shook her head and made her way back to the game of "Solitaire" she had going on the dining table. Over her shoulder, she added: 'No thanks to you, Mr Man-Flu.'

○

I mentioned earlier that I've never ranked my most enjoyable wins. A top-five I have thought about, though, is best ever series performances. While the definition of "best" can and should be hotly debated, several years immediately figure to be in the frame. In fact, on my list, four of the top five pick themselves. In no particular order, 1989: the whitewash that included the hospital ward Game 2 and the King's iconic winning try; 1995: the greatest underdog coup, perhaps in Australian sporting history; 2006: the zenith of Maroon resilience, culminating in Darren Lockyer's heroics; and 2010: the Dynasty at their peak, securing two of their three victories in Sydney. Rounding out the five is a tough task – there are numerous candidates. 1983. 1987. 1988. The 2008 and 2017 teams that prevailed despite injuries to Lockyer and Johnathan Thurston respectively. The 2020 "Worst Queensland Team Ever" (Bravo, Gallen). While every one of these (and more) would be worthy additions, my vote goes to the 2002 side.

Consider their case:

Coming back from 1-0 down to win or retain the title – at the time of writing, a feat achieved just eleven times in Origin history.

Suffering the biggest Game 1 belting in Origin history (28 points) while still winning or retaining the title.

Overcoming two of the worst gaffes in Origin history to win Game 2.

Retaining the title at Stadium Australia where, to that point, Queensland were winless in five starts.

Conjuring a shield-securing fifty metre try in the 79th minute of a decider.

All of this evidence is compelling and yet it doesn't include their most impressive achievement, the one that guarantees their inclusion in my top-five:

They saved an infant set of twins from their dangerously infectious father.

For good? No. They'd be at risk next year, and for many years after. But 2002 had shown that while I was a terminal case, there was a chance my children could live happy, healthy, productive, Origin-free lives. They could be spared the malady that was incurable in their old man.

23

Destiny's Child

July 7, 2004
Origin Game #3, Telstra Stadium, Sydney
Score: NSW 36 – Qld 14

The mug I prefer for my daily vat of breakfast tea has a paperback cover of *The Iliad* stamped on it and an arresting quote lifted from its pages:

"No man or woman, born brave or coward, can shun their destiny."

The message is not unique to Homer – similar versions of it can be found everywhere in literature, both ancient and modern. Aesop's fable *The One-Eyed Doe*, for example. From fablesofaesop.com:

A doe blind in one eye was accustomed to graze as near to the edge of the cliff as she possibly could, in the hope of securing her greater safety. She turned her sound eye towards the land that she might get the earliest tidings of the approach of hunter or hound, and her injured eye towards the sea, from whence she entertained no anticipation of danger. Some boatmen sailing by saw her, and taking a successful aim, mortally wounded her. Yielding up her last breath, she gasped forth this lament: 'O wretched creature that I am! To take such precaution against the land, and after all to find this seashore, to which I had come for safety, so much more perilous.'

In addition to supporting Homer's claim of an inescapable life path, the fable also offers the bonus moral of "Prepare as best you can; the rest is up to Providence" (a third takeaway – "Being a deer blows" – is implied, but much less relevant for this story). As a writer, I appreciate Homer's line and Aesop's fable for their sheer narrative heft. But do I subscribe to their belief? Am I a disciple of Destiny and its reign over our existence? The short answer is… kind of? Being raised Catholic – seven years an altar boy for grumpy Father Nugent at Our Lady Of Dolours Church in Mitchelton – did its best to indoctrinate me, but religion isn't the reason I'm open to the idea of a Grand Plan. Rather, it's been a handful of stones dropped with apparent purpose into my life's pond. The largest of those stones – the one whose ripples would reach every shoreline of my world – was tossed in the spring and summer of 2002. And in the eighteen months that followed, I would not only refute the disturbance, I would question the very existence of the stone.

◯

The twins were just past their first birthday when Jared's development began to be cause for concern. The red flags were noticeable on their own; next to his sister, they were floodlit like a Friday Night Football venue. Chloe's progress was by the book: crawling at nine months, standing at twelve months, saying dozens of words at fifteen months (our favourite was "shoe"; the little scamp would put on a single tiny sandal and waddle around the house proclaiming 'shoe! shoe!'). When playing with toys, Chloe ticked the necessary boxes: building Lego towers, babbling on the phone, filling a plane with people and, with sound effects, flying it around our lounge room. In contrast, Jared crawled later and took a long time to stand, preferring his alternate mode of transport: scooching around on his knees. His play tendencies with cars and trucks, however, really signposted something else going on. Unlike his sibling's use of them in the customary way, Jared would flip the vehicles upside down and spin the wheels. Over, and over, and over again.

I recognised the signs, and I'm not proud to say my knee-jerk responses were heartbreak and dismissal. The autism I'd encountered in the special schools was a colossal challenge. The sensory issues. The social aversion. The absence of communication. The difficulty of self-regulation. With a few students, there'd been aggression and violence, towards others and themselves. Were these encounters now a prelude for parenting my son? I told myself they weren't. Confirmed autism diagnoses didn't occur at twelve months; they were made at two, three years of age. And Jared's behaviours could have any number of treatable non-autistic explanations. Allergies. Hearing problems. It could even be lead poisoning. Or maybe the behaviours and delays required no explanation at all. Maybe they would resolve themselves – a situation not unheard of in the lottery of childhood progress. Maybe Jared's route to being a regular kid was just more circuitous than that of his sibling.

A visit to the GP fed my optimism. I heard everything I wanted to hear. It was too early to know for sure, there could be other reasons, things could change overnight, probably nothing to get too worked up about. Throughout the consult, Jared was fascinated by the doc's large nose, staring at it, reaching out to touch it with his finger. She took it as further proof of a child not deviating too far from the norm. Driving back home to Arana Hills, I was breathing easier. Things would turn out fine. If Destiny existed, surely It hadn't pitched me into special schools teaching as a forewarning of my own disabled child. Surely It wasn't that desperate for irony. If I wrote that in a novel, publishers would pull a hamstring running for a rejection letter.

Little by little, my hopefulness faded. A few weeks after the doctor's appointment, Jared started a nightly obsession of stacking all of his toys on his bed then sleeping beside the pile. His diet narrowed to a few basic "beige" foods. And then came the kicker: his spoken language disappeared. One day, he had a vocabulary of half a dozen or so words – 'dog', 'Mum', 'car', 'fan'; the next, they were gone. And with them went my delusion. Jared was now two years old and there was no doubt he was on the autism spectrum. A decade after my time at Ipswich and Claremont Special Schools; a decade after teaching kids in wheelchairs, kids wearing helmets, kids wearing callipers, kids using communication boards, kids who would need support their entire lives; a decade after watching parents and guardians at afternoon pick-up and wondering what their lives were like and what it took to cope; a decade after an experience I was sure I had left behind, here was an inescapable truth: I was fathering a disabled son.

Homer would've approved.

I wasn't alone in providing proof of the ancient Greek poet's warning. In Origin, Darren Lockyer – the Prince, the second coming of Clive Churchill, the new captain of Queensland – was also dealing with a destiny he couldn't shun. The best fullback in the game and the 2003 Golden Boot winner as the best player in rugby league, Lockyer had transitioned to five-eighth at the start of 2004. The shift was considered by many to be kismet. Lockyer's hero growing up had been Wally Lewis, the greatest six to ever lace a boot; it was right and proper the prodigy from Roma be the next legend to dominate in the revered jumper. I wasn't so sure. At club level, Locky had worked out the kinks quickly, steering the Broncos to a 7-4 record in the first eleven games and setting in motion a personal season that would see him awarded the Dally M for Five-Eighth of the Year. Origin, though, was an unknown commodity. With Allan Langer finally retiring for good in 2002, Queensland had under-performed in the 2003 Origin series, losing the first two games badly before a face-saving 36-6 mauling in the final tilt. Then on July 29, Ben Ikin – the incumbent Maroon pivot – announced that his 26-year-old knees were shot and that his playing career was coming to a premature and painful end. This sobering background was a wrench in the romance of Locky's move to the halves. In my estimation, the change looked more like necessity than Destiny. Still, the argument for Fate's hand made for good copy. And many believed the story of Lockyer in jersey 6 would be a procession of glorious triumph, starting with the '04 series.

It wasn't. Despite a marvellous win in Game 2 – a victory that included Billy Slater's chip-and-chase try for the ages – Queensland lost 2-1. I retain two potent memories from the decider. The first is shared by many: Brad "Freddy" Fittler in the 74th minute, final outing for the Blues, charging down Locky's kick, collecting the loose ball and crossing untouched, finger pointed to the sky; the try a dagger to Lockyer's next-Wally-Lewis birthright and the last ignominy of a night best forgotten by Maroon Nation.

(An aside: the whole Fittler "fairytale farewell" narrative largely ignores the fact that Game 3 of 2004 was Freddy's third attempt at exiting a winner: the first, the 2001 decider when Alf's return from England sent him packing; the second, the preceding 2004 game where the Blues coughed up a 12-6 halftime lead and became a footnote to Slater's magic. *Three* attempts to say goodbye! That's worse than me at Christmas! It begs the question: had the Maroons got up in Game 3 of 2004, would Freddy have had *a fourth* attempt at leaving the Origin stage victorious? Or a *fifth*? It's just as well he managed to get it done before the Dynasty came along. Trotting him out there every year until 2014 would've been tantamount to elder abuse.)

The second vivid memory is from Game 3's aftermath. Approaching midnight, I was still too bummed to sleep. Looking for something useful to do, I eased Jared's bedroom door open and tip-toed in. The scene was as suspected: every toy in the room piled up around his pillow, Jared kneeling at the foot of the bed fast asleep. By the dim glow of his penguin-shaped nightlight, I cleared his bed, picked him up, tucked him in, kissed his forehead. Retreating back to the door and surveying the scene one last time, the previous twelve months suddenly coalesced into a few seconds. I thought about special schools and spinning wheels. Big noses and lost words. Kicks charged down and fingers raised to the sky.

I thought about Destiny as we might wish it to be.

And Destiny as it actually is.

24

Plucked Out of Thin Air

May 25, 2005
Origin Game #1, Suncorp Stadium, Brisbane
Score: Qld 24 – NSW 20

'So, what happens now?' asked Simon, popping the top off his fourth Cooper's of the game.

'Golden point,' I replied.

'First time?'

'In Origin, yeah.'

'And any score wins?'

'More than likely a field goal. It's going to be a field goal-a-thon.'

'I don't know why they changed it,' said Des, chiming in. 'What's wrong with a draw?'

'Nothing, Dad! It's because we "won" in '99 and '02 on drawn deciders. If it had been the Cockroaches retaining the trophy, they wouldn't have changed shit!'

Simon hooked a thumb towards the nearby window. 'We'll know if Queensland wins well before we see it on TV.'

I nodded. In the lounge room of my youngest brother's house on Enoggera Terrace in Paddington, neighbouring Suncorp Stadium could be both seen and heard. And it was the hearing that would clue us in to the Maroons' ultimate fortunes in Game 1 of 2005. Throughout the preceding eighty minutes, the live action had remained ahead of the broadcast by a good ten seconds. At various intervals, a great zeppelin of noise would sail over our vantage, cueing us to a Queensland moment incoming. The loudest had occurred in the 78th minute; with the good guys trailing 20-19 and Darren Lockyer surging towards the Blues' ten metre line, the Enoggera Terrace living room had rattled with a seismic wave borne out of Milton. I'd greedily hoped for a winning try, but the source of the joy was almost as satisfying: a Johnathan Thurston one-pointer that scraped over the crossbar after collecting a New South Wales hand.

20-20, and headed to overtime.

I knew then as I know now: golden point is a staring contest. First to blink is in trouble. Making the opportunity count was imperative, though. If you didn't capitalise, you might not get another chance. On this night, the Blues were first to blink. After Queensland's strong opening set and a probing Locky kick, New South Wales were pinned in their own half. First tackle, minimal gain. Same for the second. And the third. By the fifth, they were still inside their 40 and in desperate need of a strong finish to the set. Trent Barrett couldn't provide it. In a sequence I ate up with more gusto than a serve of mud crab at Oxley's, the St George-Illawarra pivot poked a short grubber in behind the Maroons' defensive line then tried to con referee Paul Simpkins with a soccer-worthy dive. Simpkins wasn't fooled. We were in the box seat.

'Make 'em pay!' I declared, rising to my feet. Billy Slater then Brad Thorn took hit-ups, establishing position for the winning field goal. On the fourth tackle, when Shaun Berrigan played the ball just shy of the 30-metre line, I heard a rumble outside. Then a roar. Here we go, I thought. The prize. Thurston was tackled on the fifth and Cam Smith moved into dummy-half. Behind the line, Lockyer was set for the match-winning kick. The Smith pass was money and, despite the bevy of Blues bearing down, Locky's drop-kick was pure.

'Yes!'

'YES!'

'YESSSSS!'

It missed. A shade left of the posts. Anthony Minichiello caught the ball in the in-goal, allowing New South Wales a re-start from their 20. I slumped back down on the couch. We'd had first shot and failed; now they had the advantage. I glanced over at the window permitting passage of the Suncorp faithful's hubbub. What would be the sound of defeat? A 50,000-strong gasp, groan, howl of 'NOOOO!'? I didn't wonder for long. As Andrew Ryan rucked it out for the Blues then Craig Fitzgibbon followed suit, a firestorm of collective voice split the air over our heads. Funny, I thought. Sounds like a party. But how can that be? New South Wales is in possession; Brett Kimmorley is firing a cut-out ball to…

Us?

Matt Bowen.

Lurking in the line.

Snatching the pass away from Blue hands.

Streaking away untouched.

Game.

Over.

Amidst the fog of euphoria engulfing Suncorp Stadium, Enoggera Terrace and beyond, I marvelled at the reversal of fortune. In an instant, opportunity lost had become everything gained. And peering through my narrow, self-absorbed lens on the world, I couldn't help but feel a sense of *deja vu*, that the precursor for this moment had occurred six months earlier. In a multi-verse where literary aspiration intersected with Maroon inspiration, it was my second novel rather than the Kimmorley pass that Matt Bowen had plucked out of thin air and brought to the promised land.

When I got the email, I wasn't Matt Bowen. I wasn't thinking ahead. I wasn't preparing for success or anticipating reward. I wasn't ahead of the play, seeing the moment before it unfolded. I was oblivious, blind-sided. But, in the best way possible:

Congratulations, Darren. Most Valuable Potential *has been nominated for the 2004 Queensland Premier's Literary Awards…*

To say this news was out of left field is like saying Steven Bradbury was pleasantly surprised to cross the line first in the 2002 Olympic short track final. *Most Valuable Potential*, or *MVP* as I like to call it, was not on anyone's radar in the spring of 2004. It was barely on mine; the novel having run out the clock on its publishing journey. Writing it in 1999, hopes had been high (as they invariably are for any writer's new story). Set in Milpera and fashioned around my experiences with the migrant and refugee students in my classes, *MVP* had good bones: a pro athlete, forced into early retirement by a devastating injury, arrives at Australia's sole, stand-alone, English-as-Second-Language school to coach an eclectic group of six kids, and through the trials and triumphs, comes to understand the true nature of loss while re-kindling the possibility of new beginnings.

(Given the referencing of him in the previous chapter, you might think the "pro athlete forced into early retirement" was a nod to Ben Ikin – the truth is I conceived the character of Sean Watson several years before Ikin's sad goodbye in '03. And the horrific knee injury that cost Watson his career? It owes much, not to Ikin, but to the one suffered by Australian Opals' star Rachael Sporn in 1999. Thankfully, Sporn fared better than my character and resumed her on-court brilliance the following year.)

Initially, it seemed *MVP* might live up to its name. I entered the partial manuscript in the Australian Society of Authors' Mentorship program and, out of 100+ submissions nationwide, it was one of a dozen selected for the prize of working with an established writer for twenty hours. My chosen mentor was a Queensland author I idolised: Venero Armanno. Sitting down with Veny, having him read my story, gobbling up his advice… at that time, it was far-and-away the standout highlight of my writing adventure. And when he gave the finished draft an enthusiastic thumbs-up, it seemed like the pieces were in place for a major breakthrough. But it wasn't to be. 2001, the big agents, competitions and publishing houses passed; 2002, it was rejected by everyone else that mattered. I was gutted. How could a work of such promise deliver nothing? *Nothing?* By early 2003, I had a choice: shelve it or sign with the only destination that had shown it any love: a very small, very dodgy outfit called Narrow Press. I chose the latter, figuring *MVP* published in some shape or form was better than it sitting in my desk drawer.

Narrow did not disappoint in its dodginess. From shoestring jacket design to typos in the final print to distribution fiascos to the editor wanting his name on the cover to non-existent promotion, the publishing process was less professional than the Emus on a Kangaroo tour of Great Britain. At the end of it, though, I had a book. A lifeless book, sure, but as we've all learned from horror movies: lifeless might just be a zombie in disguise. And perhaps that zombie's awakening could be the 2004 Queensland Premier's Literary Awards. It would assuredly not be in the category the publisher had head-shakingly targeted: Best Fiction Book. If it had any shot, it would be in the young adult award – a submission I was making myself, paid for out of my own pocket. My thought process as I shoved the package into the post-box at the New Farm newsagent: maybe *MVP* could thrust its cold, dead hand out of the scorched earth and rise from the grave.

⬯

For *Most Valuable Potential* to be Matty Bowen-ed (yes, I'm making it a verb now), it had to be on the field. That almost wasn't the case. Talking to one of the judges in the wake of the book's recognition, she told me it had very nearly been discarded before reading.

'It didn't look great,' she admitted. 'We had dozens of books to consider and it seemed this one wasn't worth taking seriously.'

To my everlasting good fortune, the judge was familiar with my brother Simon's stellar work and surmised that a fellow Groth's writing wouldn't be as slap-dash as the book's presentation. Given a stay of execution, the story was read. And admired; so much so that *MVP* was a unanimous choice for the Young Adult Book Award's shortlist of three.

'Remarkable,' said the judge. 'To come out of nowhere like that… Remarkable.'

The night of the awards was a blast (think Matt Bowen's run to the try-line, finger raised, only with a far smaller crowd watching on and a lot less beer thrown in the air). Held at the State Library of Queensland, Wend and I swanned around like the fugitive couple we were, on the run from our 3-year-old twins. We chatted with the local literati, ate *tapas*, pretended to like Merlot, snapped pics with Premier Peter Beattie and former Lord Mayor Sallyanne Atkinson. At a table displaying all the shortlisted books, I found *MVP* underneath the Best Fiction winner, J.M Coetzee's *Elizabeth Costello*. Disregarding the notion that it was purposefully hiding my ugly duckling of a tome, I lifted *MVP* out, placed it on top of *Elizabeth Costello*, and took a photo to prove that this was all very real and not some waking dream.

Most Valuable Potential's golden point-styled triumph was a one-eighty degree turn for the book and for my writing career. Naively, I thought my equivalent of winning an Origin series – a contract with one of the big publishing houses – would be easier as a result. And progress did follow. I was asked to do a Brisbane Writers Festival session with Matthew Reilly immediately following the Premier's ceremony. A few months later the manuscript of my third novel, *The Umbilical Word*, impressed my soon-to-be agent. Not long after that, an Education Department grant allowed me to step away from teaching at Milpera and write full-time for a year. The biggest prize, though, would remain out of reach. Along with the Maroons in '05, I would have to endure more pain to reach the mountain top. The sort of pain that brings everything about the future into question.

25

The Sook's Last Stand

July 5, 2006
Origin Game #3, Telstra Dome, Melbourne
Score: Qld 16 – NSW 14

From the moment Jared's autism became unimpeachable fact, barriers to getting him the help he needed began to appear. Apart from the standard disability payment – somewhere in the vicinity of $200 a month, which barely covered the cost of the books we needed to read – there was no funding, federal or state, attached to an autism diagnosis. At age three, we had our son attend the Autism Queensland (AQ) Early Childhood Group: a service that helped pre-school age ASD kids develop skills for home, school and community. While the program had its positives, it was only part-time, which was at odds with the mantra that early intervention should be constant and intensive. Also not ideal: AQ was located in Brighton, a good half-hour drive from our home in Arana Hills.

When Jared was four years old, Wendy and I signed up for a course called The Hanen Approach, designed to assist parents in building an autistic child's communication through situations that arose in everyday life. Like AQ, it was mildly helpful to our cause.

But it wasn't worth the price tag, nor the lack of follow-up post-course. Wend recalled the scene at the end of the final Hanen session:

'The speaker finished and started packing up, and us parents just sat there looking around at each other. We were all thinking the same thing: what the hell do we do now?'

And then came school. Based on his assessed place in the middle of the autism spectrum, we bypassed the exclusive special school option and enrolled Jared at Grovely State School where he would mostly be in the Special Education Development Unit (SEDU) and occasionally the mainstream grade one class with one-on-one support. While the SEDU experience was symptomatic of a diseased system – the staff were more miserable fronting up there than Jared – it was the regular class that provided the tipping point for our disillusionment. In short: the money ran out. And quickly. The budget affording one-on-one support was spent before the first term was complete. With no decent Plan B in the offing, the teacher told us we had two choices: foot the bill for more aide time, or come and do the job ourselves. We were incredulous, despairing. And angry. How was this in any way faithful to the school's prospectus of equal opportunity and individualised need? More broadly, how did this sit with Australia's trumpeted ethos of a "fair go"? And was this the beginning, setting the table not just for the next twelve years in education but for the rest our son's life? It was obvious we needed better. Unlike the vast majority of Aussie families in our circumstance, we were fortunate to have a real solution, one that wasn't just papering over the cracks of a situation as hopeless as it was inescapable.

It didn't take much – a cursory online search – to figure out that Canada, though not perfect, was streets ahead of its Commonwealth counterpart. There was money. In British

Columbia, as well as standard disability payments, families with an autistic child 0-6 years old received $20,000 annually for treatment; from 7-18, they received just over $6,000. There was help. In Ladner – home to most of Wend's family, and our preferred destination if we jumped ship – classes for special needs students were fully integrated into the elementary schools and possessed superior resourcing, including permanent full-time aide assistance. Of further comfort was that a similar commitment to support carried through into secondary school, and then beyond school into the adult years. Almost before we'd closed the screen on our search, we were convinced: Canada was our future.

Naturally, there were cons amidst the pros. Leaving my family and our friends. Selling our house. Buying a new house. Finding jobs. The weather. Starting over. The devil you don't know. There was my writing, too. Although the goal of a contract from a big publisher had not yet been achieved, the foundation of a meaningful career in Australia – literary agent, notable award nomination, a building reputation – was in place. Not much of that foundation could be transferred across the Pacific. My progress as an author though, like all the other cons, was no match for the Jared reasons compelling us to move.

By late-April of 2006, our departure date, give or take a week, was set: late-May 2007.

◯

On the back of the decision, everything was tagged with a label of finality that if and when I experienced these things again, they would never be as they once were. Last Southbank visit. Last train to Gaythorne. Last summer afternoon storm. Last spring magpie attack. Last backyard cricket at Christmas. Last bodysurf at Coolum. Last Pad Thai at Bangkok Milton.

Last Origin.

My attitude going into the 2006 series was simple: win it for me. Already mourning the losses that came with our forever departure, I couldn't wear a Maroons defeat as well. Such outrageously selfish stakes weren't doing me any favours. Or the team, for that matter. Queensland was trying to avoid becoming the first state in the Origin era to lose four series in a row – assuaging my grief was an additional burden Mal Meninga's men could do without. I was in too deep, though. While it was excessive to argue a Queensland triumph would make saying goodbye easier, it was not unreasonable to suggest it could help sustain me in the early days of exile.

After the first game in Sydney, sustenance seemed out of reach. Brett Finch, late replacement for Craig Gower (stricken with coulrophobia) and Matt Orford (infected with leprosy), slotted a late field goal to sink us 17-16. In the wash-up, all the talk was that several senior players – Petero Civoniceva, Steve Price and, most notably, captain Darren Lockyer – would be facing the axe if we got done in Game 2. Unable to contemplate any departures other than my own, I had faith we'd see the best of the Maroons at Suncorp. As the game approached, Wendy bemoaned the fact I wouldn't be there in-person. I fancied the thought of going, but the fact was I hadn't been to a tilt since the twins' birth. The unending exhaustion, the belt-tightening, the challenge of purchasing tickets in an era of instant sellouts… all of it had contributed to Groth Origin Night becoming a televised rather than live event. And then there was the ever-present self-preservation factor. What if I went along to this last hurrah and we (gulp) lost? I'd be inclined to choose Siberia over Vancouver for the next chapter of my life.

My contradictory mix of spinelessness and confidence wasn't reflective of the game – the Maroons mocked the former and validated the latter with a 30-6 walloping that saw a sublime

Lockyer win man-of-the-match. Now it all hung on a decider. Already skewing sad due to the hard farewell on the horizon, I lost sleep over the question looming large: with what manner of Maroon heart would I be leaving my beloved Queensland's shores?

Full?

Or broken?

Attendance at our house for Game 3 was just family, no friends. In the lead-up to kickoff, Canada got zero mention. The tell-all had been several weeks prior and the hurt on both sides was still quite raw, to the extent we had an agreed upon, unspoken pact: let's not talk about it for one night. It was on all our minds, though. And its influence was plain to see. From the moment of my parents' arrival, they were all over the twins, asking about school, building Lego forts, guaranteeing a house stacked with Nutri-Grain (Jared's favourite) and Dixie ice-cream cups (Chloe's favourite) for the kids' next visit. When it was bedtime, eyes misted over and hugs were tinged of never wanting to let go. I also sensed the black fog of frustration surrounding my father. Like me, he was upset at the circumstances forcing our move overseas. Australia was supposed to be a friend to the battler, he'd lamented the day before Game 3. Where had we gone wrong? How had it come to this? He noted the tenet central to Queensland Origin: "We won't let you down". Couldn't that promise be delivered to his grandson and the disabled community? Was it only on the football field where it could still be fulfilled? I keenly felt Dad's exasperation. Coupled with my own and added to the titanic measure of self-interest I'd heaped upon this game's outcome, it provided context – not an excuse – for the unravelling I experienced at the 50th minute of the decider.

Things started out fine. The Maroons drew first blood in the 10th minute when Adam Mogg produced some mid-air, millimetre-perfect magic (Mogg-ic?) to ground Johnathan "JT" Thurston's chip kick for a four-pointer. In the 18th minute, stout defending snuffed out a Matt King raid, keeping the scoreboard unchanged and my palpitations manageable. An Eric Grothe Jr runaway intercept in the 25th minute brought the Cockroaches level, but it was against the run of play and didn't distract from the fact that Queensland – rank outsiders with the bookies coming into the contest – were in it up to their ears.

'A relative tried to stitch us up before,' said Dad, recalling Eric Grothe Snr's length-of-the-field effort in 1981. 'We know how that turned out.'

At halftime, the boys went into oranges locked at 4-4. I felt positive – we were travelling well. That applied to me, too. Despite the enormity of my stock in the decider's outcome, I'd handled the first 40 with admirable restraint. Watching a Flight Centre ad during the break – 'Los Angeles or San Francisco flying United Airlines return from for $1,599!' – it occurred to me that maybe I'd shouldered my goodbye grief all the way to acceptance. Maybe I'd come to terms with my departure enough to be thankful for this last footy ride regardless of the result. It was a nice thought. If attributed to the protagonist in a novel, the reader would nod their head in appreciation of such a satisfying endpoint to the character's emotional arc.

In real-life, there is no arc in sporting obsession. No growth. No reconciliation of grief. Even without the deeper meanings attributed by tragics like me, fandom is a constant recycling of denial, anger, bargaining and depression. In the second half, I was drawn to these dark forces more than I'd ever been in twenty-five previous years of Maroon mania. The fall began first set after the resumption of play. In what seemed like history repeating, Eric Grothe Jr sacrificed the family name for the good of Queensland by dropping the pill cold on the Blues' 30 then calamitously toeing it back towards his own try-line. In the scramble that ensued, Tonie "Tunza" Carroll won the race to the ball and dived over under the sticks.

'That's our Eric!' shouted Dad, as the two of us high-fived and celebrated our cursed DNA.

The anointing of Groth(e) mayhem as the ticket to glory, however, was premature. In a bunker decision that beggared belief – even Phil Gould labelled it 'ridiculous' – the video ref denied Carroll's try, ruling that Steve Price's excessive breathing on the ball during the initial tackle was an illegal strip. On its own, an officiating gaffe of this magnitude could easily be the difference between the two sides. But worse was to come. Three minutes later, with New South Wales attacking the Maroon line, an errant Danny Buderus pass saw Craig Gower lose possession. Then JT, his mental clarity brilliant under fatigue, rolled over the loose ball, touching it only with his chest and thus avoiding a knock-on. Referee Steven Clark didn't see it that way, determining Gower had propelled the ball backwards (wrong) and Thurston had contacted the ball with his hands (horribly wrong). Scrum, Blues' feed, 20 out from our line.

In the broadcast booth, Peter Sterling declared it to be 'an awful couple of minutes for Queensland'. He was underselling it. Two telling blunders in quick succession? It was a disgrace. Around the state, from Cooktown to Birdsville to Coolangatta, I could hear the outrage. It's a joke! Southern bias! They want the Cockroaches to win four in a row! They've paid off Clark to make sure of it! Although I wasn't going full conspiracy theory with the bribing of officials, I understood the sentiment. At least there was the thinnest silver lining to the cloud of controversy: the scoreboard still read 4-4.

Not for long. Next set of six, a Luke O'Donnell offload and a shift right created an overlap that Matt King took full advantage of, plunging over to the right of the posts. Compounding the turn for the worse: *another* questionable call from Clark. The tackle prior to King's touchdown, Nathan Hindmarsh had fumbled seeking to get a pass away. I was incensed now, pacing the room, swearing.

'This is an absolute travesty,' I growled. 'If these lucky pricks go on and win, there has to be an asterisk. There *has* to be!'

Then came the 50th minute final straw. A bomb from Gower hit the deck, found Steven Menzies' hands and ended up with Grothe crossing out wide. Replays clearly showed that, in his attempt to collect the bomb, Blues' fullback Brett Hodgson had muffed the catch, spilling the ball forward. With the Maroons ready to resume play at the spot of Hodgson's error, video ref Graeme West deliberated. And deliberated. And deliberated.

'Surely this decision could not also go against Queensland?' asked Ray Warren on the Channel 9 broadcast.

'I'm getting nervous now,' admitted Gould.

'They *can't* give it!' added Sterling.

West did give it. Despite its eminent candidacy for worst refereeing decision in the history of Origin, the green light came up. Lucky Pricks 14, Queensland 4. In the span of ten minutes, an unforgivable series of refereeing howlers had doomed us.

'Fuck this shit,' I announced to the room. 'I'm done.'

Backdropped by my father's infuriatingly earnest plea – 'Mate, come on… don't be like that…' – I stormed up the stairs and headed to the bedroom where I could rail against the world alone.

◯

Of all the games to serve up Origin's gravest injustice, it had to be this one. The last one. An end point that was itself a product of grave injustice. It would've been laughable if it wasn't so cruel.

Sitting on the bed, door shut to whatever additional sadism was piling on downstairs, I thought of my son sleeping in the room across the hall and fought back tears. In every consideration of the 2006 decider, I'd wanted a win for me – I realised now I wanted it for my boy. A victory for these underdog Maroons would speak words Jared might never find. The unconscionable denial of that opportunity for victory felt like it was singling him out, kicking him when he was already down. I didn't care to witness that. So, I'd bailed. What alternative was there? When the system failed and a fair shake was a mirage, when your best effort was blunted by malignant forces beyond your control, what else was there to do but walk away, live to fight another day?

I needed to articulate this to Dad. The subtext of his pleas for me to stay and watch the game had been straightforward: don't be a sook. Be brave. Stand your ground. I couldn't blame him for thinking it – my fan cowardice *bona fides* had been well established for many years. On this occasion though, he didn't understand. This wasn't the same as his annual pilgrimages to Lang Park in the '70s to endure Queensland futility – this was emblematic of his grandson's struggle for respect. This was the unfairness of life writ large on the Origin page. I was certain that when I armed Dad with this insight, he would see the method in the madness of my escape. The 2006 decider was salt in a wound I could no longer tolerate. And if he was being honest with himself, I doubted my father could either.

I checked my watch. I'd been in the bedroom around twenty minutes. The game was likely nearing the seventy-minute mark. I stood up, decision made (in my estimation, the only decent decision enacted all night). It was time to leave the fortress of solitude and head back to the living room. I would return for the sook's last stand.

Not to sit through the painful final act, mind you.

I was going to end the misery and turn the TV off.

⬭

Rejoining the watch party, I expected a blowout. Instead, it remained as I had left it twenty minutes ago: 14-4. Fair enough, I thought. Makes that asterisk much more powerful if we only lose by 10. I stood by the couch and lifted the TV remote from the armrest. No one had said a word since my return – I was fine with that. I would do all the talking after I killed the broadcast. I aimed the remote at the console, thumb at the ready. Then I paused. Ray Warren was going up a notch:

'…He goes out to Thurston… who gets around O'Donnell.'

'He goes out to Brent Tate!

'TATE! GOES FOR THE PEDAL!

'MENZIES AFTER HIM! WON'T GET HIM!

'TATE WILL SCORE! HE'LL BRING IT AROUND!

'HE'LL MAKE IT A CERTAIN SIX-POINTER!

'BRENT TATE! BRILLIANT TRY!

'THEY'RE COMING BACK!'

I stared at the screen, vaguely aware that the remote had slipped from my hand and fallen back onto the couch. I sat down. A hand touched my shoulder – it had to be Wend, though I couldn't turn my swimming head to confirm. As Clinton Schifcofske banged over the conversion, Dad's quiet voice pierced Phil Gould's blathering about 'Welcome to State of Origin!' and 'When you think you've got 'em down, they come back again!'

'Nice to see you, son. Just in time.'

There was no judgement in his tone. No finger-pointing. Simply an air of good cheer. The look on his face was actually appreciative, as if my walking back into the room had been prerequisite for the Tate try. It was then the truth dawned on me:

my father was not mistaken; he understood perfectly well. His plea for me to stay, to 'not be like that' – it wasn't an accusation of cowardice. It was a gentle reminder of the lesson I'd been taught as a 13-year-old boy, watching my first live Origin in 1983: *there was comfort in possibility*. Systems had failed – hell, they failed all the time – but a puncher's chance remained. For Jared. For the Maroons. If it was in the final ten minutes, or on the far side of the world… so be it. The fat lady hadn't sung. She hadn't even warmed up. That was reason enough to have hope.

Hope became possibility redefined in 1983.

It would level up even further in the 2006 decider.

The set of six following Tate's try, Queensland rolled forward, riding a new momentum. Our living room had come alive. Led by my father – 'Come on, lads! Get into 'em!' – everyone was now having something to say. I was silent. The misery I'd wanted to end, the food-for-thought I'd prepared to serve up… it had been replaced by humble pie. And possibility. On the fifth tackle, Locky kicked long, looking to turn the Blues around and pressure them into error. When cousin Eric Jr collected the ball and ran it back, I braced for the Groth(e)-inspired disaster that would see the Maroons grasp the available chance. He would not be the villain, however. That title was reserved for the man at dummy-half. Flanked by Peter Sterling's observation that New South Wales were slow to get back, Brett Hodgson passed out of Grothe's play-the-ball, looking to find the first receiver. It never arrived. Questionable from the second it left Hodgson's hands, the ball drifted forward and fell out of reach of the intended target.

It hit the turf.

Bounced up.

Into the midriff of an advancing player.

The player who wanted it the most, who believed he could defy the flawed powers-that-be, who'd found comfort in possibility. The player on the cusp of being forced out of the Origin arena. The player who'd put himself in position to make the most of a puncher's chance:

Darren James Lockyer.

The Queensland captain, ball clutched to his chest, broke through the desperate lunge of Blues prop Luke Bailey and found nothing but fresh air between him and the tryline.

'HE'S SCORED!' cried Sterling as Locky crossed the stripe.

'OH NOOOO!' wailed Gould as Maroon teammates Civoniceva and Carroll dived on top of their captain in the in-goal.

'BLOODY BEAUTY!' shouted Dad, leaping to his feet and spilling XXXX all over his Bobby Lindner number 8.

I stood in front of the TV, hands on my head, mouth agape, eyes a pair of billiard balls. Like my son upstairs, I had no words. My purpose in returning to the game had been to make a stand. And a stand had indeed been made. As a father, I could barely comprehend it. As a Queenslander, I should've expected it.

Six minutes remained; time enough for injustice to rebound and ruin everything. In the 77th minute, a moment of reckoning. Rhys Wesser fielded a kick ten out from his line and was set upon by a gang of Blues. They lifted Wesser off his feet, carried him back and dumped him in our in-goal, the assumed reward a drop-out and an opportunity for New South Wales to snatch victory. Referee Steven Clark wasn't impressed. Calling 'THAT'S ONE!" as Wesser was carted back, he blew the whistle. Penalty, Queensland. Was it a square-up? Was there some sense of guilt, some need for atonement governing Clark's decision? Regardless, it was the right call – an opinion echoed in Dad's two-fingered salute to the TV.

And then we were home. In a final play that brought everything full circle, Eric Grothe Jr hoofed a desperate punt downfield, only to see it go out on the full. The extraordinary full-time score: Indomitable Heroes 16, Lucky Pricks 14. With Ray Warren proclaiming another Maroon miracle, I pivoted to my father. I still couldn't speak – I could only gawp, unblinking. Dad's grin, wider than the ocean I would soon be crossing, said everything about this decider's place in Origin history. His glistening eyes, though, betrayed emotions other than glee. Reflection. Resignation. Pain. As per the unspoken pact, he wouldn't address the collective grief of our departure. And I didn't want him to. This was a night to celebrate what we had gained. Resuming the arm-wrestle with our losses could wait until tomorrow.

It wasn't at all surprising that my over-investment in the 2006 decider became a cautionary tale in self-sabotage. One could very easily argue that, given my behaviour on the night, I was undeserving of such an epic victory for my swansong. Ironic then that it was the jewel in a crown of sporting reward I wore to Canada. Every team in the country I followed, from the serious to the casual, got up in 2006 / early 2007. The Broncos capped a remarkable semi-finals run by beating a heavily favoured Melbourne in the grand final. The Australian Kangaroos outlasted New Zealand in a Tri-Nations final for the ages, Darren Lockyer scoring the winning try in overtime. The Queensland Bulls won the Sheffield Shield. The Baggy Green belted the Poms 5-0 in the Ashes then lifted their third successive World Cup trophy two months later in the West Indies. Even the Brisbane Bullets got in on the act, winning their first National Basketball League championship in seventeen years. Led by the mighty Maroons, the stars of my fandom aligned for one magical run. To this day, I'm grateful they gathered together at the start of the year and vowed "let's all do this for Darren".

While the above-and-beyond effort was deeply appreciated, no amount of supporter joy was going to soften the blow of leaving. The scene at Brisbane airport on May 15, 2007 was suitably emotional. Prior to the end moment of passing through security, we'd done the thing where you pretend this isn't happening and this isn't goodbye and we're not at the airport; it's just a regular outing with the fam, sipping cappuccinos at the Coffee Club, chatting about the unseasonably warm autumn and the potential for John Howard to finally get turfed out of office and Tassie girl Mary turned Princess of Denmark having a daughter and the comforting possibility of the Maroons going back-to-back… just another day, nothing special. The façade lasted as long as it could. Fronting the escalator that would take us away, we were all weepy apart from the twins. Chloe was clutching their little Wallace (minus Gromit) toy, so all was right in their world; Jared was bouncing on the suitcase pile and singing the Wiggles' song "Rock-A-Bye Your Bear" in his own distinctive language. I assured the folks we'd see them soon enough – there was this new thing called "Skype" that showed video of the people you were calling and didn't need a webcam. It'd be just like visiting together for real, I lied.

Dad was last in my line of hugs. We were barely keeping it together. Voice shaking, he told me we were great parents. Wendy as a mum? No one better. And you, my son – a tremendous father. Just tremendous. I thanked him and told him I'd learned from the best. Then I was heading down the escalator, careful to not look back for fear I might lose my nerve and cancel the trip. We were exiting Queensland, Wend's address for nearly twenty years, the place where our kids were born, and the only home I'd ever known.

I was scared. Thoughts of "I'm on my own now" sniped away at my conviction.

But they couldn't contend with the comfort in possibility.

They couldn't compete with hope.

26

A Question of Commitment

June 13, 2007
Origin Game #2, Telstra Stadium, Sydney
Score: Qld 10 – NSW 6

Do better for the Maroons – that was the simple fix after my faith was found wanting in the '06 decider. I needed to lift my fan game to show that, despite being 12,000 kilometres away, my commitment to the Queenslander cause could not be questioned. The perfect scenario to prove that loyalty confronted me on June 13, 2007.

Just after 4:00am, Pacific time. I was in the basement of 5214 Lynn Place, Ladner, forty minutes south of downtown Vancouver. The house belonged to sister-in-law Lee, brother-in-law Cal, and their daughter Jamie. Through their generosity, it was also a temporary home to me, Wendy and the twins. We'd been there three weeks; we would be there another five months until we bought our own place in November. The four of us were camped downstairs in the basement – a space not purposefully designed to accommodate one human, let alone any number of humans greater than one. Wend and I shared a mattress on the floor; the twins occupied bunkbeds in the adjacent space. No longer at the mercy of jetlag, they were all asleep. I was wide awake, sitting on the toilet in winter pyjamas, open laptop on my knees, live Origin score on screen.

Only the score. No game to watch, no stream to access. Just a cutting-edge 2007 webpage and a refresh icon, which I was clicking every five seconds. In ideal technological conditions, I might've been able to tap into a radio broadcast; I'd done so in Brisbane for a number of years with NHL hockey, the most recent occasion two months earlier for the Canucks' monumental 4-overtime playoff win against the Dallas Stars. These were not ideal technological conditions. The best network option in the basement was stealing the neighbours' wi-fi, which was spottier than a dalmatian with measles. If you moved a millimetre or breathed too hard or looked at the laptop wrong or sneezed or farted or did absolutely nothing at all, the connection could conk out leaving you unplugged for an indeterminate amount of time. The most reliable location for internet? The bathroom, specifically on the throne.

I'd logged on a few minutes into the second half. An earlier start was intended – maybe sometime during the first forty – but not wanting to wake the family with an alarm, I'd been relying on my internal rugby league clock to rouse me. The score read 6-6. As I cooed at the laptop, urging it to be nice and to not freeze or die or spontaneously combust, my mind's eye pictured the action taking place on the Telstra Stadium turf. Cut-out passes from Locky. Show-and-go's from JT. Probing darts from Cam Smith. Kamikaze kick-returns from Karmichael Hunt. Big hits from Tunza Carroll. Brave, front-on tackles from Dallas Johnson. New South Wales – I couldn't view them as anything other than a pack of faceless roaches scurrying about the field, pursued by a Wally Lewis impersonator with a tank of DDT. That was fine by me. I needed my imagination for the great list of things I'd left behind in Brisbane: Kangaroo Point at night, watching movies in gold class with friends, jacarandas in bloom, the taste of a Mango Weis bar… the less wasted on the Blues, the better.

I'd been in Canada under a month and already I was trending homesick and dislocated. These early days were a strange limbo. I felt stranded on an island both familiar and alien, with no means of building a raft to return home. Dawn till dusk was a procession of autism support applications and bank paperwork and real estate pages and used car dealerships and job searches. The evenings: catch-ups, drinks, card games, incessant "Crocodile Dundee" references… and more job searches. We'd arrived in Vancouver with a chunk of cash to start our new lives, but each week without a pay packet carved a little piece out of the chunk. I had no interest in teaching again – I'd experienced the best of the profession in my thirteen years – so I was applying for anything my weird CV had a remote chance of landing, putting up bomb after bomb in the hope of catching one in the in-goal.

I trusted the Maroons were exhibiting more nous than my job searches. And more stamina. Ten minutes of "The Thinker" pose on the loo had resulted in both my legs falling asleep and tingling sensations in the toes. My bladder was also full – in my excitement to tune into Game 2, I'd forgotten to take a leak before settling in. I couldn't risk shifting, though. The earlier cardinal error of clenching a buttock to get the blood moving had seen the site duly crash. Scrambling through a number of positional adjustments, service was restored with the laptop balancing precariously on my right knee and my torso twisted to the right. It was unpleasant, but effective. The dandelion spores that comprised the neighbour's wi-fi had not been displaced by a passing breeze since.

At the 63rd minute, a page refresh revealed a score change. Queensland 10, DDT Crew 6. The update was predictably light on details – all it showed was Steven Bell as the try scorer. I internally screamed with joy then told myself to settle down. An elevated heart rate might displease the network gods. I eased the cursor over to the refresh icon and waited, allowing Johnathan Thurston time to line up the conversion. My hope was that Bell had crossed beneath the black dot, but given he was playing in the centres, the likelihood was a score out wide (I would discover later that, due to a Brent Tate injury, Bell was on the wing and the touchdown had occurred as out wide as out wide gets). Not a problem for JT. For sure he'd pilot one of his patented, right-to-left, banana-bending kicks between the sticks. I gave it a few more seconds then clicked refresh. The screen blanked, bar a sad face emoji and a message that the connection was lost.

'For fuck's sake!'

The words were out of my mouth before I could swallow them down. I winced, bracing for disturbed children or an angry wife or both. No sound apart from some light snoring. I breathed a sigh of relief then gave the finger to the laptop, which was still in a standing-eight count. By the time I'd found a weak but holding signal (laptop on the floor in front of my feet and turned a smidge to the left; me still seated on the toilet but bent forward like a child waiting for his backside to be wiped), it was the 68th minute. The score remained 10-6. Assuming the accuracy of the feed – a colossal assumption, to be sure – Thurston had failed his attempt at goal. Crap. It was a big miss. I would've been a lot happier with a converted try lead.

Who was I kidding? "Happier" wasn't achievable in this situation. The final ten minutes could only be a dismal fusion of technological frustration, physical nuisance and imagining the worst. Proving my point: at the 75th minute mark with the score unchanged, I clicked, convinced the reload would show that the Blues had evened things up and now had a kick to edge in front. As the buffering rolled on, I cursed the bad news about to be confirmed. They were probably gifted a try. Fluke bounce. Forward pass. Maybe it was the bunker having another Barry Crocker a-la 2006. I tensed up as the screen took shape. Then it was complete, and the full horror of the moment was revealed:

Sad face emoji.

Connection lost.

The outburst this time came, not from my mouth, but from a limb. On a hair trigger due to the tension, my calf cramped up, flinging ninja stars across the length of my left lower body. Reflexively, I gasped, sat bolt upright on the toilet and kicked my leg out. Hoping to shock the seized muscle back into submission, all I managed to do was clip the floored laptop with my big toe. It teetered for a second then keeled over like a felled tree. Shit, I thought. That can't be good. Gritting my teeth to the ongoing agony, I reached forward, slid my hands under the stricken PC, lifted, and cradled it in my lap. The good news? The "lost connection" page was gone. The bad news? It had been replaced by a blue screen of death.

I laid the laptop back on the floor and stood up from the toilet. The cramp eased instantly. To assure recovery, I did a few stretches. Then I took a leak to make a racehorse proud, the relief immeasurable after forty minutes of a full-to-bursting bladder. I checked my watch. The game was over, result known to all but a castaway in far-off Canada. I considered the hardware at my feet.

'Laptop,' I muttered, 'I question your commitment to the Queenslander cause.'

Then I kicked it. Not hard. Not a full punt with the leg swing and follow-through. Not like the conversion JT had missed, or the one the Blues had just nailed to keep the 2007 series alive. Just a firm nudge. An Alfie-like grubber. The laptop skittered along the laminate floor for a couple of feet and came to rest at the threshold to the bathroom. And perhaps it was what the laptop had needed all along. Perhaps all the cooing and cajoling and contorting had been the wrong idea and the requirement from the outset was tough love. Like a dying star, the blue screen of death collapsed in on itself, winked out, and was replaced by something more familiar. I cautiously approached, unsure if this was just another ploy to affirm my burgeoning Luddism. I bent down, grasped the laptop and stood. Wiped my eyes and blinked. The game screen had returned in all its piece-meal glory. Clock 80.00. Score: Queensland 10 – New South Wales 6. I eased the cursor to the refresh icon and clicked. Clock 80.00. Score: Queensland 10 – New South Wales 6. I clicked again. Clock 80.00. Score: Queensland 10 – New South Wales 6. I clicked again. And again. And again. Seven times – same clock, same score. In the end, it was eighth click that convinced me beyond a shadow of a doubt that the Maroons had prevailed:

Sad face emoji.

Connection lost.

I pressed the power button, watched the shutdown and closed the laptop. Recalling my earlier kick, I inspected it for any obvious damage. There was none. Good. Along with the better wi-fi upstairs, the PC's semi-functionality was pre-requisite for the job-searching day ahead. I popped it in one of the suitcases littering the floor. Before climbing into our grounded mattress where a sleeping Wend had starfished 75% of the available space, I paused, allowing a modicum of my precious imagination to be employed on the celebrations underway. All across Queensland, they'd be going off.

At the Caxton. At the Regatta. At the Ferny Grove Tavern. In every country town pub carrying the name "Grand". In thousands of lounge rooms and rumpus rooms and bar areas and man-caves. On McConaghy Street, Dad would already be setting up the DVD recording to send across the pond. Smiling, I considered the toilet that had been my Origin venue for the past hour. It was a far cry from the Lang Park terraces and the Suncorp seats and the dozens of watch-party couches I'd occupied in the past. But for an hour at least it had helped me feel a little less stranded on the island, a little more capable of building the raft to return home.

Would there be a time when home wasn't Brisbane, Queensland, Australia? Would it ever be Vancouver, British Columbia, Canada? Not for a while. A long while. But that was fine. Whenever the tipping point, it wouldn't take anything away from my source, my origin. I would have two homes. And in a world fast filling up with sad face emojis and connections lost, two homes were surely better than one.

27

The Breakthrough

June 24, 2009
Origin Game #2, ANZ Stadium, Sydney
Score: Qld 24 – NSW 14

As the aughts drew to a close, one could barely comprehend the seismic shifts they'd ushered in. A world confidently marching into the 21st century had been rocked by events both colossal and unprecedented, and historic crossroads like 9/11 and The Great Recession and the rise of social media had made the global landscape unrecognisable by the end of the decade. In Queensland State of Origin, the 2000s had reflected the tumultuous times. The years had seen catastrophic lows and, for some, existential angst before discovering a gene of resolve previously unmapped by the Maroon spirit. For myself, the journey felt like several lifetimes. Had an aughts clairvoyant conjured the sequence of life-altering events in store, I would've assumed they were drunk. I'd survived though, along with my footy team. Entering 2009, it was time to level up.

It was time for a breakthrough.

Four titles in a row – a streak never before achieved by either state in the Origin era. With ten minutes left in the 2006 decider, the idea that we would triumph in that series, let alone the two that followed, seemed more remote than a Torres Strait Airbnb. What became apparent after Darren Lockyer's iconic intercept, however, was that this was a fledgling dynasty. Forged in the furnace of Blues' supremacy from '03 – '05, the young Maroon core – Thurston, Smith, Inglis, Slater, Hodges, Myles, Thaiday – proved to be pure steel. In 2007, they survived the Game 2 Melbourne slugfest to lift the shield; in 2008, they won without talisman Lockyer, who sat out with knee problems for the series duration. Clearly, they were a special group. In '09, the time was right for them to achieve Origin immortality.

Game 1 at Melbourne's Etihad Stadium (a game I would see months later via the Des DVD service) did nothing to suggest otherwise. Racing in three brilliant tries to lead 18-6 at halftime, the Maroons overcame a reduced bench and some fortuitous New South Wales bounces to win 28-18. Inglis was sublime, scoring two tries, setting up the sealer for Darius Boyd, and walking away with man-of-the-match honours. In the aftermath, the call from south of the Tweed was to stay the course with the debutants blooded at Etihad. Naturally, the selectors panicked, dropping Terry Campese and Anthony Laffranchi, bringing back the mummified remains of Trent Barrett, and opting for three injured players, two of whom – Michael Jennings and Craig Wing – would ultimately be ruled out. Queensland's four-peat was beckoning and the Blues seemed determined to do everything they could to oblige.

My own quest for success was not in step with the Maroons. While domestic stability had been achieved in the two years since departing Brisbane (house bought, day job secured, kids settled in school, autism support accessed), literary advancement had been much harder to come by. Agent submission of my third novel, *The Umbilical Word* – the tale of a father-to-be who sends an email to his unborn child then receives a reply – failed to land a big-house contract and, like *Most Valuable Potential* before it, I opted for a "better out than not" deal with established Queensland indie, Interactive Press. Similarly, a young adult story I'd penned, *Kid Concentrate* – a tale of two teenage cricketers who bond over family tragedy and a seemingly magical bat – had done the rounds with my agent and gone close with Random House but had failed to get over the line. These were not my hoped-for outcomes. But as is often the case with artists, hope springs eternal with a new project.

My next novel was titled *Kindling*. A suburban thriller in which an 11-year-old autistic boy accidentally discovers a tragic family secret and runs away to a fire burning on the outskirts of town, I began writing *Kindling* in 2006. I'd drafted the first eighty pages when I showed it to my agent, seeking her opinion on its progress to date. She wasn't sure fiction was the right vehicle for the material.

'Have you thought about just writing your real-life experience as an autism parent?' she enquired.

I put the novel aside and gave it a go, drafting a few early chapters. Apart from the cracking title – *Things the Fortune-Teller Forgot to Mention* – it wasn't my best effort. I set it aside as well, then decided to abandon all writing for a little while. I had too much on my plate already with the imminent move. Once we'd found our feet in Canada, I'd return to the page and attack whatever project was at the forefront of my mind.

By March 2008, I was ready to write again. And the piece I couldn't shake from my thoughts was *Kindling*. Despite my agent's lukewarm response, I sensed there was something in it that was too good to pass up. Over the next year, I chipped away at the manuscript, working on it when I could, which was often late at night when the rest of the family was asleep. By June 2009, the novel draft was complete. It felt like a winner; at the very least, the best work I'd done. Wend – always my first reader – agreed (two-thirds of the way through she warned me that if I killed the young autistic protagonist Kieran, we were done, our marriage was over. She was serious, and I very much wanted to remain her husband, so… spoiler alert…). I passed the *Kindling* manuscript along to my agent then tried to focus on things other than the fate awaiting it. Origin 2 and Maroon history-in-the-making fit the bill.

⬯

Given the *gravitas* of this game, I had to watch it live. Gone was the Lynn Place loo and laptop of 2007 – we had our own house, our own functioning wi-fi, our own telly, our own cable. One of the channels available on our cable package was Setanta, which offered a selection of non-North American sports coverage including the NRL and State of Origin. Wearing my best hang-dog look, I asked Wend if we could purchase it for Game 2.

'Do I have a choice?'

'Of course… You can choose "Yes" or "Absolutely yes".'

She sighed and nodded, perhaps still feeling a measure of benevolence towards me after I declined to kill the kid in *Kindling*. A few days later, Setanta was unlocked on our system. I was set for my first live Origin watch in three years.

As the players ran out and Ray Warren acknowledged me for welcoming him into my lounge room, I reflected on the strangeness of my spectating lot. 3:00am start. Absence of company. Dead silence of the house and surrounding neighbourhood. My attire: 2008 jersey tucked into pyjama shorts. No snack food, no beer. Not even a cup of tea. Everything I'd ever associated with a viewing of my beloved Maroons had been stripped away. It felt like I was performing an act of subversion, engaging in illicit activity, breaking the law of this hockey-worshipping land. My racing heart and churning stomach — they were appropriate. These were physiological calling cards of a criminal.

The true crime of the game was not in my clandestine witness, but the dog-act perpetrated in the 22nd minute. With Queensland cruising at 12-0, a Blues half-chance down the right-hand touchline was intercepted by a knee-sliding Greg Inglis. Before he could get to his feet, Trent Barrett — his mummified remains suddenly possessed by an ancient, evil curse — came flying in, right arm swinging with pure malice. The blow collected GI square in the jaw, all but breaking it. It was sickening, tantamount to assault. Watching the replay, Coach Groth was livid but bereft of a satisfactory outlet for expression. I couldn't shout at the TV. I couldn't stomp around the room. A quiet rant was possible, but without a crowd of listeners to nod earnestly and shake their heads and furrow their brows, there was no point. As the trainers helped a dazed Inglis from the field and Barrett was placed on report rather than sent off, I vented my frustration on a couch cushion; first screaming into it, then punching it as if it were Barrett's eminently punchable face. We'd lost our interstellar star to unpunished foul play and were down to sixteen men with an hour remaining in the game. If history was to be made, it would be hard-earned.

The Maroons went into the sheds up 18-10 after each team gifted the other an intercept, and the video ref (say it with me, now) disallowed a legitimate Queensland four-pointer and (say it with me, now) gave the benefit of the doubt to a controversial Blues try. I logged onto Facebook, gauging the temperature of Maroon Nation. People were happy with the scoreboard and apoplectic about the Inglis-Barrett incident. I started writing a post affirming their rage then gave up. My typing was far too slow — the game would be over by the time I was finished. I went to the kitchen, drank a glass of water and, in the semi-darkness of our townhouse's ground floor, considered the day ahead. If Queensland were victorious, joyful adrenaline would override my lack of sleep and get me through the workday. If we lost, I figured I had no choice but to chuck a sickie. Stomach bug was always a fine option. And not too far from truth. Phil Gould commentating a New South Wales win never failed to inspire a bout of nausea.

The second half was a literal nail-biter. Already hobbled by Inglis' inability to return, Queensland's bench was further compromised by injuries to Ben Hannant and Sam Thaiday. There were also questions surrounding the health of Dallas Johnson and Ash Harrison. In the 52nd minute, with the scoreboard unchanged at 18-10, I had to begrudgingly give Gould a rap for his accurate summation of the crisis:

'Queensland are wounded,' he said. 'They've got wounded blokes out there everywhere… They're going to have to show that old-fashioned grit to tackle their way to victory…'

History, I thought. If it was hard-earned before, it was Herculean now.

It didn't help that we weren't helping ourselves. When Billy Slater had an air-swing at a bomb in the 61st minute, gifting the Blues a repeat set, it was no surprise that our brave defence faltered and David Williams scored in the corner. 18-14 and an eternity left on the clock. I buried my head in my hands. I thought about my Canadian colleagues at the day job to whom I'd preached Maroon. I'd educated them on Queensland Origin, its background, its meaning, the significance attached to this morning's result. I'd made the necessary comparisons: 'It's Canada versus the US in Olympic hockey… It's Yankees-Red Sox in the ALCS… It's Duke-North Carolina in March Madness…' I'd corrected them on pronunciation: 'It's Muh-*rown*, not Mah-*roooon*…' When next they saw me, they'd be bound to ask: 'Did your Muuuh-*rowns* win?' I'd have to say no, we lost. And I'd have to deliver the whole sorry context because the whole sorry context was required for every conversation I had now, not just concerning rugby league. And even if my listener was a hardcore sports fan, I'd see their default Canadian deference begin to fade after thirty seconds. I'd see them shifting their feet and stealing glances at their watch. I'd see the dulling of their eyes and thinning of their lips. I'd see them questioning the wisdom of their enquiry and making a mental note to not ask about these Muuuh-*rowns* ever again. I'd see all of this because Toto and I were not in Kansas anymore, and Oz – not the Oz I'd left behind – was my world now, and clicking my heels and saying 'there's no place like home' wouldn't change my identity or my past or my accent or my son's autism or my choice to come to Canada. And it would all be that much worse because we got beat.

I reminded myself that we were still in front, and that this was Queensland's comfort zone: questioned, backs to the wall. At the end of the '80s, I'd understood: we find a way, we feast on the doubters, we win more than our fair share. In the twenty years since, I'd occasionally forgotten this truth. But not tonight, I promised the sleeping house that was my only witness. Not this team. And not this chance at history.

The cause wasn't helped by the fact that we still couldn't get out of our own way. In the 66th minute – the Maroons' first set after Williams' try – Michael Crocker spilled the ball on our 40, inviting New South Wales to attack. Desperation defence, though, held up Joel Monaghan in-goal. Then in the 72nd minute, after more self-inflicted damage from a Petero Civoniceva knock-on, we thwarted successive sets on our line, culminating in Darius Boyd snaffling the Cursed Mummy Barrett's chip-kick to the corner. Eight minutes of eternity left. And yet more calamity. A Jarryd Hayne kick-return saw Willie Tonga reel out of the contact clutching his shoulder. I looked to the heavens (aka our popcorn ceiling) and remarked to the Nick Earls collection on the nearby bookshelf that this tilt now resembled the hospital ward Game 2 of '89. The question was: Would the lightning of essential Maroon defiance strike twice?

It would. In the 78th minute, a Thurston cross-kick ended in the hands of Luke O'Donnell. Trying to stay in the field of play while Hannant and Lockyer drove him backward, the Blues' second-rower fumbled the ball. Johnny-on-the-spot Cam Smith couldn't believe his luck – in one swift movement, he scooped up the loose pill and dived over untouched. As the broadcast flipped to the exultant Queensland section of the crowd and its bevy of red wig-wearing Fatty Vautin impersonators, I danced and cheered and clapped and screamed... all without making a sound. They'd done it! Four in a row! And in the most Maroon way possible: digging deeper than any mortal team could ever do.

At lunchtime later that day, floating above my exhaustion on a cloud of victory, my pal Ray suggested Queensland's triumph was a sign of things to come:

'The Mah-rooons got the "W",' he said. 'Next up: your book, D.'

I considered Ray's eager, nodding face. My best friend at work, he was always upbeat, positive. Unlike me, he had no doubt about my writing talent or the brightness of my future. I proposed a toast, raising the leftover pizza slice I'd brought from home and "clinking" it against Ray's half-eaten Taco Del Mar burrito.

'It's Muh-*rowns*,' I replied. 'And I hope you're right.'

⬯

The email arrived in my inbox August 11, 2009.

I was on the computer stationed in our home "office". It was an office because, for the time being, the twins were sharing the neighbouring bedroom and the bunkbeds contained within. At some stage, that arrangement would change; Chloe would want space, away from Jared's disrupted sleep, hammock swinging and random harmonica playing. For now, their future four walls were a writer's garret (and shelter for a treadmill gathering dust).

I read the email again. My agent had sent a brief note, asking a question on behalf of the publisher from Hachette: Would I be prepared to visit Australia next year? I read the enquiry several more times, pulling apart the sentence, poring over every word. Then I hailed Wendy from downstairs.

'The publisher wouldn't ask a question like that,' I said to her, 'unless she was making an offer.'

'Maybe she's selling a time-share.'

'Wend.'

'No, I don't think she would ask that without an offer.' She leaned against the treadmill. 'Why not just ask your agent directly?'

I made a pained face. A query like that needed delicacy rather than bluntness. What if it *was* a time-share? God, fifteen years of rejection had made me fearful to the point of near paralysis. Everything leaned towards this being the moment of breakthrough, and still I was having trouble tapping into my Queenslander courage.

'Just ask,' repeated Wend. 'I think you'll like the answer.' She moved in beside my chair, leaned over, kissed the top of my head. 'You've earned this. You deserve it.'

My agent's reply to my reply arrived within the hour. Yes, Hachette were offering a contract for *Kindling*. I leapt up from the desk, knocking my chair over in the process.

'YOU LITTLE FUCKING BEAUTY!'

Wend and Chloe arrived at the entrance, the latter looking quite scared. I said it was okay – Daddy just found out his book was going to a great home. Chloe asked if my book was a Geronimo Stilton. I said no, but I'd definitely consider it for the next one. Following a teary hug with Wend, I posted the news on Facebook. Within minutes, there was a knock on the door. Neighbours Sheila and Paul had seen the news and dropped everything to come congratulate me. They'd brought with them the only booze they had in the house: a six-pack of coffee liqueur shots that may have pre-dated our move to Canada. They were the sweetest shots I'd ever thrown back.

At the end of the night, post the whirlwind of impromptu celebrations with family and friends, I opened the file of the *Kindling* manuscript on the computer. I smiled. This wonderful, willing collection of words. Like the Game 3 Maroons, they'd persevered, proving the naysayers wrong to break through and set a new standard. A good span of the aughts had been climbing the mountain with no guarantee of survival, let alone success; by decade's end, the summit had been reached. It was a beautiful view from the top.

How long could we stay there and enjoy it? I figured a little while at least.

For the Maroons, it would prove an understatement.

For yours truly, it would prove a pipe dream.

2022

28

Not Okay

June 8, 2022
Origin Game #1, Stadium Australia, Sydney
Second Half
Score: Qld 16 – NSW 10

In the 49th minute, when skipper Daly Cherry-Evans scores to give the Maroons a 12-4 lead, it shatters any illusion of distance between myself and the need for victory.

A win will bring everything full circle. Past, present and future. The culmination of a fifty-year fandom. The odyssey of my Queensland identity. Most important of all: one last great story written in the love language I share with my terminally ill father. If this Generation Next of Maroon upstarts can hang on, it will be the Origin yardstick by which all others are measured.

As the match comes down to the wire, my heart soars and sinks with each shift in momentum. Kalyn Ponga's brilliant cut-out ball to put Valentine Holmes over untouched sees me strutting around the living room like a sun risen rooster and the family yelling at me to get out of the way of the TV. But Holmes' wayward conversion attempt reins in my cock-of-the-walk — failing to extend the lead beyond two scores has left the barn door open for New South Wales. In the 72nd minute, the Blues barge through with a Cameron Murray touchdown, reducing the deficit to six. Then they rumble downfield again, threatening back-to-back scores, until a stroke of Cam Munster genius strips the ball from Stephen Crichton. In the 76th minute, they're back on the doorstep, only to be cruelled by the Maroons' multiple efforts and a Damien Cook knock-on.

'The scramble of Queensland… how are they holding on?' asks Cam Smith in the Channel 9 commentary.

'Oh, this is an epic!' adds Andrew Johns.

Our chance to close it out comes in the 78th minute. Ben Hunt slices through the defence, launching rockets of 'GO! GO!' from my bazooka mouth. With support left and right, Hunt need only find the right pass. He doesn't, going outside to Holmes rather than inside to Cherry-Evans. I bring my hands to my head and air the mother of all groans. Next tackle, Selwyn Cobbo is wrapped up a metre out. That was it, I announce. That was the moment.

An age of ninety seconds remains. Somehow, still up 16-10. Blues surging. Crowd screaming. Queensland disjointed. Fading. Wilting. Dane Gagai is penalised for a strip and heads drop. We've got nothing left. Everyone knows it. Time and again in the history of Origin, the Maroons have engineered folk tales. But it's not every game that the glass slipper fits or that gold is spun from straw. As the Blues take the tap and ready the kitchen sink, it's obvious our boys are done. They can't resist any longer. Their boundless courage for seventy-nine minutes — it will be for naught. New South Wales will strike at the death and steal the win in overtime.

It's too late now, but I wish I was beside Dad on the couch. I would inch closer to him, throw an arm over his shoulders. Command the game's final act to slow to snail's pace so I could tell him what needs to be said. I love you, Dad. You and Mum and Sean and Simon being here means the world to me. I'm so sorry I couldn't jag a win for us, for you. That's it, that's all. Between the lines, though, so much more: I don't want this to be our last game together, my father represents all that is good about being a Queenslander, it's a privilege to be his son, I will write about all of this tomorrow, cancer can go get fucked, some things in life are unavoidable no matter how much we try to will them away…

And he'd hug me. Get a little teary. Then he'd nod towards the game and give that subtle raised-eyebrow, tilted-head, knowing look:

'Mate, we're in front. It's okay.'

Thirty seconds left. Isaah Yeo — the Blue concussed in the first tackle of the night, who should've been taken off, who should've played no further part in the game — pokes his nose through the defence and streams forward, try-line in his sights. I cover my eyes with my hands, unable to watch.

It's not okay.

The 2010s

29

Swanning and Rampaging

July 7, 2010
Origin Game #3, ANZ Stadium, Sydney
Score: Qld 23 – NSW 18

The year after inking the *Kindling* contract was a taster of the literary big-time. It started with silence; the two months after signing on the dotted line passed without publisher contact, leading me to question whether I had landed a book deal after all. Maybe this was all a figment of my overactive imagination? Maybe it was a cruel joke perpetrated by a Nigerian prince with a big inheritance? Then in October of '09, the Hachette editor sent her generous first critique of the work and my baseless fears were quashed. The process to bring *Kindling* to the shelves of Australia was underway.

Pinch-me moments were plentiful. There were the admissions from the publisher and editor about how much they loved protagonists Kieran and Nate, about how dead wife and mother Felicity was such a beautiful and haunting character, about how the devasting ending to the novel would stay with them forever. There was a peek at the cover design for the book – always an out-of-body experience for an author. There were the pleasing advance reviews, including a five-star assessment from *Australian Bookseller and Publisher* that Nick Earls assured me aren't handed out willy-nilly. There were my author copies, catapulted across the Pacific, arriving on the doorstep in an unassuming cardboard box and doled out to an oohing and aahing inner circle (to each of Wendy's three sisters, I wrote in their copy 'You're my favourite'). All of this goodness had me wide-eyed in wonder, but it was merely a preamble to the main event of returning to Oz to "tour" the novel.

The contract money was enough for the whole family to travel with me. Wend was excited but also cognisant that the lion's share of twin-wrangling would fall on her shoulders while her showboat husband swanned around town. And the first town subject to the Groth swanning? Sydney. That felt right. Three weeks before in Origin 3, we'd won our fifth series in a row, whitewashing New South Wales 3-0 for the first time since 1995. To do so required winning twice at ANZ Stadium – a feat not achieved by the Maroons for twenty-two years. The way I saw it, it was the perfect time to be an all-conquering Queenslander in the Emerald City.

Almost as soon as our feet touched Australian soil, the swanage commenced. I was whisked away to the ABC studios in Ultimo for an interview with the National Breakfast Club, bounced over to Hachette's plush offices to meet the team, then wined and dined with a dozen booksellers, all of whom adored the novel. Next day, it was more meet-and-greets with booksellers across the city then back to the ABC for an extended sit-down with the First Tuesday Book Club. At the end of a whirlwind couple of days, the folks at Hachette were pleased. *Kindling* and I had made an excellent impression. This was how books and authors became successful. On the road to the next leg of the tour, I thought:

Can it get any better than this?

It could. At the opening night of the Byron Bay Writers' Festival, I hobnobbed with *American Psycho* author Bret Easton Ellis, survived Di Morrissey's rambling welcome speech, and had an impromptu chat with Alan Close at the surf club urinals. After hours at The Northern, accompanied by younger brother Simon (he was conducting a workshop at the Festival), I drank beers and talked cricket with ABC journo and thoroughly top bloke Steve Cannane. In front of sizeable, eager crowds, I did sessions about my journey to publication and making the literary "top grade", sharing the stage with, among others, the brilliant actress and author, Tasma Walton. Back at our hotel, I would shake my head every five minutes and say to Wend:

'Can it get any better than this?'

It could. In the Festival's "Launchpad" marquee, *Kindling* made its official entry into the world. I celebrated Maroon-style by running down the middle of the tent, high-fiving the crowd. I lifted the book high, told the assembled punters that this little ripper was fifteen years in the making, and received a big ovation. I read my favourite scene from the novel while my beautiful wife and hero father beamed with pride in the front row (Mighty Mum had volunteered to mind the twins so that Wend could attend). Post-launch, alone in the author "green room" tent, surveying the fancy grub on offer, I thought:

Can it get any better than this?

It could. Another author soon joined me in the green room. 6'4", thatch of greying hair. Familiar attire of jeans with white collared shirt and tie. A suppressed yawn that suggested a festival appearance shoehorned into a busy schedule. I did a double-take. No way! Am I dreaming? It had been a thrill to see his name in the program, but I hadn't dared to think I might encounter him off-stage, let alone by himself in the green room. I took a breath, rose from my chair and stepped forward. Be cool, I thought. But it was too big of an ask. I idolised this person, for his iconic humour, searing intelligence, brilliant writing and improvisational genius.

This was John Doyle.

This was Rampaging Roy Slaven.

It's not an exaggeration to say that Roy and H.G.'s annual Origin commentary was required listening for me in the late '80s and throughout the '90s. As well as being the perfect combination of hilarity and smarts – something I aspired to in my own creativity – it was a source of comfort. The nerves and negativity consuming me before each Maroon tilt would dissolve the moment the volume was turned down on the Channel 9 coverage, the ghetto blaster was tuned to Triple J, trumpets blasted out of the speakers, and King Wally Otto in the Soundproof Booth launched into his inimitable opening spray, letting us know 'the card table is set' and 'have the tissues ready' and 'peace is worth fighting for'. Friends and I would be in fits of laughter going through the rollcall of nicknames they'd given to players on both sides (my favourites were "Deborah Kerr" for Allan Langer, "The Burning Map" for John Cartwright, "Cheese 'n Chives" and "Salt 'n Vinegar" for the Smith Brothers, and "The Squirrel Gripper" for Martin Bella). We'd sing along to the "national anthem" – Lionel Rose's "I Thank You" – and giggle at the oblivious warbler on TV belting out "Advance Australia Fair" on mute. Then the game would begin and so, too, their incomparable play-by-play, featuring "tool action" and "date work" and "nut merchants" and "grabbing him by the cruets" and even the odd reference to Slaven's legendary racehorse, Rooting King. All of Roy and H.G.'s glorious antics should've convinced me that the vast quantities of emotion and meaning I attached to Queensland Origin were wasted. In the end, it was just footy, deserving of parody and absurdity as much as love and affection. And truth be told, I would be convinced… but only for sixty minutes or so. When the contest got down to brass tacks, Triple J would take a back seat to proper commentary, befitting the seriousness of proceedings.

Roy and H.G. were no match for my Maroon fandom excesses, but I worshipped them all the same. And now I was standing in front of John Doyle, introducing myself, prattling on about being his biggest fan, singing the praises of the "Life and Times of Rampaging Roy Slaven" cassette tape I'd worn out from a thousand listens, asking him to sign my Byron Bay Writers' Festival program. In the face of this onslaught, he couldn't have been more gracious. He signed (as John Doyle, not Roy). He asked what I was at the Festival for (my introduction had bordered on incoherence, so I suspected he had doubts about me being literate, let alone an author). When I gave the elevator pitch for *Kindling*, he nodded, congratulated me and said it sounded like a winner. I replied that it was no *Changi* – the superb miniseries Doyle had written for TV in 2001 – and he said I was too kind. And then, just as I was about to plead with him to ditch H.G. for D.G., a minder materialised at his side, giving me side-eye, and letting the great man know the location of his next session. Doyle apologised, wished me and *Kindling* well, and took his leave. I returned to my chair beside the charcuterie board, stared at the signature on my program, and looked around the green room I once more had to myself.

'Can it get any better than this?' I said aloud.

For the first time on this tour of fulfilled dreams, I was certain it could not.

◯

For the Dynasty, 2010 was the peak of their powers. In their eight-straight and eleven in twelve years, it was the only 3-0 triumph. I mentioned earlier that I rank 2010 top-five in my all-time series wins; any decent judge of Maroon performance should have it similarly regarded.

Which of the three victories is the best barometer of the 2010 team's greatness? Many consider it the 34-6 belting in Game 2 at Suncorp. I believe it's Game 3. In all my years of Queensland Origin, I've never seen a squad more driven by the "no dead rubbers" ethos. Playing away from home, shield already secured, down by five with ten minutes to go, Blues intent on grubbing their way to a face-saving win, the Maroons were undeterred. A touch of Lockyer-Slater class put us in front in the 74th minute then a shift right after an Israel Folau intercept provided the exclamation mark on a 23-18 dub.

Back in Brisbane after Byron Bay, between further commitments for *Kindling*, Des and I sat down together to watch the 2010 series in all its glory. Game 3 was the first DVD he put on. I asked him why that one. He laughed as if my query was an Irish joke he'd never heard before. His answer was simple, succinct and less surprising than Roy and H.G. comedy gold:

'It doesn't get any better than this, son.'

30

Sympathy via Satellite

July 6, 2011
Origin Game #3, Suncorp Stadium, Brisbane
Score: Qld 34 – NSW 24

Snow fell January 10, the night Brisbane drowned.

Jared, then nine-years-old, was overjoyed. Though limited in his capacity for speech, his actions shouted: 'At last!' Winter had underwhelmed to this point; the promised festival of snowmen, snow angels, snowball fights, snow forts, snow anything had fallen well short of expectation. Many had figured it to be a bad season in Vancouver. All manner of alarmist predictions had signposted the December solstice; claims abounded, trumpeting record lows and frequent storms and full shelters. For two months, Jared had waited for the white-out to come. When it finally arrived, he wasn't aware that calamity always rode sidecar with the snow, propelling drivers into ditches, cutting off electricity, and bringing assured levels of chaos to the streets. He simply gave thanks. Mother Nature had deigned to be kind.

I was not thankful. I was awash in Facebook updates.

○

Water over the bikeway now…

Many people panic buying in the supermarkets, wiping out supplies of milk, bread, fruit and meat…

Police cutting off access to my street! Shit just got real…

◯

I held a hand to my pinched forehead as the feed hummed. This was insane. The city of my youth, my family, my entry into fatherhood; the city I still considered home, the city I loved… it was suffering. Not at the hands of a sudden, unfamiliar trauma, like the earthquake that hit Vancouver Island in 1946. Brisbane's foe was experienced, proven, all too understood from forty years before: the insidious and inevitable rising of the river, slowly drowning the inner-city 'burbs the way hantavirus takes its victims by submerging the lungs in the body's own fluid.

It was just beginning.

Around dinner time, brother Simon posted photos from his downtown work at the State Library of Queensland. The first showed the river lapping at the foot of the landscaped surrounds. By the time of the second, snapped an hour later, the concrete walkways at ground level of the Library had gone under. I noted Wend's rhetorical comment – *Why aren't you going home* ☹ – and decided he needed further encouragement:

Yes, gtf home, Si…

He was doing just that, but he was stuck in a gridlock of fleeing CBD commuters. Three hours later, he received a message from Al Jazeera letting him know they were using his pics.

◯

Have been through heartbreaking morning helping with moving a friend's belongings upstairs or to elsewhere on higher ground…

OMG… Edenbrooke is being evacuated!

> *Saw footage of flooding in Milton and Oxley's / Drift Cafe floating down the river…*
> *Scary stuff…*

◯

'Your son has an idea in his head.'

Wendy's plea prised my attention away from the iPad. Jared was doing his happy dance, leaping and spinning and raising his arms and rocking foot to foot. He bounced, bum first, on the adjacent exercise ball then pressed his hands and nose against the glass back door, staring wide-eyed at the flakes cascading from above.

'Snoooow!' he said, balancing awe and delight. 'I looove snow!'

'Think I'll take him out,' said Wend, donning her winter jacket. 'Just for a couple of minutes.'

She gave a tired smile and led our celebrating son outside. I could tell she was glad to have a distraction, if only for a brief moment. I reminded myself: her roots were as deep as any belonging to me. Family, friends, stories… She had a trove of each. She'd lived in Queensland for twenty years. Given birth to our children at the Wesley. Worked for Suncorp. As written into our wedding vows, she'd cheered on Maroon triumphs and railed against the defeats. A nurtured niche in her heart would always pump to the rhythms of Venero Armanno's *Firehead* and Powderfinger's "Odyssey Number Five".

It was faltering now.

Much of her day had been spent fretting over the online *Courier-Mail* and its flood coverage. No detail had escaped her attention: the river was set to peak overnight; it was believed it could top 1974 levels; thousands of homes would be inundated; damage would be in the billions; the death toll – currently standing at thirteen in the wake of the Toowoomba and Lockyer Valley tragedies – would undoubtedly rise. Every prediction, every declaration of doom, had added another arrow to her quiver of concern. It hurt to be so far away, a hapless spectator. Sympathy via satellite left a lot to be desired.

During the morning, anxious and unable to concentrate, I'd bent the ear of anyone and everyone at my day job. Canadian colleagues were familiar with the coverage – it had been in the papers and had featured in both local and national news broadcasts for the better part of a week. They wanted to know how bad it was. I'd tried my best to communicate its magnitude:

'Imagine one third of Surrey going under…'

'Picture water covering the field in BC Place…'

'Think kayaks paddling down Robson Street…'

They'd shaken their heads in disbelief. I could see I'd brought them closer to understanding and further away from empathy. I didn't hold it against them. How could I, given my own wedges of separation: three years of Canadian permanent residence and a fifteen-hour flight?

'How are your loved ones?' had been my workmates' tentative follow-up. I'd told them my parents lived in the safe, northside suburb of Mitchelton. My brother and his family were in Red Hill; much closer to ground zero but high enough to remain untouched. Friends and acquaintances were spread far and wide across the city – most had offered assurances they were fine, some had revealed they were preparing for the worst. I'd brought the conversations to a close the same way each time:

'Keep us in your thoughts today.'

They'd nodded and returned to their flood-free lives. Purged of silence but not of guilt, I'd admonished myself for the use of the term "us".

◯

The city was empty this morning. 90% of businesses closed…
Waking up to clear skies and devastation is still on its way with the king tide…
Ipswich Mayor Paul Pisasale: 'If I find anybody looting in our city they will be used as flood markers.'

◯

Facebook was still rolling at 11:00pm local time. Amongst the torrent of Brisbane posts was detritus from my Vancouver friends. Questions about plans for the evening. In-joke innuendo between friends. Links to favourite products and movie stars and music videos. Complaints about the snow.

'This is bullshit,' I muttered. 'Get outside your bubble for a second.'

The scolding was unfair, but I indulged it all the same. Wend nipped it in the bud.

'He's going to be very sad tomorrow.'

'What?'

'Jared… He's going to be sad tomorrow.'

For a moment, I couldn't fathom the statement. He'd come in from the brief play outside contented and rosy-cheeked. He'd gone to bed with a split watermelon for a smile. He continued to randomly shout 'SNOW!' at regular intervals.

'Turning to showers tonight,' said Wend. 'It'll all be washed away in the morning.'

I put the iPad in my lap and leaned back in my chair. It was true. The winter wonderland that had floated down from the sky like manna would be gone by sunrise. My son's allyship with Mother Nature would be replaced by confusion and despair and distrust. It was unfair, but that was the way of the world. Cruel blows, delivered without logic or control, were destined to rain

219

down in life. Could we absorb them, own them, shape them into stories of courage and compassion?

I looked at the iPad screen. Captioning a photo of two teen boys paddling a gutted fridge down their suburban street were the most recent Facebook updates:

…We're high and dry with spare rooms. If anyone needs help let me know…

My place is fine. We are available for clean-up duties — if you need the help, don't be too proud, just sing out…

…Disasters like this bring the best out in people. John Farnham and Angry Anderson will come out of retirement AGAIN…

'Jared'll get through it,' I told Wend. 'He's a Queenslander.'

Of all the indelible flood images, the one that hit hardest was Suncorp Stadium. Whenever I thought about it or saw a photo — field gone, goalposts partly submerged, player races inundated, change rooms ruined — my heart ached. The image was an indictment. I hadn't been there for my city. I should've been there. No matter that I live in Canada — I should've boarded a plane, crossed the Pacific, and been on the ground before the water was gone. I should've joined the Mud Army, helping friends, supporting strangers, living and breathing Queenslander spirit. I should've come home.

I channelled the pain and guilt I felt into my new novel, *Finding Fault* (later titled *Are You Seeing Me?*). A story about Brisbane twins — neurotypical Justine and autistic Perry — who visit British Columbia for one last holiday before going their separate ways, *Finding Fault* explored much of what the floods had brought to the surface in me: loss, grief, family, distance. At its core, though, was love and resilience. As the manuscript neared completion in the run-up to Origin, it seemed like providence. Both art and football held the promise of resurrection. The Maroons would attempt to assuage the state's suffering by winning a sixth straight series, possibly in a decider at an unbowed, newly repaired Suncorp Stadium. Adding further zeal to Queensland's restorative mission was Darren Lockyer's departure; after thirty-three caps and nineteen as captain, my second favourite player of all-time was suiting up for his last dance. As for *Finding Fault*, it too represented a rebound from adversity. For all its "can't get any better than this" vibe, *Kindling* had sold poorly, in large part due to being out of sight / out of mind in Australia after the 2010 tour was done. The new work, though, could build on the fine critical foundation it had laid down. And when Hachette released *Finding Fault*, perhaps an extended stay in Oz could be arranged – a commitment I figured would please the publisher and go a long way towards righting the sales ship.

The 2011 series was, indeed, tied 1-1 when it got to Brisbane. I performed the "up at 2:30am, damn the day job" routine again. It was a must given I'd been missing in action during my state's desperate hour of need. Watching the pre-game, I marvelled at the condition of Suncorp Stadium. It looked a picture; all traces of the disaster six months previous were gone. I couldn't imagine the amount of work required to deliver the world's best rugby league venue from its watery grave. The players understood, though. They'd spoken to the rescuers. Not just in Brisbane – all over the state. In Emerald and Toowoomba and Grantham. People for whom rescuing was a job, and people who'd had the job thrust upon them. People who'd done all they could to save footy grounds and pubs and bridges and shopping centres and libraries and neighbours' houses. People who'd saved people.

Seventeen Maroons would be the rescuers tonight.

It was one of those precious, rare as hen's teeth, stress-free Origin viewings. At no point was losing a consideration – from kickoff to final hooter, I was supremely confident of victory. At 24-0 after thirty-four minutes, I even considered opening the laptop and working on *Finding Fault*. The manuscript was close to the finish line and, as was always the case with a novel nearing completion, the pull to bring it home was compelling. I resisted, though, cognisant that salvaging Queensland from the depths of its *annus horribilis* was much more important than tossing a lifebuoy to my literary career. In the 69th minute, when Greg Inglis embarrassed four Blue defenders to give the Maroons an unassailable 34-10 lead, I took special note of the mad celebrations in the stands. From my couch in far-away Vancouver, it looked a lot like catharsis.

On December 8 of 2011 – my beautiful wife's birthday – I found out that rescuing my literary career required much more than a lifebuoy. Hachette were not interested in *Finding Fault*. The disappointing sales of *Kindling* couldn't justify any further investment in my name or my work.

I was stunned. Gutted. One shot – that's all you get? No building a readership? Just instant success or bust? My agent tried to explain. The industry had changed. Less tolerance. More risk aversion. Smart phones. Social media. People were spending more time on their status updates and less time reading books. She wasn't giving up though. She submitted *Finding Fault* elsewhere and Simon & Schuster responded with enthusiasm. The publisher loved it, calling it the best manuscript she'd read in a long time. She was taking it to acquisitions: a meeting of key people in-house to determine which projects would become books and which would be turned away. I was familiar with these meetings – it was a stand-or-fall moment for your story, controlled by people you might never meet, ruled by a decision in which you had zero sway. All you could do was cross your fingers and wait for word.

The word was 'No'. Nothing to do with the story or the writing – the team at S&S loved the work. The problem was the sales numbers of *Kindling*. They were too awful to ignore. I was tainted. Sorry. Thanks – sincerely, *thanks* – but no thanks. Just like that, my bright writing future had been snuffed out.

During the low months that followed, I posted my misery online. Friends and family in Queensland rallied. You're an awesome writer, they assured me. *Kindling* was amazing. This is just a setback. There'll be other opportunities. I thanked them for their kindness while inwardly berating them for their platitude, their Pollyanna, their cluelessness about the extent of the blow.

Sympathy via satellite.

It left a lot to be desired.

Frequently, I would reflect on the January disaster to bring some perspective to my despair. Thousands of people lost businesses and homes. Thirty-five people died. A tragedy. Darren, you had a story rejected by the big end of town – that's hard. Disappointing, difficult. Maybe even unfair. But not tragic. I reminded myself of this truth time and again, trying to put my gloom in its proper place. Regrettably, it didn't take. I kept coming back to a shameful analogy:

My dream had been washed away.

(This chapter is dedicated to the thirty-five Queenslanders who lost their lives in the 2011 floods).

31

Citizen Groth

July 4, 2012
Origin Game #3, Suncorp Stadium, Brisbane
Score: Qld 21 – NSW 20

In 2012, after the crushing rejection of *Finding Fault*, I suffered an identity crisis.

Since my early 20's, I'd understood I was a writer. Writing was what I did, perhaps even what I'd been put on this planet to do. I wrote words every day. I thought about words. I talked about words. I owned completed stories and published books and cool recognitions and a bad back and a lonely wife and neglected children and crippling self-doubt. Nothing more was needed to prove I was a writer. And yet the spurning of *Finding Fault* had made me question everything I thought I knew. Famed psychoanalyst Erik Erikson would've sussed me out in a heartbeat: in the State of Origin match-up between generativity and stagnation, the latter was well and truly on top.

Following the brief period of self-pity on social media, I tried my best to hide the hurt. To the oft-asked question of 'When can I read your next book?', I replied: 'As soon as I can read it.' In solitary moments, I prayed to higher powers, pleading the case for my voice (*Come on, Goddess, I'm not writing pap… I'm writing about family and disability and otherness and acceptance… things that matter!*). I begged the universe to give me another shot. I cried a few times, in bed, quietly, while Wend slept unaware beside me. Eventually, I could stay arm's-length from the emotion long enough for flashes of useful thought. How do I get past this? What can be done to move forward? I settled on two things. First: my next novel would be a collaboration with younger brother Simon (I figured if there was more taking it on the chin, then two chins were better than one). And second: I would become a dual citizen.

The decision to naturalise felt essential. My name was hot garbage in Australia – if I was to survive my identity crisis, if I was to continue meaningfully pursuing a writing future, I needed to get published in North America. And to get published in North America, it would help a lot if I was Canadian.

(It was around this time my agent suggested I use a pen name on future works, so as to avoid the toxicity of "Darren Groth". I thought she was joking and supplied her with my preferred pseudonym: "Ruprecht van Longbollocks". She was not joking and felt a name without testicular connotations might be wise. Much water has passed under the bridge since that surreal exchange, but I still want to see "Ruprecht van Longbollocks" on a front cover someday. Ideally, a children's picture book.)

In the early stages of the citizenship process, I kept telling myself this was not at all a betrayal of my roots. I may have been on a salvage mission for my sense of author self, but my allegiance to home and heritage was in no way compromised. I was mollified by the fact that my cherished Maroons were dealing with their own identity schism. In December of 2011, Arthur Beetson had died suddenly of a heart attack at the far-too-young age of sixty-six. To every fan, but especially my father's generation, Origin without Big Artie was incomprehensible. He'd willed the concept into existence with his haymaker on Mick Cronin in 1980 – thirty-plus years of possibility had sprung from that single defining act. He represented everything we Queenslanders had come to understand about ourselves. With his passing, who were we now? Who would we be? Added to that uncertainty was the retirement of Darren Lockyer: champion, future Immortal, initiator of the unbeaten streak in 2006, image through which the current team was cast. Locky's absence prompted some to wonder if the magical run of six straight series was in jeopardy. Could the loss of a contemporary touchstone be overcome? It was a valid concern. When Wally Lewis retired, we'd gone down in the three series following. When Allan Langer retired – same result; three series defeats. With another Mount Rushmore Maroon hanging up his boots, was it New South Wales' time to dominate, as they were so fond of telling everyone? Could this group maintain the Dynasty identity?

They could, and they did. In Game 1, a second-half clinic in defensive resolve and a correct call by the video ref to award a Greg Inglis try in the 73rd minute saw the good guys prevail 18-10. Game 2 in Sydney did not go our way – a Cooper Cronk sin-binning and injuries to Billy Slater and Corey Parker aided the Blues' winning effort – but a stirring comeback hinted at Game 3 glory. The Suncorp decider didn't disappoint. With five minutes remaining, and the scores locked at 20-20, Cronk – elevated from the bench with Locky's goodbye – etched his first entry into Origin folklore with a 40-metre drop goal that proved the difference in the contest.

Whether it was the looming naturalisation ceremony in October, or my parents visiting for the second time since our move overseas, Wend and I went Maroon troppo for our viewing of the Game 3 triumph. As it wasn't live (we were watching the DVD Dad had brought over), knowledge that the result had gone our way only added to the festive atmosphere. We donned our jerseys. Put up banners and flags (including one on the car, which was ultra-confusing for the locals). An ornamental cane toad wearing the revered "6" jumper sat pride of place in front of the TV. In the hallway, I created a Queensland "Wall of Fame", featuring printed portraits of The King, Artie (rest in power), Alf, Big Mal, and the greatest of them all, Desmond Eric Groth, kitted out in the sweep guernsey of 2010. Snacks included a mix of the locally sourced and items brought over in the folks' "care package": Savoury Shapes and Chokitos and Macadamias and Jatz crackers with kabana and Wendy-made lamingtons and the very unlikely but delightful addition of Weis Bars (sadly, the stock at Jarry's Market in Ladner Village would be short-lived). It was kitschy, it was overkill. It was probably a knee-jerk response to my desire for Canadian citizenship. It was perfect.

As Cronk's winning field goal sailed between the uprights and Dad launched into an impromptu rendition of "You Can Count on a Queenslander", it occurred to me how testing the victory had been. Before the opening whistle of the series, the Maroons were shouldering Beetson's passing and Lockyer's absence. Then, respective dummy spits from Ricky Stuart and the Sydney press over the refereeing in Game 1 meant they were needlessly saddled with officiating favouritism. In the decider, they rallied from an early 8-0 deficit. They wore the constant niggle of the laughably named "Bruise Brothers", Gallen and Bird. They endured two pulled-from-their-arse plays by the Cockroaches to level up at 20-20: Brett Morris' juggling catch for a try and Todd Carney's conversion from the sideline. Finally, they survived Mitchell Pearce's attempt at an equalising field goal in the final minute. They stood tall through all the trials and showed they were every bit the Dynasty of the previous six years.

Watching new captain, Cam Smith, lift the shield, I recognised the example this team had set for me. Hard times weren't a reason to doubt your identity.

They were an opportunity to affirm it.

My swearing-in ceremony took place on October 12, in an auditorium at the Surrey Citizenship office. It was a melting pot; around eighty or so new Canadians from every corner of the globe were on hand, each with their own story to tell, many with a group of supporters in the gallery. The mailed instructions in the weeks prior had made a point about dressing up for the occasion — consequently, I was wearing my best suit, collared shirt, tie and patent leather shoes. I also had a backup item more befitting my style: a Vancouver Canucks jersey, famed "16" of captain Trevor Linden, bought in 1995 during my working visa stay. I wasn't sure if I'd throw it on, but I'd brought it along in the event the moment felt right.

After Queensland's Origin win, my perspective on becoming a dual citizen had fully shifted from fearing disloyalty to embracing necessity. I was doing this out of pure pragmatism, to keep my writing dream alive. It wasn't personal — it was just business. Totally fine. That all changed when the ceremony commenced. I thought about the premise of our move to Canada: to give Jared a better chance in life. I thought about how well he was progressing with all the extra support now available to him. I thought about the Milpera kids I'd taught and how fortunate I was to have a choice of where to live. I thought about how much Wend enjoyed being back with her family. I thought about Chloe and the exciting prospects that lay ahead for their burgeoning visual artistry. I thought about how lucky I was to have been adopted into the wonderful Fraser clan. I thought about how the magic of *Kindling* being signed by a big publisher had happened only after leaving Australia. By the time the singing of "O Canada" came around, I was choked with emotion.

And then my name was being called to accept my certificate and the congratulations of the citizenship judge. Without hesitation, I ditched the suit jacket and pulled on the Linden jersey. As I mounted the stage, the gallery – largely made up of locals – cheered and applauded as if it were the lower bowl at Rogers Arena, or the licenced terraces of Lang Park. The smiling judge, noting the response, asked me if I had a jersey for him as well – I told him if I'd known, I would've had my beautiful wife bring her prized Gino Odjick "29" along. He laughed, shook my hand, welcomed me to Canada, and directed me to the gallery with a hearty, 'Go Canucks!'.

That evening we had a party at our place to celebrate my new status. Family and friends were focused on one question:

'How do you feel?'

My throwaway response: 'Like a proud "Canozzie".' But the true answer was more complex. I'd entered into naturalisation as a way to resuscitate my literary career and by the end it had delivered much more meaning and substance than a simple transaction. It had reminded me to be grateful; as a husband, as a father, as an in-law, as an immigrant. And, yes, even as a writer. Was my identity crisis done? Not entirely. The shadow of questioning would cling to my heels until the next instance of positive author news came my way. Until then, I could look to the many gifts in my life – among them the 2012 Dynasty-extending Maroons – and know that I was a privileged citizen of this world.

32

The Fork Taken

July 17, 2013
Origin Game #3, ANZ Stadium, Sydney
Score: Qld 12 – NSW 10

Dear reader, if you know little to nothing about North American sporting culture, you may not be familiar with a man called Lawrence Berra. Better known by his nickname "Yogi", Berra was a catcher for Major League Baseball's New York Yankees from 1946 to 1963. While his career as a player and manager was stellar – he was a Baseball Hall of Fame inductee in 1972; if I was to make a Queensland rugby league comparison, it would be Johnny Lang – Yogi Berra's real legacy lies in the unforgettable off-beat quotes he produced throughout his lifetime. 'It is what it is.' 'The future ain't what it used to be.' 'Baseball is 90% physical; the other half is mental.' 'Always go to other people's funerals; otherwise, they won't go to yours.' He's even credited with first saying: 'It's *déjà vu* all over again.'

My personal Yogi Berra favourite is: 'When you come to a fork in the road, take it.' Legend has it the quote originated from directions he gave to his best mate about the location of his house, situated at the end of a through-way that split into two. Whichever route you took, whatever choice you made, you ended up at your destination: Yogi's pad. While unintended as wisdom, the quote has assumed an almost mythical sensibility. People have shared it in books better than this one. Argued for its place on statues and plaques. Written essays and blogs dedicated to divining its latent insight into the human condition. Whatever meaning you ascribe to the statement, I've landed on it as the best descriptor of the Queensland Dynasty's defining quality. I think it also sums up the acts of faith that saw my beleaguered *Finding Fault* manuscript finally get over the line, revive my literary fortunes, and raise them to heights I'd never imagined.

In the Channel Nine "Stories of Origin" podcast episode "The Dynasty", Andrew Johns argues the primary reason for Queensland's eight-year dominance was that we had champions in the key positions. While there is undeniable truth to this claim, Johns' tone in the piece – a heavy dose of forlorn resignation – hints at inevitability, that the Maroons' greatness was fated, fully formed from the outset. He appears to lean towards the theory of champions being born rather than made. I lean the other way. I believe the all-timer statuses acquired by Darren Lockyer and Cameron Smith and Johnathan Thurston and Greg Inglis and Billy Slater and Cooper Cronk were just as much the result of hard work as God-given talent. And through that hard work were forged the wrought mindsets to elevate them above every other Origin nucleus that preceded them: unshakable belief and absolute trust. Such were The Dynasty's superpowers, they were never paralysed by decision. The moment was never too big. The adversity was never too great. When challenged, they believed, and they trusted.

When they came to a fork in the road, they took it.

All but the most ardent contrarian would agree the pivotal fork taken was in 2006 when Locky intercepted Brett Hodgson's errant pass. But by no means was it the only instance. 2007: carry an 11-game winless streak into Telstra Stadium; bury it with an effort coach Mal Meninga labelled 'special' and 'backs to the wall'. 2008: already without the injured Lockyer, replacement Scott Prince suffers a gruesome broken arm fifteen minutes into the Sydney decider; press on with trademark resilience before getting home on the back of JT-Slater magic. 2009: series won, Justin Poore assaults an unconscious Steve Price in a Game 3 all-in; payback is extracted with legal ferocity, sending a message the affront would be added fire for next year. 2011: lose Johnathan Thurston at a key juncture of Game 3; march on undeterred to secure the series. 2012: get taken to the brink by a resurgent Blues; crown a new hero with Cooper Cronk's field goal for the ages.

2013 would prove to be the final year of The Dynasty's glorious run of consecutive victories. Ironically (or perhaps fittingly?), their last fork taken in the streak would be a streaker. Up 12-10 in the decider with three minutes left on the clock, Cam Smith darted down the blind inside the New South Wales 30, released Corey Parker, then steamed onto the lock-forward's offload before being tackled a metre short of the line. With the Blues defence shot to ribbons, the Maroons shifted right to a rampaging Matt Scott who plunged over near the posts to put the result beyond doubt. Only, there was a problem. A pitch invader – naked bar a pair of white tennis shoes and a solid tan; pursued by Security, Police and likely the ghost of Ron McAuliffe – had interfered in the play prior to Scott crossing the line. Queensland's destiny had been disrupted and the Blues had one last chance to end their worship of the Washington Generals. Viewing the incident, my reaction was: *Christ, the Cockroaches will even use a* streaker *to not lose again!* But The

Dynasty would not be denied. In the final seconds, with the invader being frog-marched off to the paddy-wagon, a desperation cross-field kick from New South Wales captain Robbie Farah yielded nothing more than winger James McManus being bundled into touch. That was all she wrote. Maroons 12-10. Eight straight.

Yogi Berra couldn't have kept this team away from his house if he'd wanted to.

⬯

By the start of 2013, *Finding Fault* was no longer on my radar. I was working with younger brother Simon on two new novels: one I'd drafted in the early 2000s called *Kid Concentrate* (later, *Concentrate*), the other a from-scratch story titled *Wake* (later, *Infinite Blue*). I was enjoying the collaboration; it was back-to-basics, revelling in the act of writing itself, free of any definitive expectation. I was open to the idea of the Brothers Groth becoming bigger than the Brothers Grimm, but in terms of my life plan, it ranked just above winning Mr. Olympia and becoming lead singer of AC/DC. On the very rare occasion I thought about *Finding Fault*, it touched upon those Dynasty superpowers of belief and trust. I believed the story was good. And I trusted that somehow, some way, someday, it would get a chance to show it was good.

In early 2013, somehow, some way, someday suddenly became a little more substantial. Unbeknownst to me, my stalwart agent had been sounding out contacts across the pond and one of her targets had shown keen interest. I was stunned. Wary, too. I'd made fragile peace with the fact of *Finding Fault* coming up short. Now, there was that heartless peddler of misfires and mirages: hope.

In the spring, I met with the contact. He loved *Finding Fault* and wanted to represent it — and me — in North America. I said I'd have to think about it and laughed like a kookaburra. He also felt the current adult version of the work might not be the best fit; in his estimation, it had more potential as a young adult novel. He wanted to know if I was agreeable to making a change.

I paused. Here was a fork in the road. I could be the precious author and refuse to compromise my original version. Or I could explore the proposed changes and find something new, maybe even something better. Either way, it ended at the same destination: my new North American agent sending it out to publishers.

'Sure,' I replied. 'What have I got to lose?'

I didn't lose anything. I didn't gain anything either. The new young adult version of *Finding Fault* – which I liked a lot with its late-teen protagonists and revamped third act – failed to pick up a deal on the continent. Okay, Hope, I thought. Can you please leave me alone now? But that sadistic dick was not done with me. The agent had spoken with the Harper Collins Canada publisher, who was willing to do an "editorial consult". If I was willing as well, perhaps it could lead to signing on the dotted line. Another fork in the road. "Consult" was code for more changes. As had happened previously, I could acquiesce and the story could end up improved. Or I could stick to my guns, claiming further changes without the promise of a contract was like buying an engagement ring for a blind date. Either way, it ended at the same destination: Harper Collins having a second look.

'Sure,' I replied. 'What have I got to lose… apart from hope?'

The outcome of the consult was not a signature on the dotted line. I listened to the ideas presented, went away, made the alterations I thought were necessary and delivered the manuscript for the second look. The feedback? Not even close. The publisher wanted the novel overhauled, stripped back to the beams. Without that, there was no way forward. Right, Hope, I thought. Can you please leave me the fuck alone *now*? But that torturous arsehole was still not done with me. And this time it would be an even worse punishment. Up to now in the sorry, stagnant odyssey of *Finding Fault*, all the momentary ascensions from the ashes had been generated by external forces – the Simon and Schuster acquisitions meeting, the North American agent coming on board, the consult with Harper Collins. This new seed of hope was (gulp) sprouting from within. This new fork in the road had been paved by yours truly.

'In Oz, it was rejected by the adult fiction publishers,' I told Wend. 'But this is a new manuscript, a young adult work. Maybe it can go out again?'

'What have you got to lose?' she asked.

'My sanity,' I replied.

After informing my agent of the new opportunity, she put *Finding Fault* back in the hands of the big Aussie presses, only this time with their young adult publishers. Soon after submission, Random House responded with considerable enthusiasm. The catch (say it with me, now): they wanted the story changed. The climax ended a little too abruptly – the suspense could be drawn out for longer. Was I open to re-jigging it? Receiving the news, I laugh-cried. Or cry-laughed. One of the two. I was bone-tired. Bending your artistic vision without assurance of any reward for the effort… it was death by a thousand cuts. But no amount of bloodletting would shift reality. This was the gig. Like State of Origin, there is no mercy in publishing. If I needed any more proof in my career – and I didn't – the fruitless journey of *Finding Fault* had provided it. In the end, the only fallback was the superpowers of the Maroon Dynasty.

Sure, I thought, replying to my agent, letting her know I'd make the changes. What have I got to lose?

Apart from my belief and trust?

◯

On a late November Sunday afternoon, I decided to watch Dad's DVD of the 2013 decider again – a little belated birthday treat. When the streaker arrived on the scene with two minutes to go, I thought about fast-forwarding through the delay then opted to let the tape run. I quickly opened the laptop and checked my inbox before play resumed. There was an email from my agent. She'd received word back from Random House.

They were making an offer.

Swallowing the lump that had instantly formed in my throat, I put the laptop aside and watched misty-eyed as the Dynasty once more scaled the summit. Like 2009, I was joining them. It had been two-plus years of false dawns and futility, but at last, I was back in the big-time.

The final fork in the road had been taken.

I'd made it to Yogi Berra's house.

33

Icarus, Grounded

June 18, 2014
Origin Game #2, ANZ Stadium, Sydney
Score: NSW 6 – Qld 4

This is what my fan experience has devolved into here in Vancouver:

The day before the game, I try not to think about it too much. It's a task made exponentially easier by the fact no one here knows or cares about rugby league or State of Origin. The things that make it unavoidable in Bris-Vegas – rampant media reporting of the team's preparation, the water cooler discussions, the palpable tension and excitement, the colours and jerseys worn around town – these are reserved for hockey in the Great White North. If I'm feeling brave, I might manufacture a little buzz by mentioning the game in conversation with workmates, folks I've already relentlessly indoctrinated into the Maroon cause (imagine the scene: I'm entering a second hour of Wally Lewis' greatest performances while the polite Canadian listener mouths 'KILL ME' to every passer-by). In general, though, I stay mum about the contest. Best to keep it on the DL in case we lose and next day I'm the one pleading to be put out of my misery.

After the day job shift, I come back to a home geared up for "*that* time of year". Wendy knows the game is looming, courtesy of friends and family on social media. She appreciates my concerted efforts to keep the evening as normal and Origin-free as possible – again, an endeavour greatly assisted by the fact it's not in our faces. She also knows it all goes out the window if Queensland wins. The day after a victory, living with me is like a 24-hour episode of footy "Jeopardy" where I am host, contestant and live studio audience, and every question is about what happened during the eighty minutes:

'Hello and welcome to Jeopardy! Tonight's categories are: "Heroes in Maroon"… " Ref Blunders"… "The Game's Turning Point"… "New South Wales Sucks"… "It's Great to be a Queenslander"… and last but not least, "We Won, But I'm Still Pissed at those Ref Blunders"…'

The twins' sense of Origin's creeping presence is by osmosis. Chloe is a huge Queensland fan, but only as it relates to "Masterchef Australia" contestants. Jared's understanding is limited, though his affection for his birth state is evident in the Ferny Grove train videos he watches on YouTube, the photos of Des and Kath he loves to scroll through, and his willingness to join in the "QUEENSLANDER!" chant anytime I let loose. I've reconciled with the knowledge that, barring some unfathomable turnaround, the Groth Maroon lineage ends with me. It's just as well. What Dad handed down was something honourable and pristine, the fan equivalent of a white dove. What I'd be gifting my kids is a scrub turkey.

(A brief aside about being fine with the lack of a Maroon successor. I read an article a number of years ago that has stayed with me; it concerned an American university professor who was father to a profoundly autistic son. Told in first person, it detailed the professor's efforts to fulfill the only wish he had as a parent: that he and his boy could go to a baseball game together, sit in the stands, eat a hotdog, and stay until the final out. The prof was working hard to fulfill his dream, constantly engaging in baseball talk and showing it on the TV, offering different foods in the hope of expanding his son's limited diet, focusing on the valuable life skills of sitting still and attentiveness to task, mitigating the meltdowns that frequently dogged his efforts. There was a long way to go and there'd been precious little progress to date – a state of affairs the academic seemed quite bitter about. He'd been denied so much as a dad. Why couldn't he have this one thing? The article was intended to illicit sympathy, and I confess it did so with me. Not in the way the professor might've hoped, however. I didn't feel at all sorry for him. Only his son.)

With the evening's Origin avoidance done, it's off to bed, usually sometime between 11:00pm and midnight, around three-plus hours before kickoff in Australia. This is where the benefit of being a remote Maroon devotee is meant to come to the fore. While the battle rages in Oz, I will be at peace, blissfully asleep, heart rate within a healthy range, blood pressure unencumbered with the peaks and troughs of Maroon fortunes. Sounds good in theory. In practice, it's laughable. Mind swirling with game reverie, I have trouble settling down. When the curtain finally drops, the sleep is anything but blissful. I dream about dreadful things, some of them possible (us getting belted), others just for kicks (a Blues' Zamboni turns the field to ice and we have no skates). I will stir awake during the wee hours, often more than once. If it's late enough – after 5:00am – the compulsion is to check the final score. Win or lose, it will end any chance of drifting off again. I don't check the score.

When at last I'm properly up with the sun, it takes a second to find the courage to Google the result. If I'm feeling particularly fragile, I'll ask Wend to look it up on my behalf. We won? "Jeopardy" time! Days' long delight, multiple viewings of the eighty minutes and gleeful gorging on the Sydney media's inevitable meltdown. We got done? Maybe a cursory look at the headlines. Definitely feigned ignorance (It never happened. You hear me? We didn't lose because IT NEVER HAPPENED).

I know what some of you are thinking: Darren, you're cheating. You're flouting the accepted rules of sports fandom. More than that, you're attempting to get around an inescapable truth: you can't live authentically after the fact. That's fair. I have never watched a Maroons loss in Canada. Not one. Some of that is due to the luck of Dynasty domination; the vast majority is by choice. Quite obviously, an infallible Queensland rugby league team is a mirage. It's a biased, harm-reduced, alternate reality. And I accept that. In this one indulgent corner of my existence and identity, I am swallowing the *soma* of Huxley's *Brave New World*. I am softening the path, smoothing the way. Because my wings are only pretend, made from feathers of convenience and bound by the wax of comfort, I'm not Icarus flying too close to the sun.

I never leave the ground.

⬥

In the run-up to the 2014 series opener in Brisbane, during a late-Spring workout at the day-job gym, I came to a realisation: my alternate Origin reality was now the norm rather than the exception. The last live game I'd watched? The 2011 decider. Everything since had been either triumph on tape delay or defeat immediately tossed in the bin. Hot on the heels of this new understanding came a commitment to stay the course. Barring the most exceptional circumstances, the Maroons would continue to be sure things from now on. No longer would I risk visiting the frontlines of my state's annual war.

In hindsight, I might seem prescient. I had an inkling before the 2014 series that the Dynasty's unbeaten streak would end. In a genuinely competitive two-horse race, to have prevailed so often was already in defiance of probability. At some point, the Blues would have enough go their way to eke out a victory. Even unparallelled greatness has a "best before" date.

The night of Game 1 met the standard of patchy sleep and restless thought. In the morning, with a flinchy face and one eye closed, I looked up the score. New South Wales 12, Queensland 8. A quick skim of an ABC article revealed Cooper Cronk had broken his arm in the tenth minute. There it is, I thought. The circuit-breaker. The Dynasty had withstood all manner of hardship in eight years – this devastation might just be a bridge too far. And it was. For Game 2, another tempestuous night was followed by a fearful sun-up glance at the result. New South Wales 6, Queensland 4. I gave the coverage a tad more attention than Game 1, mainly to celebrate this Maroon outfit which, in many quarters, was being hailed the greatest team in Australian sporting history. In amongst the bouquets were clutches of weeds: hilarious claims from delusional Sydney scribes that it was time for payback.

'Not so fast, tossers,' I muttered and closed the book on Game 2.

Three weeks later, the Game 3 morning search revealed a very different scoreboard: Queensland 32, New South Wales 8. Needless to say, I watched this one. Three times. After revelling in all of it – the smash-up, the half-time parade of former players instrumental to the streak's early years, the sight of the Blues having to lift the shield after being walloped, the suspicion that this unrivalled Maroon team wasn't yet finished – I thought about this curated Origin bubble of "wins only" I'd created, this safe little grounded-Icarus space I'd carved out. There was definite appeal in expanding its borders beyond football, into other more hallowed areas of my life. Foregoing challenge, eschewing suffering, ending unpredictability, boiling the world down to only those things that make you feel good or offer you consolation or affirm your outlook on life… it was a seductive prospect. Take Jared's situation. Now that he was in a better system with proper support – had been for seven years – I could dine out on that success, feasting on the cleverness of our move to Canada. So what if the bill of our son's long-term future was still to come? Same goes for my aging parents. I could continue marvelling at their apparent indestructibility, touting their fine genetic stock and the excellent care provided by their longtime GP, Dr. Loh. The very real signs of decline – Dad's recent diabetes diagnosis and Mum's brush with breast cancer in 2008, among others – it was far preferable to turn a blind eye to those.

And then there was the writing. Here I stood, a new book released in May with Random House Australia. *Are You Seeing Me?* was its title now after *Finding Fault* was abandoned during editing. I could adopt an "all good" mindset, set up an environment where only the positive filtered through. Easy-peasy at this early stage. The physical object was a thing of beauty. Early reviews had been glowing. Publisher and agent were pleased. No sales figures yet to ruin everything. *Are You Seeing Me?* You betcha! What I'm seeing is solid gold! Never mind that this novel was in the very same position as its hobbled predecessor, *Kindling*: author living overseas, unable to support it in-person all year round. Forget that this return to the big-time would in all likelihood be as short-lived as the last occasion. In my Origin-styled literary career construct, I would be safe and sound, protected, never flying too close to the sun, never crashing back to Earth.

Never leaving the ground.

34

Icarus, Soaring

July 8, 2015

Origin Game #3, Suncorp Stadium, Brisbane

Score: Qld 52 – NSW 6

Following the 2014 series defeat, the Dynasty had every right to fix themselves to their *terra firma* of Origin history. Eight straight. Best side ever. Immortal status secured for Lockyer, Smith, Thurston; probably Slater and Inglis as well. If they'd all retired from representative footy and spent the rest of their days wearing Groth-brand rose-coloured glasses, dwelling only on their many glorious victories, Maroon Nation would not have begrudged them their decision. The players, though, weren't content with a risk-free legacy. They sat with the discomfort of 2014 and were determined to don their wings again. There was more flying to be done.

In Game 1, they withstood the pull of gravity. Accused by the Sydney press of being too old (Question: when will Cockroach journos come up with something new? Answer: when Hell freezes over, thaws, freezes over again, and hosts the Winter Olympics…), Queensland played a strong road game, winning the arm-wrestle, dominating field position and leaning on their peerless poise-under-fatigue to get home 11-10, another Cooper Cronk field goal in the dying stages salting it away. Of particular satisfaction was the Blues' rank ineptitude prior to Cronk's one-pointer. Camped in the attacking 20, they had multiple golden opportunities to slot their own game-winner; instead, a series of brain explosions saw Michael Jennings kick a grubber dead and the Maroons receive seven tackles. The Dynastic ones duly executed the set to perfection and the game was ours.

My feeling going into round two: the series smelled of a sweep. New South Wales had blown it in Sydney; they'd needed to win, they'd done enough to win, they'd had the perfect chance to win… and they'd lost. You couldn't let an opportunity like that slip against a legendary squad, no matter how old they were. And now the scene shifted to Melbourne – an advantage for the Maroons with all the Melbourne Storm influence in the side. The evening of Game 2, I went to bed confident the shield would be regained. For seven hours, I slept like a Lone Pine koala, free of any calamitous dreams. In the morning, I woke to find Wend already up and dressed. She asked if I wanted to know the score. I lifted my chin, told her I was good to check on my own like a big boy, and dived into the online search.

New South Wales 26, Queensland 18.

I stared at the iPad screen, frowning, confused. Couldn't be right. Must be "stuck" in the second half. I'd endured live feeds getting stuck from time to time on the ESPN site. Very frustrating. I glanced over at Wend – she was refusing to look my way. Hesitantly, I hit the refresh icon. Same score. And the clock showed full-time. I let my head fall back on the pillow. No. No! NO! What had happened? How had we lost? Forgetting my own rules of disengagement for defeats, I began to read the reviews.

Of all the painful content, one *Sydney Morning Herald* piece stood out. It reported that early in the match, young Blue tearaway, David Klemmer, had called Queensland elder statesman and walking offload, Corey Parker, a "has-been". Later, as New South Wales' game-long niggle and cheap-shottery began to produce an edge that would see them home, Parker shouted at Klemmer to 'show some respect', prompting a thoughtful, nuanced response from Klemmer: 'Get fucked, you cunt!'. The author considered the incident indicative of the Blues' new winning attitude and a prelude to their inevitable dominance in the years to come. By the finish of the article, I hated everything. Klemmer's antics. The journalist. The glib tone of the story. Most of all, I hated that it might all be true. Were a New South Wales player pleading for respect in the midst of a losing battle, I'd be licking my chops for the next tilt.

Next to its sedate, self-confident predecessor, the night of Game 3 was unrecognisable. I tossed and turned in bed, unable to shake my feeling of dread. Why had the Dynasty brethren assumed this risk? Why hadn't Smithy and JT and Hodgo and GI and Billy the Kid and Coz Parker all called it a day after 2014? During the streak, they'd been Michael Jordan on the Bulls – in 2015, they might be Michael Jordan on the Washington Wizards. For eight straight years, they'd been Ali versus Foreman – in 2015, they might be Ali versus Berbick. The thought of such an ignominious downfall made me nauseous.

At some point during the late hours, I managed a fitful sleep. I dreamed I was driving the Maroons' team bus to Suncorp, taking wrong turns and stalling at traffic lights, doing my best to prevent the players getting to the stadium. At the Caxton Street Hotel, an apoplectic Chris Close kicked me off the bus and plucked a new driver out of the surging crowd: my father. Wearing his old Queensland Railway Institute jersey and ignoring his eldest son,

Des shook Choppy's hand and climbed into the empty driver's seat. He saluted the crowd with a couple of toots on the horn, kicked the bus into gear and took off at a hundred clicks an hour, determined to make up for lost time. I gave a limp wave and turned to face the angry Caxton mob — it was at this perilous point I woke up in a sweat, sun streaming through the bedroom window.

I couldn't look at the score. I couldn't ask Wend. I needed a few hours to steel myself for the melancholy-in-waiting. Around mid-morning, the not-knowing finally crossed my threshold of intolerance and I opened up the iPad.

'Crash and burn, boys,' I muttered as the search loaded the result. 'What's the damage?'

I stared at the score. Twin waves of emotion swamped me; first shock, then awe. I rubbed my eyes and put on my glasses, though I didn't need them for reading.

Queensland 52, New South Wales 6.

'I'll be buggered,' I whispered. 'Sky's still the limit.'

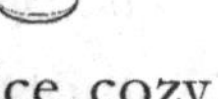

Here's the thing about being a nice, cozy, safe Icarus on the ground: at some point, Life tosses you into the air and forces you to fly towards the sun. When it happens, it's easy to assume the worst. I get it. Avoiding a fall — that was the whole point of fastening yourself to the earth in the first place. But now you're airborne, whether you want to be or not.

What if you soar?

Maybe the sun isn't so hot after all. Maybe the wax on your wings doesn't melt. Maybe you start to like having your head in the clouds.

Maybe you climb higher than you ever thought possible.

In October of 2014, *Are You Seeing Me?* was signed by highly regarded Canadian press, Orca. It wasn't quite the big-time but it was a big moment, made possible by my decision to naturalise and the persistence of my North American agent. I was pleased. Seven years after our move, I was finally establishing a writing foothold in my adopted home. And, lo and behold, I could support the work! It wasn't enough of a breakthrough to risk cock-eyed optimism, but at least I was now open to being less of a killjoy. Maybe the book could sell enough in North America to not flatline my career?

Of course, death-by-sales was still a very real threat in Oz. If *Are You Seeing Me?* was to avoid going the way of *Kindling*, it had to make a splash on the 2015 Australian literary award circuit, preferably one of those cannonball drops that soaks passers-by and leaves very little water remaining in the pool. With sights fixed on the new year, I was caught out by the book's first recognition in December: *Are You Seeing Me?* had been chosen as one of Booktopia's "2014 Books of the Year". Further burnishing this unexpected gold star was Booktopia's inclusion of me in their "Favourite Australian Authors" poll – a lovely, mystifying decision that ended appropriately with my straight-sets elimination in the first round. As a new calendar of Aussie landmarks went up in the kitchen of our Ladner townhouse (January was the Opera House… Brisbane beggars couldn't be choosers in Canada…), I wondered if the Booktopia love was a joyous one-off or a thrilling sign of things to come. Providing a quote for the front cover of the novel, the great Nick Earls had communicated his belief that *Are You Seeing Me?* had the potential to change my author life, maybe even my life in general. I'd thought he was just being nice. Had he truly seen something exceptional in the book? As a Queensland literary icon, I figured he would know.

Easy, big fella, I told myself. Keep your feet on the ground.

February produced more goodness. In an email replete with exclamation marks, the publisher informed me the novel had been selected as an outstanding work by the International Board on Books for Young Adults (IBBY). Among fifty chosen worldwide, *Are You Seeing Me?* was one of two successful Australian entries in a submission of one-hundred-and-fifty-nine books from twenty-seven countries. It's an amazing achievement, she wrote. You should feel very proud. I was proud, but as it had been with the Booktopia nods, I was still afraid to admit we had lift off. Only one recognition would allay that fear and guarantee a different outcome to *Kindling*: the Children's Book Council of Australia "Book of the Year" Awards.

The CBCAs are the State of Origin of youth literature in Australia. Not only do they carry unrivalled prestige, they're an economic powerhouse, driving sales to schools in every corner of the country. Selection as a "Notable" is like making the Maroon squad as eighteenth man. Selection as a "Finalist" or "Honour Book" or "Winner" means you're in the run-on team. It's the pinnacle of the field, best of the best. It always lifts a career. It often defines a career.

The 2015 CBCA lists were to be revealed on social media the morning of April 14. I knew it was happening, but due to the time difference, I was on Dad dinner duty – nachos! – so I wasn't paying close attention to the announcement. I figured if I made the cut, someone would let me know. Chopping up the capsicum, I heard my phone ping a few times in quick succession.

'Dad,' said Chloe, not looking up from the couch and their Mario Kart-ing on the Rainbow Bridge. 'When did you become popular?'

I checked the messages, half-a-dozen in all. They were congratulating me and linking to the CBCA site. *Are You Seeing Me?*

was a Notable selection. They were also letting me know the Finalists would be posted in ten minutes. Dazed by the news, I reverted to type. Notable is great, but not a game-changer, I muttered to myself, popping the nachos in the oven. Be happy with being a Notable. It's all you're going to get. This effort to temper expectation and not risk disappointment lasted ten minutes. Hustling the twins to the dinner table, my phone blew up, pinging like a pinball machine. I sensed what had happened, but I feigned ignorance, tweeting out: 'What's going on? Cooking nachos for the kidlets. Did I miss something?' More pings, each delivering the news that I was in the Maroons' run-on team:

Are You Seeing Me? was a finalist for CBCA Book of the Year.

Feeling I needed to respond immediately to the dozens of well wishes, I started sending out replies: *Thank you! I can't believe it! You're too kind! So grateful!* I was twenty messages deep when Chloe interrupted, tapping me on the shoulder.

'Dad, there's smoke coming out of the oven.'

Oh shit. I dropped my still pinging phone and raced into the kitchen. Without thinking it through, I flung the oven door open on the now cremated nachos. Within seconds, the smoke alarms triggered, filling the house with a wailing that sounded suspiciously like "BAD DAD! BAD DAD! BAD DAD!" Five minutes of mayhem ensued. Door slamming. Fan buzzing. Tea-towel waving. Phone pinging. Me shouting. Chloe sighing. When finally the crisis was averted, I flopped down in a chair, a little voice whispering in my still-ringing ears:

Welcome to Origin!

Baptism of literal fire aside, an unassailable truth was now apparent: I had burnt the nachos, but not my Icarus wings. I was off the ground. I was in the sky. I was flying beneath the glare of the sun.

The soaring would continue unchecked through 2015. Following the CBCA shortlisting, *Are You Seeing Me?* would be nominated for six more Australian gongs, including the Prime Minister's Literary Awards and, like *Most Valuable Potential* eleven years earlier, the Queensland Literary Awards. Published in hardcover by Orca in August, the book was a surprise finalist in Canada's Governor-General's Literary Awards and the BC and Yukon Book Prizes a few months later. It was also a selection in the "White Ravens" – an annual list by the International Youth Library in Germany that profiles the world's best books for young people. The knock-on effect of these successes hit home when the focus shifted to my next novel. My agent said I was "hot property" and that surreal tag was confirmed when both Penguin Random House (the two giants had merged earlier in the year) and Orca paid a premium and signed my next work on spec. I could scarcely fathom it – being signed on spec was a privilege known only to the bankable authors, the sure things.

In early 2016, *Are You Seeing Me?* jagged a big win on home soil: best YA novel at the South Australian Literary Awards. The publisher felt it was the perfect opportunity to come back and support the book in-person and I gladly accepted an invite to Adelaide Writer's Week where I hung with the likes of Lauren Groff and Kate Grenville and Magda Szubanski. For the award acceptance, I revived the footy-style celebration I'd enjoyed at the Byron Bay Writers' Festival, running through the crowd, distributing high-fives. Between sessions, a meeting with Random House and my agent conveyed exciting news on the overseas rights front: the book had been sold to Turkish publisher, Pegasus. There was also significant interest in several other territories, including the UK. As the whirlwind week came to a close, I had to acknowledge: in the last eighteen months, what *Are You Seeing Me?* had achieved was no longer just my Maroon call-up. It was my version of the Dynasty.

Gratifying as it all was, I understood it couldn't last. This was not my innate grounded-Icarus kicking in – it was the immutable laws of physics. Great heights must inevitably be followed by descent. What goes up, must come down. Not to say that great heights can never be attained again. They can. But only after a reset, a moving on from what had first propelled you into the stratosphere. The Maroons would submit proof of this in 2016. For the first time in their illustrious decade-long reign, they would lift the shield without Mal Meninga as coach, the great man having stepped aside for Kevin Walters. Queensland was resetting. And so was I. By the time the series wrapped with a 26-16 win in Game 2 at Suncorp, my literary energy was wholly and solely on my new novel, *Living for Martel Maddux* (later titled *Exchange of Heart* in Australia, and *Munro vs. the Coyote* in North America). Additional marvellous things might still be in the works for my little *Are You Seeing Me?* dynasty, but by the end of 2016 they belonged to a sky already conquered.

35

All Good Things

June 21, 2017
Origin Game #2, ANZ Stadium, Sydney
Score: Qld 18 – NSW 16

When I first started penning *Exchange of Heart* – the tale of a grieving high-school exchange student who finds healing as a volunteer at an assisted-living residence in Brisbane – one question became a jumping-off point for the project: If my son were to move into a care home, what would I want it to be for him? In real life, far removed from the fictional page, the topic of Jared's adult future was scary as hell. I didn't want to think about it more than I absolutely had to. Enabling this avoidance was the Canadian school experience. Though not without its challenges, our time in the BC Education system had been positive – unquestionably better than the sliding doors outcome had we remained in Queensland. And because of this run of good years, I'd been lulled into forgetting that school eventually comes to an end. By 2017, that end had appeared on the horizon. Jared was approaching the mid-point of his Senior Vocational program at Delta Secondary; following his Grade 12 equivalent in 2019, there was the option of an "over year", which many intellectually disabled students participated in. After that, he would be out in the big, bad world.

Not surprising then that this imminent seismic shift should seep into *Exchange of Heart*. Exploring adult disability in the novel allowed me to keep the emotion and fear at arm's-length. It also permitted me to play God and shape things as I would want them. The assisted-living residence central to the story – I named it "Fair Go" – exhibited everything to make it a caregiving utopia: agency for the residents, kind and dedicated staff, beautiful grounds, fine facilities, modern technology, respect, passion, empathy, advocacy, laughter, friendship. I couldn't hope to make the world perfect for my lad when he left school, but I could offer an aspirational vision we could all strive for.

An era coming to an end was not just narrative fuel for the new book, it was the book itself. The day of its release would be the last gasp of the *Are You Seeing Me?* golden run. No longer could I live large on past achievements – I was now in the hands of an untested follow-up, starting over, living and dying with its unique journey and burden of expectation. In Australia, I figured *Exchange of Heart* would realise one of two fates: further success leading to a lasting mark on the literary landscape, or a *Kindling*-like comedown returning my career to the doldrums.

So often the case throughout my many years of fandom, I found solace in my footy team wrestling with challenges that spoke to my own. History shows the 2017 Origin series was the final go-round for Johnathan Thurston, Cam Smith and Cooper Cronk. No one knew for sure it was their last in the lead-up – Cronk would make the announcement in December; Smith, famously, would pull the pin three weeks out from Game 1 in 2018 – but I had a sneaking suspicion all three would depart (I actually thought Billy Slater might bail as well, especially after being overlooked for Game 1).

South of the Tweed, they'd been clanging the death knell for the Dynasty since 2014; at long last, the prediction would come true. The greatest Maroon team of all-time, victors in ten of the last eleven series, would hope to summon the sublime once more before bowing to the only opponent that could've bested them: Father Time.

Permit me to muse for a second on appreciation. It's a constant theme in life that us humans have trouble acknowledging the best of times while they're happening, and that it's only after they've ended, only through the stark lens of hindsight, that we recognise how good we had it. While I'm not immune to taking salad days for granted (see above: Jared at school), I've also sought to consciously nurture a position of gratitude in the present. Key to this commitment is a pair of devices common to the writer's toolbox: noticing and imagining. When something or someone stands out in a good way, I make an effort to notice. And to further my appreciation, I imagine the contrast, that same something/someone when circumstances have soured, their time no longer touched by Midas. Used together, noticing and imagining have helped me better recognise the need for prompt thankfulness. What you are reading is a prime example. Every day, fathers die suddenly, and the sons left behind can offer only belated tributes to their memory – courtesy of Des' generous cancer prognosis and successful treatment, I was in a position to be spared that lifelong regret. I took notice of the extraordinary opportunity I'd been afforded. I imagined the contrast, a host of horrible alternatives that could've otherwise denied the opportunity. Thus, with a grateful heart, I began to write. Now, as I sit at the keyboard typing this sentence, closing in on this book's conclusion, the privilege I feel is even more pronounced.

The Maroons are masters at ensuring you appreciate them in the present. They're specialists at standing out, classically after letting you imagine the worst. When you think you've seen skill, they show you a miracle. When you think you've seen passion, they show you a ragdoll. When you think you've seen belief, they show you a Neville. When you think Queenslander spirit has been distilled down to its essence, they reveal yet another element to its chemistry. When you think you've seen it all, they show you something new.

2017 might've been the definition of "all good things…", but the Dynasty, and specifically Johnathan Thurston, was going to show you something new to appreciate on the way out.

I was shocked by the Game 1 score. I thought we might lose without the injured Thurston and the inexplicably snubbed Billy Slater, but a 28-4 smackdown? At Suncorp Stadium? Worst Maroon home loss ever in the Origin era. No surprise then that I didn't watch the game or read the reports. I went about my ruined day comforted only by the fact that the series wasn't over and that JT and Slater would be back for the re-match in Sydney.

I experienced my usual restlessness the night of Game 2. And, naturally, another bad dream. I was in the warm-up sheds for the Maroons, strapping the players' various injury concerns. When it came to JT's shoulder, I told him I had special tape that would guarantee he got through the eighty minutes okay. I dug around in my "medical kit" — it was a backpack I'd won in a raffle at local Ladner pub, the Sundance — and pulled out a wedge of butcher's paper. I opened the paper and inside were a dozen slices of black forest ham. Without a word of dissent from Thurston or Kevin Walters or anyone else in the Maroon sheds, I proceeded to strap the future Immortal's shoulder with ten dollars' worth of cured meat. When I was done, I asked JT how it felt — he gave me a thumbs-up and then, seeking to further reassure me, peeled off the slice securing his clavicle and gobbled it down. As omens go, it wasn't one that inspired confidence.

I woke just after 5:30 in the morning, I didn't want to wait — I needed to know straight away. Wiping the sleep out of my eyes, I fired up the iPad. The first headline read "Maroons Keep Origin Series Alive, Win Game 2 18-16". I screamed internally with glee, eased out of bed so as not to disturb Wendy, and tip-toed downstairs to watch the Sportsnet recording I'd set up the night before. Watching the first half, I couldn't reconcile what I was seeing with the final result. Things had started well enough with Val Holmes' wing acrobatics giving us the early lead, but after that it was all New South Wales. They put us to the sword, running amok through our flimsy edge defence, scoring three tries in thirteen minutes to lead 16-6. Then, in the thirtieth minute, JT reeled out of a tackle on Tyson Frizell, clearly favouring his shoulder. There wasn't a chance in hell he would stay on the park till the final hooter.

'Should've used bacon,' I grumbled as the Channel Nine commentary team rightfully hinted at the game being lost.

It was after this obvious blow to our chances and the Blues' bombing of another try soon after that I felt compelled to pause the tape and check the score online again. It hadn't changed: the Maroons still victorious, 18-16. I shook my head. How on earth had we turned it around? To date, it had been one-way traffic; 16-6 could easily have been 30-6. Had Andrew Fifita lost his marbles and got himself sent off? Had dysentery run through the Blues' room during the break? Had some other deli meat given JT's shoulder a new lease of life? Making a cup of tea at half-time, I was fascinated to see the second 40. Although I knew it all worked out in the end, I was eager to see the extraordinary after imagining the worst. I was keen to deliver some appreciation.

Ray Warren hadn't been fooled by the Blues' dominant display. Coming back for the resumption of hostilities, he warned that Queensland had done 'some of the Houdinis of rugby league'. Would Thurston be part of the escape act? In the forty-sixth minute, with the Maroons under the pump and forced into a line drop-out, sideline reporter Darren Lockyer, who'd been watching his former teammate struggle since the Frizell tackle, suggested JT was merely "out there" and that "no doubt the Blues will target him". He was still out there in the fifty-second minute when Josh McGuire burst into the Cockroach backfield, setting the platform for a brilliant round-the-corner pass from Will Chambers and a Dane Gagai saloon passage to the line. He was still out there as Queensland turned up the defensive intensity in the final 20, hoping to induce a fatal error. He was still out there in the seventy-sixth minute when a shift left led to a superb Michael Morgan flick pass and the Gagai equaliser. And he was still out there a minute later, lining up the conversion, five in from touch, believing he could win us the game.

Would win us the game.

Did win us the game.

Arm hanging, the pain such that the adjustment of his headgear – a key aspect of his goal kicking routine – was torture, JT aimed the ball to the right of the sticks then watched as his trademark bend brought it back on line and over the black dot. 18-16. I was speechless. This was a new benchmark for courage. Beyond Bob Lindner playing on a broken foot and Trevor Gillmeister climbing out of his hospital bed and Paul Bowman making three tackles with a shattered knee. All I could do was stand and applaud.

In the after-game analysis, a dejected Andrew Johns tagged the inability to target the wounded Thurston as 'the dumbest half of football New South Wales have played'. I lapped up the *schadenfreude*. And I couldn't have agreed more. The Blues had failed to notice and had lacked imagination. Consequently, the appreciation of closing out the series had passed them by. Three weeks later in Brisbane, the Dynasty took care of business for the eleventh time in twelve years, winning the decider 22-6. That they did so with Thurston on the sideline and Cameron Munster making, arguably, the best Origin debut since Artie Beetson, saw many suggesting that the Blues' pain might never be relieved, and that Queensland Origin was the exception to the rule of "all good things…". An ABC article I read following back-to-back watches of the tape commenced with: *It is the end, so why does it only feel like the beginning?* As much as I wanted to believe that the Dynasty could survive the loss of Immortals and would triumph forever, I wasn't buying it. In my heart of hearts, I sensed we were set to return to our natural state: underdogs, outsiders.

Written off.

◯

Exchange of Heart was published by Penguin Random House in Australia on October 14. Three days later, it was released in North America by Orca under the title of *Munro vs. the Coyote*. In some ways, it felt like *Are You Seeing Me?* had never happened. Here I was, beset by the same Australian conundrum as before: no year-round author presence on the ground, no ability to personally assist the bottom line, no guarantee the work would fly. For all the victories of *Are You Seeing Me?*, there was no mortgage on lasting author success in my homeland. I had to earn literary Origin selection all over again.

One might argue it was my natural state.

36

The Worst Conclusion

November 18, 2020
Origin Game #3, Suncorp Stadium, Brisbane
Score: Qld 20 – NSW 14

It's been said before, but it bears repeating: Queensland *is* Origin. We are the reason it exists. We are the reason it has thrived. We are the reason it's the biggest and best sporting rivalry in the nation. We are the story. New South Wales? A mere side character, present in the narrative only as a device, a vehicle for the hero's journey.

It's easy to assume the most compelling evidence of Maroon centrality lies in the miracles and the fairytales and the escapes, our consistent ability to overcome insurmountable challenges. For sure these iconic moments seed Origin's pride of place in the Australian sporting landscape, but they're easy flowers to pick. It's also convenient to suggest the best proof of Queensland's pedestal is the Dynasty. Here in North America, winning too much is a drag. With the exception of the victorious supporter base, fans are turned off by the same result year after year. The Belichick-Brady Patriots, the Joe Torre Yankees, the Ken Holland Red Wings, even Jordan's Bulls… all of them overstayed their welcome to the point of, if not disdain, then certainly indifference. Not so with our domination from 2006-2017. People couldn't get enough of Queensland's reign. Record crowds. Record TV ratings. Record sponsorships. Record merchandise sales. Every year, most of Origin's audience favoured Maroon glory and Blue pain. Were it up to us non-New South Welshfolk, our upper hand would've been *ad infinitum*.

For my money, Queensland as Origin's bell-cow is best demonstrated when we lose. During every low ebb – '85 and '86; the post-King years; the 2000 drubbing; the after-Alf years – our struggles ran roughshod over the New South Wales storylines. Is Maroon spirit gone? Can we still compete? Will Origin survive? Will rugby league survive? These tropes were back in vogue at the end of the decade. Series wins in 2018 and 2019 saw the tiresome southern pundits at it again, elevating the Blues to the role of protagonist. They peddled "revenge" and spruiked "our turn" and hawked "Dynasty 2.0", oblivious to the irony that talking up a new age just further entrenched the Maroons as the standard. The perfect illustration of this was the 2019 decider. In describing James Tedesco's eightieth minute try to win the series, the consensus media assessment was that the Cockroaches had 'done a Queensland to Queensland'. While this simultaneous Maroon worship and Blue minimisation was delightful, it wasn't enough to make me watch the loss or read any post-game analysis. My commitment to Origin-good-vibes-only was unwavering. And by 2020, it seemed less a choice and more a necessity.

Things had taken a distinct downturn. *Exchange of Heart* bombed on the 2018 Oz award circuit, including the all-important CBCAs. Sales were disappointing. And when Penguin Random House passed on my next project, it was apparent much of the Australian progress achieved by *Are You Seeing Me?* had been reversed. The

North American edition of *Exchange of Heart – Munro vs. the Coyote* – provided some relief. The novel managed to garner two major Canadian recognitions: nominations for the CCBC Amy Mathers Award and the OLA White Pine Award, both of which can be considered Origin-esque for prestige and commercial value. But those quality nods were soon taken off at the knees – Orca didn't want to sign my next project either. They'd honoured their agreement to publish *Infinite Blue* in 2018 (the novella I'd written with brother, Simon) but that was it; they were stepping away from the books I liked to write and had found success in – young adult literature – to focus on books I didn't write and had no track record in – the children's market. I was crestfallen. In what seemed like the blink of an eye, I'd gone from publishing security on both sides of the Pacific to author without a home. Hot property to vacant lot.

More heartbreak was in store. I'd written a new novel in 2019 – it would later carry the title *Boy in the Blue Hammock* – and I was certain it was a cut above. Handing the manuscript over to my North American agent, I harboured hopes of recovery. My career in Australia might've been dropped to the reserves, but there was recent top-grade Canadian success to lean on. And this novel was next level, better than anything I'd written in the past, better than anything I might ever write in future. In February of 2020, inconceivable word came back from my North American agent: he didn't want to take it forward. He believed the work was too flawed to warrant sending it out. I was crushed. Too flawed? Can't be! This is a cut above! Next level! Better than anything past or future! It was a disaster. Now, I not only had zero publisher support, I had zero prospects as well. My literary career had unravelled and the best stuff I'd ever penned was destined for the scrap heap.

At the time of my agent's rejection, I recall thinking I'd contracted some disease of misfortune, some contagion of calamity. Soon enough, I would discover the disease was real, and the misfortune and calamity were global. On March 11, the World Health Organization declared the spread of Covid-19 to be a pandemic. By the afternoon of March 16, with the province of British Columbia moving at a rate of knots towards lockdown, I was furloughed indefinitely from my day-job. As uncertain days blurred into weeks and uncertain weeks blurred into months, my general dispiritedness was compounded by concern for my son. Covid was a frightening spectre looming over all of us, but the thought of Jared getting sick was unbearable. There'd already been verified stories of ill intellectually disabled people being denied ventilators; later, more appalling revelations would come to light – statistics revealing Jared's community was six times more likely to die of Covid, documented evidence of the intellectually disabled being assigned "Do Not Resuscitate" wristbands without consent. Even without these horrors, the worry was crippling. Then there was his mental health. He couldn't comprehend the massive changes going on. One minute he'd been enjoying the fun final months at school, the next it was replaced by... nothing? No classroom or transit or bowling or aerobics or group outings? Just home and Zoom sessions and puzzles and masks and boring days with his father? By summer, his considerable patience had worn razor thin. Possessive of the language to sum up his feelings, he would've told me: 'Dad. This. Is. The. *Worst!*' Without the means of such verbal expression, Jared used what he had at his disposal: distress. Meltdowns became a near-daily occurrence. I tried to explain what was happening, to let him know that change – *good* change – was coming. *Before the year is finished, there'll be routine again. Dad will be back at work. And you'll be in a "day program" with adult friends. It'll be more fun than school! Well, when the lockdown measures relax and they're allowed outside the building, it'll be more fun than school… Things will get better soon. I promise.* None of my reassurance made an impression. After a while, I surrendered, exhausted. When the meltdowns predictably came, I would soothe him best I could, saying 'I feel ya, mate' (I couldn't) and 'I totally get it, bud' (I didn't).

By November of 2020, no more adversity was needed to gild this stretch as the worst of my life, both personally and professionally. But there was one more coat hanger to the head incoming. Just after Remembrance Day, Dad and Mum got on a video call with me, Sean and Simon. Dad didn't muck around: he had cancer. Multiple myeloma. It attacked the blood and the marrow. It was terminal. The words had little time to hang in the air before they were swatted away in typical, brightside-Des fashion. They'd caught the cancer early. Very early. So early that he didn't need chemo. So early that he might have a decent number of years left. Not so bad, hey? Could be a lot worse, yeah? Dazed, us three sons nodded. I can't speak for Sean and Simon, but for me, everything said after "terminal" faded into the background.

When I got off the call, Wendy took me into her arms and asked if I was okay.

'Maybe?' I replied. 'Are *you*?'

I knew her answer. Her beautiful mother, Dorothy, had died in December 2017 after an eight-month battle with pancreatic cancer. Dad's call, despite its silver linings, had dangled her over the abyss of those black days.

'Ask me later,' she said. 'I'm going to make you a cup of tea.'

The day after the call, I realised my "maybe" response to Wend's check-in had been generous. Something in my soul had become unmoored. Projecting into the future, I felt the difficulties encountered the last couple of years were now par for the course.

I was middle-aged, in the waning phase of my existence, the "central character confronts obstacles" second act of my story arc. Positives would still come along. Jared would join his program. My father was okay for now. The pandemic would end. I might even get good author news again. But they wouldn't alter the overall outlook: the ledger of life would now echo the words of Olympic founder, Pierre de Coubertin, skewing a little more towards the struggle than the triumph. And it made sense. I'd lived fifty relatively charmed years – the time had come to pay the piper.

Trouble was a neighbour now.

The worst would keep knocking on my door.

◌

And the door of the 2020 Maroons.

Heading into the series – for the first time ever, it was being staged in November – Sydney journalist Dean Ritchie labelled the Queensland squad 'the worst in 40 years of Origin'. Like my father with a cancer diagnosis, the Maroons responded with customary pluck and defiance, bucking their plus-8.5 price tag pre-game and coming away from the Adelaide Oval with an 18-14 upset. In Game 2, though, they more than lived up to the derogatory label, getting embarrassed 34-10. Heading into the Suncorp decider, former Cockroach skipper Paul Gallen doubled down on Ritchie's original claim, saying the tag of worst ever was 'fair'. While I appreciated the fire Gallen's declaration would light under the boys, my negative headspace wouldn't allow for optimism. When I looked at this Maroon team – full of debutants and no-names and compromises and honest toilers and last resorts – I didn't see a series win. I didn't see the protagonist overcoming the obstacles. I didn't see 1989 hospital ward heroics or 1995 Nobodies or '06 hand of Locky. I didn't see a footy respite from my woes. I saw a squad like me: beaten down and out of their depth. I saw what I'd been conditioned to see the past few years: the worst.

I went to bed the night of Game 3 in the pre-requisite state: grumpy, bone-weary, worried for the world, worried for my father, afraid Jared might wake up distressed during the night. Wendy asked if I'd set up the PVR to tape the decider. I told her I had.

'You don't sound too enthused,' she said. 'That's not like you.'

I huffed and nodded. 'These days, I'm not like me.'

Her face a well of bottomless compassion, she kissed me on the cheek then rolled over.

'Queenslander,' she said, turning out the lamp on her nightstand.

Despite myself, I smiled and nuzzled her shoulder. We'd been married twenty-five years. This past July, our intention had been to celebrate the milestone in New York – the pandemic had put paid to that idea. It had also torpedoed plans of a family get-together in Vancouver; given Dad's situation, we'd probably never get the chance again. *Situation.* I couldn't come up with a better word than that? This was why my writing career had tanked. Given Dad's *circumstance* – Jesus, no better; maybe worse – what were the odds I would see him in the flesh again? Slim? None? Yes, they'd caught it early. Yes, the prognosis was encouraging. Yes, Dad was putting on a brave face. But this was cancer. This was a *terminal* situation, circumstance, whatever. This time next year, he might no longer be with us.

I did dream that night. I was playing for Queensland. Strange as it sounds, I'd never before dreamt I was on the field in the Maroon jumper. The ground was the old Lang Park with its concrete terraces and Caxton scoreboard. My teammates were an eclectic bunch: Wally Lewis, Darren Lockyer, Tony Currie, Barry Gomersall (playing, not reffing), Matthew Hayden, Jacki

MacDonald, Thea Astley, Canadian buddy Andrew, and the giant Matilda mascot from the '82 Commonwealth Games. My jersey number was "69" (even in the bleakest of times, my subconscious remained steadfastly immature). After a few hit-ups and tackles, I looked at the score. Down by two with two minutes left on the clock. I approached Locky and told him there was only one person who could win it for us: Desmond Eric Groth, everyone's mate in the stretched number "8". I called to the sideline: *Dad! Get on the park! It's time!* No answer. I began a search, lifting off from the Lang Park turf and hovering over the sell-out crowd. *Dad! We need you! Now!* It occurred to me he might be where we'd watched our first live Origin game together, the incredible 43-22 massacre in the 1983 decider. I floated over to the spot, halfway up the Milton Road hill. No sign of him. Only a human-size pile of used Violet Crumble and Cornetto wrappers. I went to call out again but was stopped by the final hooter. I looked back towards the field – to a man (and a mascot), my teammates were slumped on the field, spent, defeated. We'd lost. I swore, threw my head back and found myself staring at the faint outline of the light fixture on our townhouse ceiling.

The bedroom was dark and chilly. Outside, the rain drummed the overhang above our front door. Atmospheric river season was in full swing and the Lower Mainland winter – a grey, drizzly ordeal at the best of times – was set to be a Covid second-wave marathon of mental fortitude. On my phone was a news notification I hadn't requested. Seven-hundred-and-seventeen new cases in BC yesterday. Eleven new deaths. I deleted the notification. At some point, I had to figure out how to shut those bloody things off. Add it to the to-do list for today, alongside applying for more EI and washing my hands twenty times and coming up with Plan B, C and D for Jared and having my first drink at one minute after midday. Oh, and also add to the list discovering the sorry fate of

Queensland's worst ever team. I looked at the time. 5:38am. The decider was over. I wasn't ready for the inevitable result. It was too early — there was a whole day available for courting despair. Avoiding Google, I checked my email. There was a new message from Dad. In my addled condition, I'd forgotten Des wasn't averse to sending a message post-game. Invariably, the subject heading he chose was a giant spoiler. This one, borrowing from the famous tourism slogan, took the cake:

QUEENSLAND! WORST ONE DAY, PERFECT THE NEXT!

I dropped the phone on my chest, lay still and closed my eyes, trying to identify what I was feeling. I couldn't. I was engulfed by an ancient, pixelated memory that was now suddenly in high definition.

The night of the first Origin in 1980.

For the longest time, the means by which ten-year-old me had found out we won was a mystery. I figured Dad told me next morning, or I read it in the *Courier-Mail*, or I saw it on TV. Now, it had come back to me with a clarity both startling and soothing.

I am awake. The only light in my room is supplied by the dim bulb in the hallway. Dad is sitting at the edge of my bed. He must've arrived home just this minute because he's still wearing his brown leather jacket with the woolly collar, the one that only comes out on Brisbane's coldest nights. He smells like the footy — beer and grass and sweat. And cigarettes, even though he doesn't smoke. He's clutching the rolled-up game program in his hand. His grinning face seems to possess its own source of light.

'We won, mate,' he whispers. '20-10.'

I go to sit up but he pats my leg, tells me to lay back down. He apologises for waking me up — he'd just wanted to let me know.

'They called us a joke,' he says. 'They reckoned the game would be a non-event, the worst...'

I wait for him to finish his sentence, but he doesn't. He just side-tilts his head in his subtle "told you so" way and gives a little shrug of the shoulders. Then he taps my blanket with the program, tells me to sleep well and says goodnight. As he exits the room, he assures me we'll watch the game together tomorrow.

◯

I opened my eyes, grasped my phone. Suppressing the urge to cry, I opened Dad's email and began to read. It was a summary of his thoughts – the pivotal players, the key moments. He'd singled out skipper Daly Cherry-Evans for special praise; DCE had 'stuck it up 'em!' with his victory speech. Naturally, there'd been a reference to the worst Queensland team ever. Dad signed off saying he couldn't wait to send the DVD over.

Later in the day, after I'd revelled in Val Holmes soaring for the corner and Cam Munster's double-kick magic and Harry Grant wreaking havoc through the middle and the 12-man grit in the final five minutes, I replied to my father's message. I declined to tell him (yet again) that DVDs were as redundant as a Blues' Dynasty. Instead, I requested he send over a Betamax cassette tape.

37

To Be a Queenslander

'Mate, we're in front. It's okay.'

Thirty seconds left. Isaah Yeo – the Blue concussed in the first tackle of the night, who should've been taken off, who should've played no further part in the game – pokes his nose through the defence and streams forward, try-line in his sights. I cover my eyes with my hands, unable to watch.

It's not okay.

Shouts:

'NOOOOO!'
'AAARGH!'
'WHAAAT!'
'WOWWWW!'
And then Dad's unmistakable contribution:
'YOU LITTLE BLOODY RIPPER!'

I open my eyes and peer through splayed fingers. On the TV is a riot of Maroon celebration, much of it under the crossbar of our own posts, near enough to the spot where Yeo was certain to score. Ignoring similar levels of festivity in the living room, I snatch the iPad from the table and scroll the stream back a few ticks.

'Hey!' barks Simon, jumping to his feet. 'What are you doing?'

'I want to see that final tackle again.'

'Again?' asks Sean. 'I'm not sure you saw it the first time.'

Mum nods. 'He was covering his eyes. He's still a little boy after all these years.'

'Thank you, Mother,' I reply. 'I'll get you to change my nappy after this.'

She shakes her head. 'Ooh, you're bold.'

I hit "Play". For the second time in two minutes, Isaah Yeo barrels towards the line. Despite the joy I've just witnessed, my thoughts spiral like a corkscrew. Oh, God! He won't be stopped! He can't be stopped! And then a panel sequence from a comic book ensues: Kalyn Ponga hits him front-on, wraps him up a-la Alfoil Man, and wrangles him to ground. Yeo finishes within breathing distance of the stripe. The clock runs out before he can play the ball. Cue the encore of Maroon elation.

I shift my attention from TV to couch. A jubilant Dad is standing. I move in front of him, and he raises his hand for a high-five. I oblige then grab him for a hug.

'Phew… It's okay,' he says.

'It's better than okay,' I reply. 'It's everything.'

A few hours later, I drive Mum and Dad to the airport. It's a gorgeous, sunny day; one of those summer gems that stamps Vancouver as the ultimate fridge-worthy postcard. We don't talk much along the way. It's reminiscent of when I left Brisbane in 2007: no one wants to say goodbye out loud and get swallowed up by the earth. At Departures drop-off, I insist on handling the suitcases, waving away Dad's protests. I find a trolley and load up, all the while careful to avoid eye contact with my parents' crumbling faces. Then I pull both of them into an embrace, assuring them we'll be over to Australia for a visit next year, guaranteed. The tears in my eyes speak to the tenuousness of the promise. We exchange 'I love yous' and Dad wants one more hug. I ask him if we'll win the series. Bloody oath, is his reply. When I get back home from the airport, I watch the Maroons' victory three more times. At the end of the third viewing, I silently thank the players. The gift they provided – they'll never know how precious it is.

In the days following the family's departure, I feel their absence. I also feel a tremendous sense of gratitude. So many wonderful memories of our time together, not the least of which was their attendance at the launch of my new novel, Boy in the Blue Hammock. *Bought by BC's own Harbour Publishing in July of 2021, my best work to date had survived the scrap heap and found a good home. I'm still a long way from returning to the literary Origin arena, but at least I'm playing again. And if you're playing, there's comfort in the possibility that you're a chance.*

A month after his return to Brisbane, Dad comes down with a bad respiratory illness he contracted at a family wedding. The likely source? His seventy-nine-year-old younger brother, Roy. Des is laid out for a week, frequently watching old Origin tapes to keep his spirits up. Across the family, there is grave concern. Will this escalate into a full-blown health crisis? Will this super-charge the cancer?

Is this the beginning of the end?

The worry is still front and centre at the time of the 2022 series decider. I go to bed that evening assuring the Goddess that if it's a choice between Dad getting better and a Maroons victory, there is no choice to make. Hell, I'd welcome a return to the 1970s if it meant my father going into remission. In the morning, I discover Queensland has prevailed in yet another classic. Two of ours – Selwyn Cobbo and Lindsay Collins – and one of theirs – Cameron Murray – knocked out in the first three minutes. Behind early but back within two by the break. An old-school punch-up between Dane Gagai and Matt Burton early in the second stanza. A sixtieth minute flash of Kalyn Ponga brilliance to edge us in front. And then the signature moment, the one to live forever: with the Blues coming to steal the shield, Ben Hunt charges down Nathan Cleary's kick and races eighty metres — the last ten with a finger pointed skyward — to put the result beyond doubt.

At the end of my second watch of the game, I FaceTime Dad. It's early morning in Brisbane and I'm anxious, unsure of my father's health status, fearful that the Goddess may have rejected my prioritising of Dad over the Maroons. He answers. The relief is immediate. He is bright. He is hale. He is present. He is without his hearing-aids and, thus, deaf as a doorpost. But he is fully recovered. The face may be old and weathered, but I recognise this man. On a historic July 8 night in 1980, he sat on the edge of my bed and told me we'd won.

I ask him how he's going — he says he feels great.

To be a Queenslander.

The Night of Gordie's Revenge

The Bull is once more restless – there is much to be atoned
It wasn't just a game we lost but 'the way we lost', he moaned
And when the man called "Harrogant" sent him to the bin
The Blues, Maroons and crowd alike, could not work out his sin
Then Bill, three days later, admits he made a blunder
The Raging Bull is seething – 'I'll tear those Blues asunder!'.

We know we didn't play that well – now, that's part of history
But tonight, at ANZ you know, our play won't be a mystery.
The engine room will be much tighter, PJ will run amok
We'll be giving Alf a ton of room to run wide of the ruck
The silky flow of Lockyer, will come into the fray
No, Blues, we ain't lost it – Gordie's mob can really play

So go you bloody Queenslanders! And give it to those Blues!
Feel the Raging Bull's ire and shake them to their shoes!
Make 'em feel the way we felt at Stadium Australia!
Make 'em feel that they're outmatched, make 'em feel that they're a
failure!
Yes, Joey Johns and his "Wizened" Blues will know of Gordie's hunger
They'll feel the weight of this great State, the boom of Maroon thunder!

Des Groth (2001)

You Still Don't Get It! – a Message to the Blues

You wrote it in your paper, that your Blues are now supreme
The Dynasty is over and you now have reached your dream
You say you have the passion to bury Queensland pride
We say – you still don't get it – our spirit never died

From Cape York to the Isa, and from Birdsville to the Coast
We're as passionate as ever, no need to shout and boast
We love the game each single week, not once or twice a year
We're always there to cheer them on – on that, you'll have no fear

Have you walked a lonely Queensland street on that special
Wednesday night
Where there's lights in every window but everything is quiet?
Have you heard the whole street then explode with a mighty
healthy roar?
You'll know it's not unusual – it's just Queensland in to score

It's alive in every living room, in every club and pub
From Torres Strait to Surfers and out there in the scrub
Around a distant campfire on a crackling radio
Maroon passion alive and well in case you didn't know

Queenslanders know what pride is – we wear it on our sleeve
We don't need your opinions 'cos we know what we've achieved
Just look up the statistics and you'll realise it's true
Maroons never waste a chance to belt a bloody Blue

You may have won this series (and not by much, you know)
But, hey, you need to make it eight, just seven more to go
There'll be no Gallens in your tank and your Bird will leave the flock
So batten down the hatches: here comes a mighty shock

Queenslanders never lose it – we've had it all the way
It's embedded there forever, until our dying day
Our passion for our boys to win – your pay, well, you can bet it
For all you folk south of the Tweed, well, still…
YOU JUST DON'T GET IT!

Des Groth (2014)

Ode to Des Groth's 60th
(The Greatest Origin Story Never Told)

Game Two was now done, the ledger one-one,
We faced a grim situation.
All the pundits agreed our most desperate need
Was a source of great inspiration.

The experts sat down, names were thrown 'round,
To whom we entrust our mission?
Lammy knew the ropes, he'd carried our hopes
In true Queensland Kumul tradition.

Julian O'Neill? Yes? He could cause the Blues stress
With his cabaret from the casino
At just under a ton, Chicken George could still run
And Greg Brentnall's still frightened of Geno.

Don't forget the King, he'd provide one last fling
If Fox let him off for a minute.
And if Big Artie chose to go in search of his toes
We'd be unbackable odds to win it.

'Dally M!' shouted one, 'He could probably run
with a few strings attached to his femurs.'
'Or Alf!' cried a second, 'He's the man I reckon,'
(But we weren't the impossible dreamers)

Then Benny weighed in with an unheralded grin
That damn near fractured his face
'Gentlemen,' he declared with his features repaired
'Let me introduce our Game Three ace.'
~
'He's a former star of A-grade QR,

Played fullback right through to front row.
The speed of his hands matched a teenager's glands
And his hits made the Sunlander slow.'

'He's exited the fold, now sixty years old –
He spends his time blowing the froth,
Gents, I'm no liar, our decider messiah
Is the "Mitchelton Mongrel" – Des Groth!'

In the week that ensued, the press boiled and stewed
Had the mighty Maroons pulled the right rein?
And when Des got a cramp on the bus ride to camp
It seemed "all to lose, nothing to gain".

But the great man relaxed, told the journos to get faxed
As the bonding session reached its twelfth slab
'Don't sweat boys,' he slurred, 'The brass hasn't erred…
Now – who's gonna call me a cab?'

And his teammates – they listened, their eyes they fair glistened
As Groth's words burrowed into each heart
This "everyone's mate" with the stretched number eight
Could lead if they all played their part.

He taught them the coat hanger, the gouge, the scrote-banger
And the timetable from Ferny Grove
And Choppy just smiled as he held them beguiled:
'We're gonna do these bastards – 'ken oath!'

~

Sunday came calling, the masses were sprawling
Over ANZ's aluminum expanse
The ask that they shared, the question they dared
Could Groth conjure one last dance?

Well, no sooner posed, than the answer disclosed
From the kickoff into the fray:
He chipped on the first, reclaimed on the burst
And on six-decade legs zoomed away!

The tone was now set; every Blue would forget
His first half on that magical eve.
The step, jink and dummy; that unstoppable tummy
And the thirty-eighth minute corner-post heave.

Would the second dig differ? A bang then a whiffer?
Perhaps if the Pope's flying Mir…
Eight tries and ten goals, seven sausage rolls
And all without spilling his beer!

And when the final hooter soared, and the Bookies' Club roared
The score line read 200 – nil
The "Man of the Match" bowed, both humble and proud
And thousands fell silent and still:

'To all of you folks, and these sixteen great blokes -
This is the best day of my life.
And now I must go, the train leaves in a mo;
There's ironing to be done for the wife.'

Darren Groth (2002)

ABOUT THE AUTHOR

Photo by Chloe Groth

Darren is the author of nine novels including *Kindling*, *Are You Seeing Me?*, *Exchange of Heart* and his most recent North American work, *Boy in the Blue Hammock*. He is a South Australian Literary Award winner, a two-time finalist in the Queensland Literary Awards, and a past nominee for numerous other prestigious prizes, among them the CBCA Book of the Year, the Prime Minister's Literary Awards, The Text Prize, and the Governor General's Literary Awards in Canada. He has written for newspapers, magazines and literary journals including *The Courier-Mail*, *The Sun-Herald*, *Mamamia*, *The Lifted Brow* and *Syntax*. He will always believe Queensland was robbed by Mark McGaw's match-winning try in Game 1 of the 1987 State of Origin series. He lives in Vancouver, Canada.

ACKNOWLEDGEMENTS

I want to thank the people who took hit-ups to help get this book written: first reader, Wend; Des and Kath; Sean and Simon; Michael Gerard Bauer; Charlie Moore; Victoria Bushnell; Claire Kamber; Andrew Staehling; Robbie Vergara; and Michael Connell.

My longtime partner in the literary halves, agent Tara Wynne — I appreciate your support. And a prop forward-sized thank you to Carolyn Martinez and the Hawkeye team for their Wally Lewis-like vision in seeing promise in this work, and their Queenslander spirit in bringing it to market.

Darren

If you enjoyed *Marooned: A Memoir of Fandom, Fatherhood, & the Far Side of the World*, you'll also enjoy:

The Umbrella Men Project by Albert Jamae
Where There is a Will by Michel Vimal du Monteil
Head Grenade by Troy Henderson
The Angels Wept by Jack Roney
Identity by Peter Long

Book reviews can make or break a book. If you liked what you read today, please do consider posting a review on Goodreads or your favourite forum.

Marooned: A Memoir of Fandom, Fatherhood, & the Far Side of the World
is available at hawkeyebooks.com.au
and all good bookstores and libraries.